Football in Sheffield

Text copyright 2016 M Liversidge, C Eyre
Photographic copyright
M Liversidge, G Leary, 2016

The rights of M Liversidge & C Eyre as author and league information supplier of this work has been asserted by them in accordance with the Copyright Design Patent Act 1988
All rights reserved.
No part of this publication may be reproduced, stored in a retrieval system or transmitted in any form or by any means electronic, mechanical, photocopying, recording or otherwise without the prior permission in writing of the copyright holders.

Published and printed by M. Liversidge
Copy proof checked by E J Huntley & Les Payne

Where to start . . .

Our local teams, Sheffield Wednesday, Sheffield United, Sheffield FC (the oldest football club in the world) and Hallam FC who play their home games on the oldest football ground (Sandygate) in the world, have all been very well documented and their many various achievements noted.

Even though these clubs receive a passing mention within the pages of this book, we will concentrate on the local Sheffield Leagues in which teams representing steel works, public houses, working men's clubs, old boys' associations, churches, ex-school teams and youth clubs played their football. With no monetary gain on offer, their incentive, aside from the end of season winner's medals was simple: a deep and shared love of the beautiful game.

The book includes images of well over one hundred Sheffield area football teams, medals and trophies for which the local men and boys have competed for over the last one and a half centuries. These medals and trophies have been brought together by contacting some of the players mentioned but by also approaching members of families who still have the medals and trophies their fathers and grandfathers won and which are still cherished by their descendants to this day. Thankfully, these families invariably have a postcard or image of their menfolk in a team photograph and have let me use them within this book.

Local league and cup winners are given in some detail (hopefully, correctly) as well as details/images of various league handbooks and programmes, and there is a rich collection of local ephemera, Sheffield newspaper clippings, illustrations and advertisements from local publications.

Images have been taken from old postcards, cigarette cards, newspaper articles and other local sources and have been used to try to provide an overall view of the local football scene in Sheffield and district over these 150 plus years.

Sheffield Works League: Haig League Division One Trophy

Oughtibridge War Memorial (Black/Orange stripes) versus Norton Oaks

Index

Junior League:
Winners Medal 1902-03
won by Sale Memorial

Stannington Village (Red/Black stripes) v Redmires

Introduction

Few can deny that the city of Sheffield has played a hugely significant role in the development of the beautiful game. Sheffield was the first to have organised football cup matches, the first city to stage a floodlit match, the first city to boast team named United, and can also boast the world's oldest football ground (Hallam FC's Sandygate) and the world's oldest football club (Sheffield FC) who also incorporated the first football rules

As the City of Sheffield grew in the 19th century, absorbing the surrounding land, there became a need for more recreational areas, football pitches, cricket grounds, bowling greens, swimming pools and golf courses etc. Between the middle of the 19th century and 1920, Sheffield was one of (if not) the most rapidly growing of all British cities. Within this time period our city had become one of the most important centres in the country for both Football and Cricket.

With half-day Saturdays granted to the working populous, recreational sports became increasingly popular and hundreds, if not thousands, of teams organised football games and eventually leagues to provide an outlet for the competitive needs of the young, and not so young, men of Sheffield and the surrounding areas. Before the 1850s local heroes were generally jockeys, bare knuckle fighters, runners or walkers who took part in very long distance races. From the 1860s our folk heroes became footballers or cricketers.

From the middle part of the 19th century onwards, Sheffield football thrived and local league players were selected on many occasions to represent the England National team; including William Edwin Clegg and his brother John Charles Clegg (who appeared in the very first international ever played,) Billy Mosforth of Sheffield Albion, John Hunter of Heeley FC and John Robert Blayney Owen of Owlerton FC who gained his solitary England cap on 7 March 1874 against Scotland. John Hudson, also earned one cap for England, wearing the captain's armband and leading his country to a 7-0 victory over Ireland in February 1883. The aforementioned John Hunter also captained his country on one occasion, in 1881, and, after being transferred to Blackburn Olympic in 1882, he won an FA Cup Winners Medal in 1883. Blackburn's 2-1 victory over Old Etonians in this final effectively brought to an end the southern and aristocratic teams, domination of the FA Cup, a defeat from which the likes of these gentlemen teams never really recovered and they never won the trophy again.

The turn of the 19th century and first few years of the 20th century saw our city's larger teams Wednesday and United, dominate the FA Cup and League championships winning the League and Cup seven times between them in a nine-year period.

Within the city itself, lower leagues had arisen, among them the Licensed Victuallers League where the public houses in a certain area competed for some superb trophies and medals (see page 16). This era also saw the birth of the Sheffield Challenge Cup, the Wharncliffe Charity Shield, the Minor League, the Sheffield Association League and the Clegg Shield, a school trophy, which is still competed for within Sheffield and which is the oldest School Football Trophy in the World.

The first 14 years of the 20th century saw the amount of local football teams grow rapidly and local sponsors poured money into these newly formed leagues. Sadly, the First World War brought to an abrupt end the sporting activities of young men throughout Britain. The war to end all wars, as it was called, also ended many of the leagues that had been formed and flourished. Many of the young footballers who enlisted never came home and vast numbers of those who did, returned with varying degrees of injury that left them unable to take part in any sport. Other physically fit but mentally traumatised lads also never played again.

Normal service slowly resumed and the local football league scene eventually thrived once again with the local steel producing companies introducing six new leagues, each with two or three divisions. These were, in order of standard: **Works Premier, Works Minor League, Haig League, Beatty League, Raleigh League and Drake League.** These leagues only allowed players who worked at the relevant steel company to play for their teams. For many years it was impossible to play in the aforementioned leagues unless employed within that industry. It was not until the 1960s that the steel manufacturers' league committee relaxed its rules, and even then only a little. To prove this point, the printing company for whom the author Michael Liversidge worked in the early 1960s used to print for Hadfields group of companies and one day whilst delivering some ordered print work he was asked "where's tha' play lad, in goal, up front or a tha' a defender?". He told the inquisitive gent, who he discovered was the Hadfield first team manager, what position he played and was told, "Well, tha' does print work for us so tha' can play for us. Come dahn to the Bawtry Ruad ground on Saturday, we're havin' trials." Michael never did go for those trials but ended up, some 12 years later, playing for Hadfields first team in the Hatchard League and stayed with them for many, very happy years.

Local pubs and clubs, old boys clubs as well as large Department Stores such as Cole Brothers, Brightside and Carbrook, and Atkinsons also all had teams playing in the various leagues - all seemed well and then......World War Two. This was not only a global catastrophe but another desultory period for the local Sheffield football league scene as young men, once again, signed up for war in Europe and once again, like it had 25 years earlier, some leagues never resurfaced in the late 1940s when peace returned to a newly re-designed Europe.

The very late 1940s through to the 1960s saw Sheffield football leagues once again entice more teams and get young men back to playing on a Saturday afternoon. Football, in the early to mid 1960s, was now seen regularly on British TV with Match of the Day on the BBC on Saturday nights. The interest was growing so much in Sheffield that teams who were forming had to sign on to a three year waiting list just to get a council owned ground/pitch such as Concord, Longley, Graves, Parson Cross parks. Any other bit of spare land the council deemed fit to put a couple of goalpost up were soon snatched up. Jimmy Childs, a construction company, flattened the top of Wincobank Lane rubbish tip so that 2 pitches could be laid there. Quite a few other companies flattened areas and let the pitches to the council.

In 1966 when England won the World Cup, interest in grassroots football throughout the country was at its height. Nowhere more so than in and around the Sheffield region. The Sheffield and Hallamshire County Football Association had just started to allow legalised Sunday football to take place and leagues were starting to add more divisions to their leagues. The beautiful game was flourishing and continued to do so for about another 20 years.

This interest, since its peak in 1967-75, has very slowly dwindled and now in the year 2016, about 90% of all the leagues we will mention and illustrate throughout this book are now defunct with only a few of the Saturday Leagues remaining, invariably with different sponsored names.

The Sheffield Sunday Leagues have stayed the distance a little better but even these have started to diminish. **The Sunday Alliance League** and **The Regional Sunday League** which merged to be the **Regional Alliance League** only a decade or so ago, has now disbanded and the league's remaining teams are now playing under the banner of the **Meadowhall League**. Therefore two/three more leagues have forever disappeared. These Sunday leagues have also had name changes to accommodate the names of new sponsors.

The few **Saturday** Leagues that are still surviving in the city are:
The County Senior
Wragg Football League (over 35s)
Sheffield Fair Play League
South Yorkshire Amateur League

The Sunday Leagues that have survived are:
Meadowhall Sheffield and District Sunday League
Blades Sunday Sport League
Sheffield Imperial Sunday League
Sheffield and District DB Sports U18/21 Sunday League.

To be fair there are a vast amount of local **junior team leagues** all under 17 still going strong but some of these seem to be more for the parents than the youngsters, a large amount of whom do not carry on with football once they reach the age of 17.

When a league does disband or just ceases to have enough sides to justify carrying on, the history of that league can soon be lost forever.

Sadly, the Sheffield and Hallamshire County Football Association do not save these details (why not?) and therefore they are lost to us forever. An individual, like myself, can try and trace these leagues through old newspapers, handbooks and archives etc. But not every league that appeared in the Library archives or the Green'Un newspaper showed end of season positions, therefore, sometimes league winners or cup winners cannot be deduced from a mid-season table with many games still to play.

Chris Eyre, a friend, football historian and S&H Referee, has supplied me with a large amount of Sheffield leagues information that he has collected over the years and without this information this book would not really have been possible. For his unselfish generosity I am eternally grateful. Many of the photographs are old postcards I own, photographs I have taken over the years and more recent images are from **Graham Leary,** an old friend and excellent local league photographer, who has kindly let me use some images from his vast collection.

I hope the book will give you a small glimpse into the history of Football in and around Sheffield .

Meadowhall League Cup Final 2010 at Bramall Lane, between Royal Earl FC and Packhorse Inn FC which Royal Earl won 2-1

The Football leagues in Sheffield, Saturdays:

Works Leagues:
Premier League, Minor League,
Beatty League, Haig League,
Drake League, Raleigh League.

The Works Premier, Beatty, Drake and Minor Leagues had 48 teams, 12 in each league and the Haig League had three division with around 10 - 12 teams in each section. All these games and fixtures were organised by the steel industry or associated companies.

Some of the steel companies who had teams in the leagues were: Arthur Lees, Davy United, Intal Works, Firth Vickers, Flathers, Jessop-Savile, Shardlows, Osborns, Bramahs, Brightside Foundry, Hadfields, Laycocks, Brown Bayleys, Atlas and Norfolk, Sheffield Waterworks, English Steel, Edgar Allen, Davy Brown, Firth Brown and many more.

Some of the companies had up to four sides throughout the various leagues.

Other Saturday Leagues in and around Sheffield: c1950s/1960s/1970s

Yorkshire League: Three divisions of about 16 teams in each section. Played within the Yorkshire boundaries.

County Senior League: Two divisions of about 14 teams in each section. Played within the South Yorkshire boundaries.

Sheffield Amateur League: Two divisions of about 14 teams in each section

Sheffield South Yorkshire Amateur League: Four divisions of about 12 teams in each section

Hatchard League: Two divisions of about 16 teams in each section

City League: One divisions of about 12-14 teams

Junior League: One divisions of about 12 teams

Friendlies League: Fluctuated between 5-8 divisions of about 10-12 teams in each section

Sheffield Sports and Athletic League: Three divisions of about 12 teams in each section

Wragg League: One divisions of about 15 teams

Intermediate League: One divisions of about 14 teams

Sheffield Thursday Friendlies League: Two divisions of about 10 teams in each section

Sheffield Thursday Amateur League: Two divisions of about 10 teams in each section

Sheffield Midweek League:
One divisions of about 10-12 teams

Attercliffe and District League:
One divisions of about 10-12 teams

The seven following leagues. Not sure amount of teams in divisions or amount of divisions they had

Heeley and District League:
Association League:
Public Parks & Recreation League:
Hope Valley League:
Holbrook and District League
Wharncliffe League
Penistone League

The Church/Religious related leagues

Sheffield Bible Class League: Two divisions of about 12 teams in each section

Sheffield Churches League: Two divisions of about 12 teams in each section

Sheffield Sunday School Football League: One division - This league was established, in 1887 with Carbrook Reform being the first winners of the Shield (see page 148 for the first 50 years winners of this shield).

Sheffield Free Churches League:
Two divisions of about 12 teams in each section

Catholic League: Two divisions

The Sheffield School Trophies

Clegg Shield,
Wednesday Shield and United Shield

These school knockout shields were supplied by the Clegg family, Sheffield Wednesday and Sheffield United for varying age groups of school children.

Sheffield Cup Competitions

These were the larger cup competition that encompassed many leagues:

The Sheffield & District Challenge Cup,
The Sheffield Senior Cup,
The Sheffield Junior Cup,
The Sheffield Junior Shield,
The Wharncliffe Cup,
The Tinsley Charity Shield,
Kelley Hospital Cup and many more.

Sunday Football in Sheffield

In 1963/64 the inauguration of the Sheffield and District Sunday League (now Meadowhall League) began and the first winners were **New Inn**.

This league was limited to 44 teams in 3 or 4 divisions. **The Sheffield Sunday Regional League** was the next to be formed and others **The Sunday Imperial League** and **The Sunday Alliance** soon followed. In fact Sunday football eventually became more popular in Sheffield than the Saturday Leagues.

Chapter One
Sheffield and district players through the eras

Players through the eras: 1870s

The star-shaped medal (shown bottom right) was awarded to **The Wednesday** footballer and politician, **WILLIAM EDWIN CLEGG** (1852-1932), and was sold at Bonhams, Chester, as part of its Sporting Memorabilia sale on 1st June 2011. It was sold to a "private Sheffield-based buyer" for £1,800. It was awarded for W. E. Clegg's participation in the first ever **Sheffield Challenge Cup**. The medal, which was discovered in a box of assorted items taken into Bonhams' Exeter office by a local client, attracted a pre-sale estimate of between £1,500 - £2,000.

Image from 2nd March 1878 after The Wednesday beat Attercliffe FC 2-0 in the final of the second ever Sheffield Challenge Cup. Third from left back row is William Clegg and to his left, (fourth from left) his brother Charles.

W. E. Clegg played a significant role in the formation of Association Football. William was the second Wednesday player ever to be capped by England.

The Wednesday 1875-76
Standing WE Clegg, JC Clegg, W Wilkinson, E Bowling, J Morton, I Gregory
Seated J Housley, WE England, WH Stacey, W Horton, G Anthony, J Hunter

The honour of being the first Wednesday player to earn an international cap went to his brother, Charles Clegg, who appeared for England in the very first International, a 0-0 draw, against Scotland .

After retiring from football through injury William was elected the Lord Mayor of Sheffield (1898) and was often referred to as the 'uncrowned King of Sheffield'.

William Edwin Clegg was awarded this medal (below) for winning the Sheffield Association Challenge Cup on 12 May 1877, when The Wednesday defeated Heeley 4-3 at Bramall Lane in front of 6,000 fans.

It was the first ever trophy won by **The Wednesday.** It was noted there was occasional snow during the game and with the game ending 3-3 in normal time, extra time was needed to settle the final.

Clegg, later opened the Hillsborough ground, and played a significant part in the early formation of the game of football, not only in Sheffield but also throughout Great Britain.

William Clegg became a solicitor and probably his most memorable client was the notorious Sheffield criminal and double murderer, **Charles Peace**.

Although the career of William, both on and off the pitch, is often overshadowed by the impact his older brother, **Sir Charles Clegg,** had on the game, it is no less impressive than that of his, slightly, more famous sibling.

W. E. Clegg,

Challenge Cup Winners Medal 1876-77

Players through the eras: 1880s

JOHN (JACK) HUNTER (1852 - 1903) was an English footballer who won the FA Cup with Blackburn Olympic in 1883 and made seven appearances for England between 1878 and 1882 playing at half back.

Hunter was born in Sheffield and worked as a butcher and silver cutler in the city whilst playing for various clubs, including **Sheffield Heeley, Providence, Sheffield Albion** and **The Zulus**.

He won all his seven England caps whilst playing for **Sheffield Heeley**, a club he originally joined in 1870. His first international appearance was at Hampden Park, Glasgow against Scotland on 2 March 1878. Although England "fielded a side they thought capable of defeating the Scots, ...(they) returned home with a humiliating 7-2 defeat". He was next selected in March 1880 for matches away to Scotland (lost 5-4) and Wales which resulted in a 3-2 victory; this was Hunter's only victory in his seven England appearances.

He was again selected the following year for the two Home Internationals. In the match against Wales, played at Alexandra Meadows, Blackburn, on 26 February 1881, he was appointed captain, but Wales achieved their first victory on English soil with a 1-0 success. For the following game, Hunter retained his place but lost the captaincy to Norman Bailey of Clapham Rovers. In the match, played at Kennington Oval, London, on 12 March 1881, England suffered yet another "humiliating" defeat as the Scots returned North with a 6-1 victory.

Despite England's poor performances against the Scots in this period, Hunter was again selected for the Home International matches in March 1882. In both these matches, England conceded five goals going down 5-1 at Hampden Park, Glasgow on 11 March and 5-3 at the Racecourse Ground, Wrexham two days later. These two defeats brought Hunter's international career to a close.

After a short spell with The Wednesday, Hunter was appointed manager of a public house in Blackburn where he joined the Olympic in 1882 as both player and coach. Blackburn Olympic had been founded in August 1877 and soon evolved into one of the finest sides in Lancashire. Hunter, an astute coach and tactician, taught the Olympic players the art of the passing game. Hunter coached a team of tradesmen and weavers to overcome the dominance of local rivals, Blackburn Rovers, and the amateur teams of southern England to win the FA Cup in 1883.

It was Hunter who decided to take the team to Blackpool for a few days' relaxation prior to the final, which had been unheard of previously.

In the final (against Old Etonians played on 31 March 1883 at the Kennington Oval), Hunter played at centre half and helped to keep the Old Etonians forwards at bay thus allowing the fitter Olympic side to come from behind to claim the cup with a 2-1 victory after extra time.

FA Cup Winners Medal 1883

Hunter remained with Olympic until mid-1880s when he joined Blackburn Rovers.

Below: Postcard featuring Blackburn Rovers F.C. Trainer: J. Hunter standing on far right of picture.

After a short spell playing for Rovers, Hunter became assistant trainer and groundsman at Ewood Park, as well as working as a licensee in Blackburn.

From 1897 Hunter had a short spell as coach of Cheshire side New Brighton Tower, helping that team rise from the Lancashire League to a brief period in the Football League.

Sadly, John Hunter died of consumption on 9 April 1903.

Players through the eras: 1890s

Sheffield-born **TOMMY CRAWSHAW** was a legendary captain who not only led **Wednesday** to consecutive League Championships in 1903 and 1904 but also helped the Owls to FA Cup wins in 1896 and 1907 – earning a unique place in club history as the only Wednesday player to win two Cup winners medals.

But all this was after he had served an earlier part of his footballing life with three other teams of that era.

He first played for local Sheffield team **Park Grange** in the late 1880s until 1891 when he then joined an **Attercliffe FC** team that was consistently "always there or thereabouts" in Sheffield Cup competitions. He stayed at **Attercliffe** until 1893 when he moved on to a Manchester league side **Heywood Central**. His last match for Heywood Central was a Manchester Senior Cup Final which they lost 4-2 to **Bury**. He then agreed to join **The Wednesday** who were fast becoming one of the top sides in English football.

Crawshaw enjoyed an outstanding career at **Wednesday** as, in addition to the previously mentioned honours, Tommy also led the Owls to the **Division Two Championship** in 1900 - in the club's first season in their new home at Owlerton – and won many representative honours, ten full caps for his country and played many times for the **Sheffield Football Association**. He was a huge favourite with **Wednesday** fans, first at Olive Grove and then at Owlerton.

During **Wednesday's** Cup winning season of 1906-7 Tommy celebrated his 36th birthday, and it was his vast experience that helped the team through to the final at Crystal Palace where, although underdogs to **Everton**, Crawshaw helped his team record a glorious 2-1 victory. The 1907-08 season would prove to be Tommy's last as a first team player. After making 13 Division One appearances in 1907-8, his loyalty over the years was rewarded with a free transfer in April 1908. His final game was a memorable one:, a 2-0 derby win over The Blades!

T. CRAWSHAW. SHEFFIELD WEDNESDAY.

Crawshaw moved on to **Chesterfield** and later **Castleford** where he played on until around 1910.

In the 1911 census, Tommy and his wife Jane and their five children lived at the **Shrewsbury Hotel**, 109 South Street in Sheffield (pictured). Thomas is described as a licensed victualler.

Tommy later owned a newsagent's shop in Bramall Lane, of all places, then he went back into the brewery trade and became landlord of the **Sportsmans Group** public house near Hillsborough and then onto **The Yorkshireman** in the City centre. Tommy passed away in 1960 while resident at the Wharncliffe Hospital, Bradfield. He was 87.

This is one of Tommy's ten England Caps. This one was won in season 1896-1897 whilst playing against Scotland at Crystal Palace.

Players through the eras: 1900s

ERNEST (NUDGER) NEEDHAM was a legendary team captain, who not only led **Sheffield United** to two FA Cup wins but also to the Blades' only League Championship title in 1898. He also won 16 England international caps.

Remarkably, though, he played more years in the local Sheffield and district leagues than he did as a professional. He played in local leagues before he signed for Sheffield United in 1891 (Ernest was initially signed from **Staveley Town**) and later returned to local football for another 13-15 years after his professional retirement in 1910.

The image, to the right, of a central cigarette card and nine medals, illustrate the range of medals he won between 1911 until 1927.

He won medals for the Sheffield and Hallamshire FA Challenge Cup and the Sheffield and Hallamshire Association League, both pictured at the bottom of this page.

He also won a Chesterfield Royal Hospital Cup Winners medal in 1920 and a Runners up medal in 1923 and winners medals in the Derbyshire Senior League in 1920 and in the Byron Cup in 1927.

He also won a medal during the First World War when he was with the **King's Own Yorkshire Light Infantry** as Pte. Needham. A medal won whilst playing for **Woodthorpe F.C.** is shown beneath Nudger's cigarette card in the main picture.

Players through the eras: 1900s

W. BROADHURST played his football for the **Great Britain Hotel**, (pictured below), a public house that used to stand on John Street, which runs alongside Bramall Lane, facing the Blades ground.

W. BROADHURST'S two medals are highly unusual in the fact they are 15 carat gold. This was, to my knowledge, otherwise sacred to just the English FA Cup Final medals.

Both these medals are crafted by top quality goldsmiths. **The Sheffield Licensed Victuallers Association,** with its medals and its two distinctive trophies being of such high quality, illustrate the standard to which some of these local leagues aspired.

The **Great Britain Hotel** won the **Sheffield Licensed Victuallers League** in 1906 and have their name engraved on two very expensive trophies pictured, (both were sold at Sotheby's for over £7,500 in May 2002). Who sold them?

Other team names that are inscribed on this mighty trophy were the **Bird in Hand** (Broughton Lane, Attercliffe), three-time winners **Bellefield Inn** (Upperthorpe, St. Philips area), **Prospect View** (Gleadless Road) and the two-time winners **Industry Inn** (possibly Darnall or the public house on Dunlop Street, Carbrook - not 100% sure which one).

Winner Medal 1906-7

Winner Medal 1907-08

Sheffield Licensed Victuallers Trophy

Sheffield Licensed Victuallers Shield

Players through the eras; 1910s

WILLIAM (BILLY) LLOYD made over 80 appearances for Sheffield Wednesday (**The Wednesday** as they were then known) and scored 7 goals.

William was born in 1885 and he signed for **The Wednesday** in early 1906, aged 20. After serving his apprenticeship in the reserves he got his first team opportunity on Boxing Day 1906. Sadly, this game was called off because of snow and, instead. he made his first team debut three days later on the 29th December. He played 6 games for the first team in that first season and was the travelling reserve for Wednesday's 2-1 victory over **Everton** in the 1907 FA Cup Final at Crystal Palace, the much used final venue before Wembley was built.

During the same 1906-07 season, Lloyd won the medal opposite when playing for The Wednesday reserves in the final of the Challenge Cup at Bramall Lane.

Lloyd owned a tobacconist shop in Hillsborough whilst still playing for the Owls.

His army service was with the first battalion of the York and Lancs Regiment seeing action in Greece and Turkey. The First World War years effectively ended his playing career as he was not demobbed until 1920.

His final game for **The Wednesday**, sadly, was their record 10-0 defeat at Villa Park on the 5th October 1912.

He later played for **Rotherham County** after receiving a free transfer from **The Wednesday** in May 1913.

The Sheffield Challenge Cup is second only to the FA Cup as the oldest cup competition in English football.

This medal was bought on ebay from a distant relative of William Lloyd.

This medal was awarded to William (Billy) Lloyd for winning the Sheffield Association Challenge Cup in season 1906-07. THE WEDNESDAY reserves defeated SHEFFIELD UNITED 2-0 at Bramall Lane.

Players through the eras: 1910s

CLIFFORD OLDFIELD won winner's medals in the **Wragg League** and **Wragg Challenge Cup** in 1905 and 1906 respectively and a **Hatchard Cup** runners-up medal in 1907. He also won a **Holbeck League Senior Challenge Cup** medal in 1913-14. He is pictured (right) in his British Army uniform. I am led to believe that when he returned, after the end of the First World War, thankfully physically unharmed, he returned to playing local league football again in 1919.

I would imagine he was still trying to forget the horrors of what he had witnessed and getting back to local Sheffield area football probably helped him to regain the feeling of some normality.

So many teams were decimated or worse by the injuries their young players received during their wartime service in Europe. Quite a few leagues never resurfaced after the loss of so many players who did not return from the front or who carried injuries too severe to pick up their local league football lifestyle again.

Clifford was a coal merchant from the Darnall area and in later life, was the licensee at the Attercliffe Non-Political Club (non-pots) and afterwards at the Lansdowne (pictured below) on London Road.

In the later part of his life Clifford ran an off-licence on Porter Street.

A photograph of Clifford looking resplendent in his Army uniform.

Wragg Challenge Cup 1905-06

Wragg Challenge Cup 1906-07

Holbrook Senior Challenge Cup 1913-14

Hatchard Cup Runners up 1906-07

Players through the eras: 1920s

JOE BEER, who played for **Thursday Amateurs,** was a runner-up in the **Sheffield Thursday Amateur League** in the 1924-25 season and he followed this up a couple of seasons later with a winner's medal in 1926-1927. Whilst researching these teams and leagues in the Sheffield Local Studies Library, Joe Beer's name appears in the Green 'Un on many an occasion describing what a robust and talented young midfield player he was (they called them wing halfs or inside forwards in the 1920s / 1930s).

One article even describes him as the lynchpin of his team, **Thursday Amateurs'** regular success.

These medals were awarded to Joseph Beer for winning the Thursday Amateur Football League in 1926-27 season and also his runners up medal for season 1924-25 season.

GREEN'UN Snippet

Joe Beer, the sturdy little left half of Thursday Amateurs took the eye in the the Thursday League Cup Final tie which was played at the Pheasant ground in Attercliffe/Carbrook

THURSDAY AMATEURS.

PLAYED 2 HOURS 50 MINUTES' GAME AGAINST MEXBOROUGH.

Back row (left to right):—E. Lofthouse, W. Anderson, H. Chadwick, B. Davis, H. Sandham, A. Baverstock.
Front row:—L. Kay (secretary), J. Lawson, J. Brookes, A. Jones (captain), J. Beare, B. Rosenberg, and J. Davis (trainer).

An old press cutting showing Joe Beer seated on the front row second from right. Note that in the Newspaper they have incorrectly spelt his name.

Players through the eras 1920s

HARRY BRIGGS was a player I actually know nothing about other than the fact his medals came in to be valued at Leslie Cass jewellers on Surrey Street, Sheffield some years ago.

The manager at Cass's contacted someone he knew who was interested in purchasing local football medals and arranged for the two parties to meet up.

The two gentlemen agreed a deal and the new owner of the medals agreed for them to be used in this book.

Shown right and below are three lovely **Holbeck & District League** and **League Cup** winners medals that were won by Harry Briggs in the 1920s.

Coleridge Road School playing fields, Attercliffe/Darnall area of Sheffield

Players through the eras: 1930s

E. SKINNER who played for **Brunswick Methodists** (pictured) was a winner of the **Sheffield Churches League** in 1934.

The Brunswick team had an Ardath cigarette card produced which extolled their achievements. Ardath produced a set of 100 Yorkshire football cards in 1936 - some 15 of these cards depicted Sheffield teams, all of which can be seen throughout this book.

Skinner was scouted by Plymouth Argyle but, when he was offered a full-time contract by the Devon club, he turned them down because he had a safe and secure job in Sheffield.

Skinner is the very tall player third from right on the back row.

This medal was awarded to E Skinner for winning the Sheffield Churches Football League in 1934.

Medal in its original presentation box from Vaughtons Ltd, Goldsmiths, Birmingham

These small cigarette cards were produced by ARDATH tobacco and show the Brunswick Methodists team of 1935. On the reverse of these cards it gives details of players who went on to the professional game, trophies won over the years and other snippets of relevant information.

Now very collectable items - this was a single card from a full set of 100 cards showcasing football in Yorkshire.

Players through the eras: 1940s

ARTHUR EATON was a young man who signed Junior forms for **Huddersfield Town** in 1946 and then, two years later, moved on to **Sheffield United's** books. Although a very good footballer, Arthur never played first team football for these two famous clubs.

His initial signing-on letters can be seen at the bottom of this page.

Before and after his unfulfilled journey into the world of professional League football with these two well-established top flight teams, he played in the local leagues of Sheffield.

Three of the medals shown in their original boxes (right) were won whilst he played for Thorncliffe Rec. in the late 1940s and early 1950s.

His medals can be seen displayed across this and the following page:

Handsworth Cup Winners 1938 (lapel pin)

Intermediate League Winners 14-16 years 1937-38

Wharncliffe Charity Cup Winners 1947-48

Hatchard League Champions 1951-52

Association League Winners 1952-53

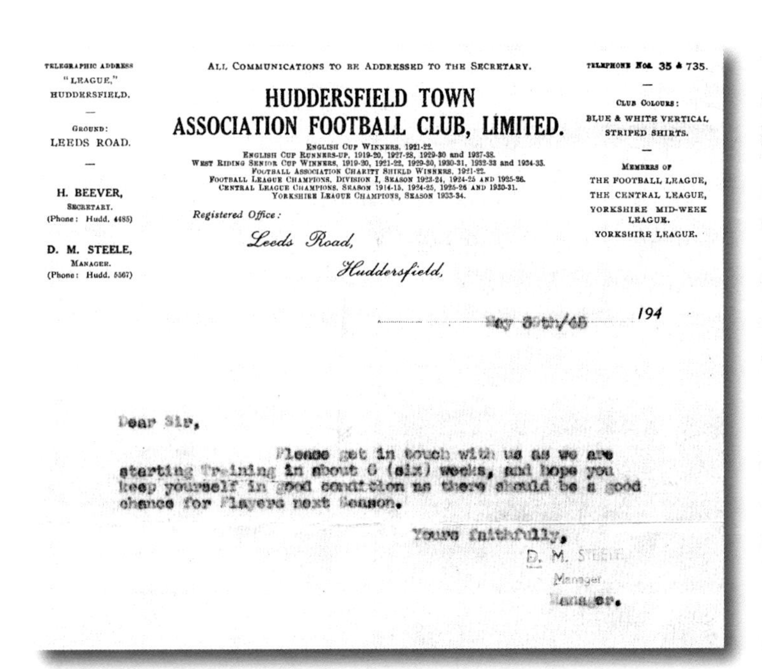

TELEGRAPHIC ADDRESS "LEAGUE," HUDDERSFIELD.

GROUND: LEEDS ROAD.

H. BEEVER, SECRETARY. (Phone: Hudd. 4485)

D. M. STEELE, MANAGER. (Phone: Hudd. 5567)

ALL COMMUNICATIONS TO BE ADDRESSED TO THE SECRETARY.

HUDDERSFIELD TOWN
ASSOCIATION FOOTBALL CLUB, LIMITED.

ENGLISH CUP WINNERS, 1921-22.
ENGLISH CUP RUNNERS-UP, 1919-20, 1927-28, 1929-30 and 1937-38.
WEST RIDING SENIOR CUP WINNERS, 1919-20, 1921-22, 1929-30, 1930-31, 1932-33 and 1934-35.
FOOTBALL ASSOCIATION CHARITY SHIELD WINNERS, 1921-22.
FOOTBALL LEAGUE CHAMPIONS, DIVISION I, SEASON 1923-24, 1924-25 AND 1925-26.
CENTRAL LEAGUE CHAMPIONS, SEASON 1914-15, 1924-25, 1925-26 AND 1930-31.
YORKSHIRE LEAGUE CHAMPIONS, SEASON 1933-34.

TELEPHONE NOS. 35 & 735.

CLUB COLOURS: BLUE & WHITE VERTICAL STRIPED SHIRTS.

MEMBERS OF THE FOOTBALL LEAGUE, THE CENTRAL LEAGUE, YORKSHIRE MID-WEEK LEAGUE. YORKSHIRE LEAGUE.

Registered Office:

Leeds Road,
Huddersfield,

May [illegible] 194

Dear Sir,

Please get in touch with us as we are starting Training in about 6 (six) weeks, and hope you keep yourself in good condition as there should be a good chance for Players next Season.

Yours faithfully,

D. M. STEELE
Manager
Manager.

SHEFFIELD UNITED CRICKET & FOOTBALL

CLUB, Ltd.,

Mr. R. Hollingsworth,
Secretary,
Thorncliffe Welfare F.C.

Jan. 5th.
1948.

Dear Mr. Hollingsworth,

Arthur Eaton (O.R)

I am instructed to ask if your Committee would be pleased to allow us to offer the above-named Player of your Club a trial in our Yorkshire League or Central League team(s) - after you are finished with the Junior Cup competition.

If permission is granted, perhaps you would be further good enough to arrange for me to have an interview with the Player.

With thanks in anticipation and best wishes to you and the Club during the new year.

Yours truly,

J.E. Davison.

Secretary-Manager.

Players through the eras 1940s/50s

ARTHUR EATON'S medals are displayed on this page

Handsworth Cup Badge/Pin won in 1937-38

Intermediate League 14-16 Winners Medal in 1937-38

Association Cup Winners Medal, won by Thorncliffe Rec 1952-53

Wharncliffe Charity Cup Winners Medal won by Thorncliffe Rec 1946-47

Hatchard League Champions in 1951-52 won by Thorncliffe Rec

Players through the eras: 1940s-1950s

DON HOLLAND, who played for **Hallam Football Club,** was one of four brothers who played in local Sheffield football leagues in the late 1940s and early 1950s. **DEREK, TONY** and **TREVOR HOLLAND** were the other three.

Don, though, was probably the best of these four brothers and actually won a **Sheffield Association League** winner's medal in the 1949-1950 season and a **Senior Challenge Cup** winner's medal in the 1950-51 season, both whilst playing for Hallam.

These two medals are probably the most prestigious honours that could be won whilst playing in the local Sheffield senior leagues.

Brother Derek kept goal for the PWD (Public Works Department) team. His team photo and medals can be seen on the relevant team and medal sections later in the book.

Don Holland pictured on front row second from right

Players through the eras: 1950s

In **The Sheffield Thursday Amateur League**, some 30 years after the aforementioned **Joe Beer** (page 19) won this league title, a **J. MCLEOD**-who played for **Brightside and Carbrook FC**-won or finished runner-up in six consecutive years and also managed to finish runner up in the **Tinsley Charity Shield** in 1954.

B&C FC must have been a very good side to produce a top two league finish for six consecutive seasons.

They also managed a Cup Final appearance in the **Tinsley Charity Shield** a competition that, I am led to believe, attracted a great number of entrants.

Tinsley Charity runners up medal

Thursday League runners-up for season 1950-51

Thursday League winners for season 1951-52

Derek Dooley on the extreme left of this 1950s photograph of the Brightside and Carbrook football team. I would imagine Mr Mcleod is one of the players within this photograph.

Players through the eras 1960s

PAUL CLARK played for the **Sheffield Boys Club select team** when they reached and won the Gillette sponsored **National Boys Club Final** in 1960, which was played at Craven Cottage, the home of **Fulham FC**, who were in the top Division of English football at the time.

Images can be seen of the team photo, the match programme and the young men receiving the Winners Trophy.

Sheffield Boys Club select XI

PAUL CLARKE – 1951 -1982 (in his own words)

I first played in what might be called a match in 1951 when my school Malin Bridge played Parkside Road School in Hillsborough Park. A teacher from each school set out markers to indicate the playing area and two posts at each end acted as the goals. The game was a goalless draw although I was certain I had scored with a header but the teacher refereeing the game decided it would have gone over the crossbar had there been one.

I went to Firth Park Grammar School in 1953 and during the next five years played in the Under 14 and Under 15 teams and, in my last year, the 1st X1. We had regular fixtures throughout the season playing other grammar schools. All the games were on a Saturday morning and although there was no league to compete in home, and away fixtures were arranged and played on pitches which were clearly marked although only very rarely did the goals have nets. We really looked like a team wearing the school colours. The shirts had buttoned up fronts and sleeves. We provided our own shorts and socks in a variety of shades. In those days football boots had studs which you nailed into the sole and quite often would lose a stud or two as the season progressed. We travelled to away fixtures by public transport with a teacher in charge and different members of staff would act as referee for the home games. Most of our matches were in or around Sheffield but we had fixtures against the grammar schools of Barnsley, Maltby and Chesterfield. One of the Chesterfield team was Bob Wilson who went on to become a big name in the game as a goalkeeper for Arsenal and Scotland before becoming a TV pundit.

My teammates during those years included Jim Smith, who was to make a name for himself in later years as manager of several clubs including Blackburn Rovers, Birmingham City, Newcastle United, Oxford United, QPR and Derby County. Another to become involved in the professional game was Dave Allen who was for a time Chairman of Sheffield Wednesday and currently holds the same position at Chesterfield. One term there was great excitement when Jimmy Hagan came to the school and supervised four training sessions. Jimmy was one of the stars of the Sheffield United team and had played internationals for England.

Firth Park School team, Paul is seen on front row second from right

On leaving Firth Park I played my football with Hillsborough Boys' Club. I had been a member at the club since I was 12 and was looking forward to the chance of playing in one of their teams. My first season was in their under 18 second team although I made a few appearances in the first team towards the end of the season. The following season 1959/60 I was a regular in the first team and this was to be the start of three successful years. Our home ground was on Wadsley Common, a somewhat remote part of Sheffield. The pitch was not good like most of the others we played on and generally speaking changing facilities were basic. There were no such things as showers although on a few grounds there was a hosepipe available to wash any muddy boots. The team was a particularly strong one and we won our league. The cup competition we took part in was the Youth Challenge Cup and involved clubs from other leagues. We reached the final and our opponents were the youth team run by Rotherham United FC. This prompted the organising committee to arrange for the final to be played at Millmoor, Rotherham's football league ground. We had our own small group of regular supporters, principally dads, but this game attracted a large crowd made up predominantly of people who had come to see the young Rotherham United hopefuls. Most of them went away disappointed as we won 4-0 and I was thrilled to score one of the goals.
Several of the team, including myself, were selected to represent Sheffield in the National Association of Boys' Clubs cup competition. Run on the same lines as the FA Cup we played through several rounds in different parts of the country. We reached the semi-final and were drawn at home against Durham the match taking place at Bramall Lane. I had played well in the early rounds, scoring twice, but had not been on form for the quarter final played in Wolverhampton and was dropped for the semi. However when the squad reported to the SUFC dressing room an hour before kick-off it was clear one of the team was carrying an injury and I was back in the team. I had a better game and set up the only goal in our 1-0 win. Bramall Lane was still a three sided ground used for both football and cricket and the match was played under floodlights. I was playing on the left wing and after just a few minutes the ball went out for a throw in and I instinctively ran after it only to suddenly find myself running on to the cricket wicket in almost complete darkness. Our final opponents were London Boys' Clubs and the final was played at Craven Cottage the home of Fulham FC. Although I travelled down to London with the squad the team chosen for the final was the one originally picked for the semi so, having played in every round, I watched the final from the trainer's bench. In those days substitutes had not yet been introduced. Once again Sheffield won 1-0 and we returned home with the trophy and I also received a winner's medal.
Some consolation came when I was chosen to be one of three players from Sheffield to be part of the Yorkshire Association of Boys' Clubs party to undertake a tour of Germany in the summer. This was a representative group and included boys from Leeds, Huddersfield, Hull and Middlesbrough. We met up in London to travel by road and ferry to the German region of Westphalia. The first two days we stayed with families but after that we were accommodated at different athletic centres and I was amazed at the facilities and coaching available for all types of sport. Our first game was against Dortmund. We hardly knew one another and played like it. We were soundly beaten.
We moved on to Winterberg and this, for me, was the highlight of the tour. Winterberg is a major winter sports venue. It was also the location of a large British Armed Forces camp. Posters around the area advertised the match against Yorkshire-we even saw one indicating Germany was playing England. We received great support from hundreds of British soldiers at the match and ran out winners England 4-Germany 2 a score to be repeated in the World Cup six years later. All the squad had a chance of playing at some stage and I did not take part in the final game which probably accounts for the fact that I can't remember either the location or the result.
Back home the Hillsborough Boys' Club team moved into an Under 21 league which we won for the next two seasons. However there was no cup competition for this age group so we were entered for the Sheffield Junior Shield, an open age competition. We were losing finalists in 1961-62. There was thought given to continuing the following season in one of the many open age leagues but it was the right time to move on and make way for the next era of Hillsborough Boys' Club teams who continued to be successful for some years.

Paul's Father, Thomas, also won local medals, winning the Works Premier League 1938 and 1939 and also the Darnall Medical Aid trophy pictured below.

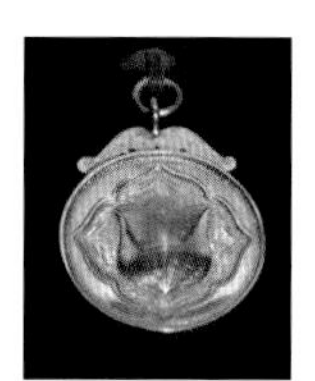

Two medals presented to T Clarke for Works Premier Division II in 1937-38 and 1938-39
Left: A personal trophy for Darnall Medical Aid Cup

Players through the eras: 1970s-80s

MIKE LIVERSIDGE first played in local football in Sheffield in the **Bible Class** and **Junior Leagues** in 1963. Throughout the 1960s and 1970s he played in the **Friendlies League, Sports and Athletic League, Hatchard League, County Senior League, Amateur League, Yorkshire League, Wragg League** and the **South Yorkshire Amateur League.**

On Sundays he played in the **Sheffield & District Sunday League, Sunday Imperial League** and the **Sunday Regional Alliance League.**

Football teams he turned out for were **Brightside, Carbrook United, The Bird in Hand, Woodhouse West End, Hadfields, Saint Thomas Mores, Bayfield, Saddle** (pictured below), **Grimesthorpe, Roman Ridge, Waterworks, Pheasant, Three Tuns, Park Wanderers, White Hart, William Hill,** and **Old Blue Ball.**

He could probably add another 50 plus appearances for various local teams. When he had no game on a Saturday or Sunday he just took his boots and without fail ended up playing for a team who were short of a player. Without a car, at that time, the venues would have been Concord, Longley or Parson Cross Parks. These three parks had about 50 pitches between them and out of the hundred or so teams you could always find a club that were in need of a player, or two.

His final game, at the ripe old age of 54, was in 2004 when he broke his leg in the last game of the season for **William Hill FC** (**Sunday Regional Alliance League**).

Over the years Mike won **Wragg League** and **Wragg Cup** winner medals in the 1970s. Played in a **Sheffield Junior Shield** final and after a 2-2 draw with **Maltby** (a game in which a penalty was missed) lost in a closely fought replay. These trophies and runners up tankard were won whilst he played for **Woodhouse West End WMC** Football Club.

He also won **Sunday Imperial League** winner's and runners up medals during the 1970s, as **Park Wanderers FC** and later renamed **Three Tuns FC** progressed from the Third Division to the Premier Division. He also appeared twice in losing sides in **Sunday Imperial League Cup finals**.

Saddle FC

Players through the eras: 1990s-2000s

After suffering ruptured cruciate ligaments Mike was told that he would probably never play football again. At 28 years of age that was a very distressing period, not made any easier by going through three operations on his left knee over a two-year period.

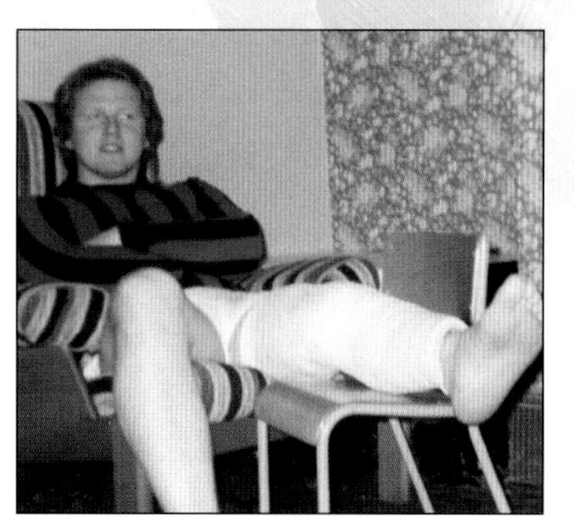

A benefit game for Mike was organised and played between Saddle Select XI and a **Johnny Quinn's All-Stars XI** which included United and Wednesday players such as the England Internationals **Peter Swan, Gerry Young** and one-time England, Sheffield Wednesday & Leeds manager **Howard Wilkinson**.

After undergoing physiotherapy to try and strengthen the injured leg, he decided to try playing again, which was, against medical advice. He returned to his old teams The **Saddle** on Saturdays and the **Three Tuns** on Sundays. Unfortunately, after a few games when the knee would swell up, Mike soon realised it was obvious that it was perhaps best that he followed his Doctor's advice. Mike decided to stop playing, which he did for about 10 years, before trying again in the 1990s turning out for a couple of sides, when they were short of players, before getting back to playing regularly on Sundays for **William Hill FC**, for whom his son Mark played. Billy Hills, as they were affectionately known to the players, played their games in the **Sunday Regional Alliance League.** He played and managed this team for a good few years until just before his 54th birthday, in 2004, when another injury, a broken leg, put an end to his footballing participation enjoyment for good.

Wragg League award for KO Cup and below Wragg League winners trophy

Saddle Select versus the Johnny Quinn All Stars

A Benefit Match in aid of
MICK LIVERSIDGE

ALL STARS XI

VERSUS

SADDLE SELECT

KICK OFF 3.00p.m.

ON

Sunday 2nd April 1978

ON THE

Brightside & Carbrook Ground
Bellhouse Rd. Shiregreen

Promoter Mr Edward Cox — Programme 10p

Four Sunday Imperial awards for Division One, Two and Three and Cup finals between 1974-1977

Tankard presented to the runners-up in the 1971 Sheffield Junior Shield final

Chapter Two
Local Sheffield and District Teams

Three Tuns 1977 with Sunday Imperial League Division One Trophy

Images of local football teams
spanning over 130 years - dates given if known

Dungworth (in white sleeves) outside the Royal Hotel, Dungworth

Stannington Football Club c1940-50. Photographed with the Crown and Glove public house looming in background

Dinnington Miners Welfare, Junior Cup Winners 1956-57 season

Edgar Allen, first winners of the Tinsley Charity Shield in 1918-19

Goldthorpe United, 1903-04

Marlcliffe, finalists in Sheffield Junior Friendlies League 1913-14

Anston Reading Room Football Club 1926-27

Brightside Church who played in Sheffield Bible Class League c1950s

Target (public house team) 1908-09 season

Sheffield Cold Stores 1911-12

Meadow Hall Football Club 1916-17

Arbourthorne Comm., Tinsley Charity Shield winners 1971

Attercliffe Baptist Football Club 1901-02

Central Thursday, League Cup Final winners in 1951

Brown Bayleys, 1927

Storrs United football team 1908 (Stannington area of Sheffield)

Brightside and Carbrook, circa 1950s - Derek Dooley on the left

Woodhouse West End WMC won Sheffield Junior League in season 1929

All Saints

Corkers

Langsett

Dore Football Club 1935-36 with Sheffield Amateur League trophy

Unknown Sheffield football team image taken from a postcard produced by an Attercliffe printer circa 1914

Stannington Village Football Team c1920-30s

Gower Albion Burngreave area 1908-09

Daniel Doncaster of the Haig League circa 1959-60

Handsworth Rovers multiple trophy winners in 1907

Heeley Red Lion circa 1999

Kilnhurst Town outside the Pavilion on the recreation ground, season 1944/45 winners of the Rotherham Charity Cup.

Hemsworth Villa circa 1982

Heeley Church 1913-14

Worrall winners in 1952 of the AJ Sanders trophy at Niagara ground

Kimberworth Wesleyans 1907 displaying a list of their achievements

Jonas Colver (Premier 11) probably Works League - season 1923-24

Sheffield Transport reached the final of the Billy Butlins Trophy, a national tournament. STFC lost the final tie 2-1 in London in 1971

Norton Woodseats pictured in the early 1950s

Sheffield Boys football team in the late 1950s - Gordon Banks, goalkeeper, within a decade of winning a World Cup Winners medal in1966

Oughtibridge 1919-20

Langsett

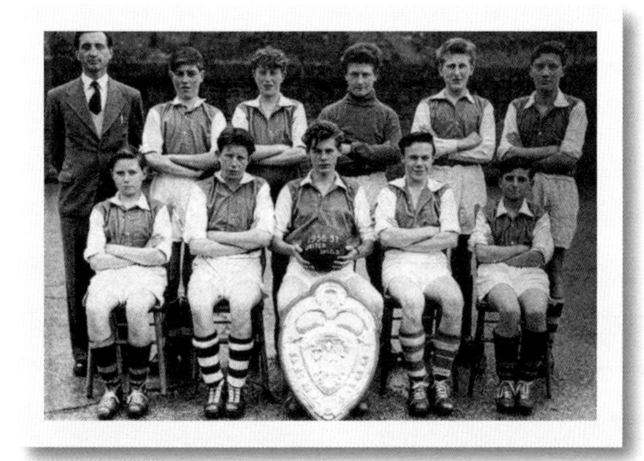

Morley Street School team who won the United Shield (pictured) in 1957

Greenhawk who played in the Sunday Regional League in the 1970s

Sheffield Public Works Department circa 1966

Western District Sorting Office, winners of the Postmans cup 1908

Tinsley Methodists, c1920s

Steel, Peech and Tozer (Phoenix) 1917

Parson Cross, circa 1960s

Park Youth Club football team in the 1950s

Parson Cross with trophies. One of the cups was for winning the Sheffield Amateur League Div. 1 1957-58

Sheffield Football Club - Whitbread County Senior League Cup winners 1988

Attercliffe Police Football Team 1914

Jack in a Box, Tinsley Trophy winners 2015

Brinsworth Athletic, 2001 with Rotherham Charity Cup

Walkley

Wadsley Bridge Spts. A, Friendlies League Div 5 Champions 1970-71

Hadfield Sports 1930

F.P.O.B. 1916-17

Hallam Football Club

Wadsley Bridge W.M.C.

Norton Woodseats 1953

Woodhouse Mill WMC winners of three trophies - Sheffield Junior Cup, Aston Nursing Cup and the Kelley Cup all in 1949-50 season

Worrall FC captain receiving the AJ Sanders trophy after beating Royal Standard in the final at the Niagara ground Hillsborough 1952

Hillsborough Tabernacle with Sheffield Adult Schools Shield 1911-12 George William Crookes Swift - third from left middle row

Graves Park FC, winners of the A.J. Sanders trophy in the early 1960s

Birchinlee Football Club 1908-09

Tinsley Wire Industries, in 1959 they won the National Wiredrawers Cup

Abbey Glen, circa 1940s

Carbrook Elementary School team with trophies for the 1937-38 season

Sheffield Public Works Department Football Club

Mosborough United Football Club shown in season 1897-98

Waggon and Horses

Totley Football Club 1909.

Rotherham YMCA, members of the South Yorks Amateur League-winners of league in 1935-36. Image from an Ardath tobacco produced photocard

Ravens FC, members of the South Yorks Amateur League. Image from an Ardath tobacco produced photocard

Brunswick Methodists, winner of the Free Churches League in 1934. Image from an Ardath tobacco produced photocard

Woodthorpe Amateurs, of the Public Works League 1935-36. Also Champions of Rudyard League. Image from an Ardath tobacco photocard

Stocksbridge Church Football Club, winners of the Sheffield Minor League title in 1914-15.

Woodbourne Alliance members of the Intermediate League. Winners in 1935-36. Image from an Ardath tobacco produced photocard

New Stubbin - winners of the Sheffield Amateur League in 1934-35 season. Image from an Ardath tobacco produced photocard

King Edward VII School - in 1934-35 season 'King Teds' scored 181 goals. Image from an Ardath tobacco produced photocard

Cole Brothers - formed in 1880s as the Morning Star FC. Play in Thursday League. Image from an Ardath tobacco produced photocard

Crookes Congs, Winners of the AJ Sanders trophy 1936. Competed in Friendlies League. Image from an Ardath tobacco produced photocard

Fulwood Champions of Amateur League and Junior Cup in 1936. Image from an Ardath tobacco produced photocard

Burlington Sports, members of the Public Parks League. Image from an Ardath tobacco produced photocard

Abbeydale St Peter's - Sheffield Adult League and Sheffield Church League. Image from an Ardath tobacco produced photocard

Balfour was made up of workers from the Capital Steel Works and played in the SYAL. Image from an Ardath tobacco produced photocard

Upper Heeley WMC won Heeley Challenge Cup in 1935. Play in City League. Image from an Ardath tobacco produced photocard

S & E Co-op Sports play in the Sheffield Thursday Friendlies League. Image from an Ardath tobacco produced photocard

Sheffield City Police, Thursday Friendlies League. Six times Yorkshire Police Lge Champs. Image from an Ardath tobacco produced photocard

Lopham Street Methodist Football Club

Sheffield Bankers, members of the South Yorks Amateur League. Founded in 1890s. Image from an Ardath tobacco produced photocard

Sheffield Teachers, members of the South Yorks Amateur League 1935-36 season. Image from an Ardath tobacco produced photocard

Unknown Sheffield team possibly from the Heeley District of Sheffield

Oak Street - Team originating from the Heeley District of Sheffield

Arbourthorne EA A pictured in 2011

Attercliffe United winners of three trophies. Sheffield Minor League, Darnall Medical Aid Cup and the Tinsley Charity Shield. Season 1922-23

Heeley Valley Road Sunday School team 1916-17

Hallam

Carbrook United who played in the Sheffield Friendlies League 1965-67. Home ground Pitch 14 Concord Park, Shiregreen. Note: A player short

Bird in Hand - South Yorkshire Amateur League 1968-69.

Saddle - first game in Amateur League 1977. Team known previously as St Thomas More of the South Yorkshire Amateur League 1975-76

Three Tuns Taverners 1977, Sunday Imperial League Div. 1 winners with trophy

Anston Utd 1933-34 with Aston-cum-Aughton Cup

Grenoside Church 1913-14, Bible Class, Junior Cup and unknown trophy

Hathersage Football Club in 1934 with G H Lawrence Cup

Public Works Department Football Club

Hallam Football Club - pictured in the mid 1950s this team play on the oldest known football ground in the world.

Whitby Road School, Darnall - season 1952-53

Public Works Department - Derek Holland goalkeeper

Pack Horse FC - Meadowhall Sunday League Cup final runners up Jamie Cooke of Arctic Monkeys fame is 3rd from left on front row.

Royal Earl - Meadowhall Sunday League Cup final winners defeating Pack Horse opposite - game played at Bramall Lane

Corkers

Sheffield City Surveyors - in the mid 1960s this team won Works Premier League and Arthur Lees Cup in three consecutive seasons

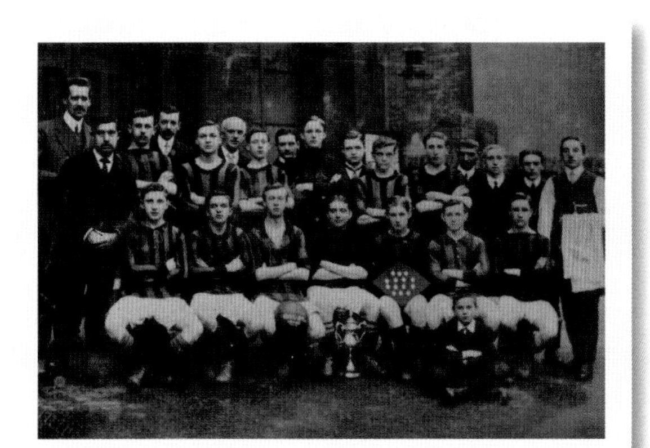

Oak Street - Team originating from the Heeley District of Sheffield.

Old Blue Ball, Hillsborough - Sunday Regional Alliance League

Tramways Football Club, First Eleven, 1908-1909

Dronfield Town U21s

Hackenthorpe of the Meadowhall Sunday League

Mosborough A of the Meadowhall Sunday League

Coleridge Road Council School, Tinsley Charity Shield winners

Beighton Miners Welfare

Intake Ball Inn

Mosborough United season 1897-98

Newhall Road Junior Football Club (School team) 1957

Hillsborough Tabernacle picture supplied George William Crookes Swift

Handsworth Turf Tavern one of the most successful sides in the Meadowhall Sunday League, Cup and League winners

Hillsborough Tabernacle picture supplied George William Crookes Swift

Rawson Spring, Meadowhall Sunday League-League Cup winners

Heeley Friends 1912-13

St James

Totley Sports Football Club outside the Little John public house in Hathersage after winning the Dore Shield in the late 1930s.

William Hills Football Club 2004 Sunday Regional Alliance League

Wadsley Bridge WMC

Unknown team- image taken from a Sheffield postcard

Chapter Three
Medals and Trophies

Sheffield and District football local league medals

N.U.R.O.F. Shield Winners Medal

Thursday League Runners-Up Medal 1950-51

Minor League Winners Medal 1922-23

T & D League, Sheffield F.C. 1924-25 won by George Loukes

Rotherham & Dist Sunday School Football Lge 1920-21 won by R Charnock

Osborn's Football Knockout Cup Winners Medal 1920

Intermediate League 16-18 Winners Medal 1931-32

Attercliffe and District Challenge Cup Medal 1905-06

Sheffield and District football local league medals

Sheffield Works Beatty League Winners Medal 1948-49

Sheffield Works Premier League Winners Medal 1948-49

Sheffield Churches Football Senior League Winners Medal 1933-34

Reservoir Football Club Winners Medal in 1901, unknown competition

Thursday Amateur League, Runners-Up Medal won by Joe Beer 1924-25

Sheffield Amateur League, Runners-Up Medal in 1906-07. W. H. Hobday

Thursday Amateur League, Winners Medal won by Joe Beer 1926-27

Sheffield and District Works Sports Association Premier League Medal

Sheffield and District football local league medals

Beatty League Winners Medal 1950-51

Hatchard Cup Medal 1919-20

Junior League Runners-Up Medal 1919-20 presented to H. White

Sheffield Thursday League Medal, Whitworth F.C.- G. T. Bott 1893

Penistone & District Football League 1934 won by F. Caffrey

Gold Medal - Hallam Football Club 1925 - WTW

Sheffield Licensed Victuallers - League winners 1907-08 presented to W Broadhurst of the Great Britain Hotel, John Street

Sheffield Licensed Victuallers - League winners 1906-07 presented to W Broadhurst of the Great Britain Hotel, John Street

Sheffield and District football local league medals

Senior Challenge Cup Winners Medal 1933-34

Sheffield Free Churches League Winners Medal 1905-06 won by T W Smith

Senior Challenge Cup Winners Medal 1950-51
won by Don Holland who played for Hallam

Association League Winners Medal 1949-50
won by Don Holland who played for Hallam

Senior Challenge Cup Winners Medal 1942-43 War Time game

Amateur League Runners-Up Medal won by F Couldwell of Hathersage

Sheffield Works- Raleigh League, Runners-Up Medal 1925-26

Wharncliffe League Winners Medal 1901-1902 won by S Bright

Sheffield and District football local league medals

Hope Valley League Runners-Up Medal 1945-46 awarded to P Frith

Sheffield Works Drake League Winners Medal 1927-28

Amateur League Winners Medal, Tinsley Church 1909-10

Minor League Winners Medal for 1908-09 won by H Jenkinson

Sheffield Works - Beatty League 1919-20 won by Habershons Sports Club

Sheffield Sports and Athletic League Winners 1921-22

Wragg Football League Runners-Up Medal 1921-22

Heeley and District League Winners Medal 1901 won by J Hornbuckle

Sheffield and District football local league medals

Clegg Challenge Shield Medal 1923-24 - J. Popplewell, Hillsborough Club

Clegg Challenge Shield Medal 1914-15 - H. H. Bailey

United Challenge Shield Medal 1918-19 - E. Haslehurst

Clegg Challenge Shield Medal - G. E. Greathurst

United Challenge Shield Medal 1912 - F J Smith

Clegg Challenge Shield Medal won by G. Loukes

Wednesday Challenge Shield Medal 1912 - F. Foster

Wednesday Challenge Shield Medal 1932-33 - A. F. Bell

Sheffield and District football local league medals

A group of four trophies presented by the Sheffield Sunday Imperial League for Winning and finishing Runners-Up in the 1st, 2nd and 3rd divisions, all won by Park Wanderers

Wragg League Winners and League Cup Winners Trophies 1971 won by Woodhouse West End WMC Football Club

Tinsley Charity Cup Competition - Runners-Up medal 1951
Won by K Macleod whilst playing for Brightside and Carbrook Sports

Sheffield and Hallamshire Junior Shield Runners-Up Tankard 1971

Thursday League - Winners Medal 1951-52
Won by K Macleod whilst playing for Co-op Sports

Drake Knock Out Cup Winners 1919-20 won by Edgar Allen F.C.

Sheffield and District football local league medals

Penistone Cup Medal-Competition Winners

Association League Medal 1919-20

City League, Runners-Up Medal for 1938-39 won by A. Thornhill

Sheffield Parks League Champions Medal, 1939-40

Haig League Division One Runners-Up Medal 1968-69

Sheffield Works - Beatty League Winners Medal

Junior League Runners-Up Medal 1931-32 won by E. Ogden

Attercliffe FC presented this medal on Christmas day 1894 to W Smith for services rendered

Sheffield and District football local league medals

Amateur League Winners Trophy 1939-40

Sports and Athletic League-Senior Winners Medal 1964-65 won by E. Hill

K.R.M. - A & D League Winners Medal in 1901-02 won by J Hornbuckle

Sheffield Works League Runners-Up for 1913-14 won by J. Angus

A.S. Lee Cup
A cigarette lighter engraved to H. Hopkinson dated 1945-46

Intermediate League 16-18 Winners Medal 1928-29

Intermediate Cup 16-18 Winners Medal 1942-43 - War Time

Sheffield and District football local league medals

Carbrook Challenge Cup
Runners-Up Medal presented to T Eyre of Worksop Town in 1891

Carbrook Challenge Cup Winners Medal

S&H County FA. Invitation Challenge Cup Medal 1936-37

S&H County FA. Junior Challenge Cup Winners Medal 1937-38

Sports and Athletic League - Premier Division Winners Medal 1938-39

Sports and Athletic League - Premier Division Winners Medal 1937-38

Association Cup Winners Medal, won by Thorncliffe Rec 1952-53

Wharncliffe Charity Cup Winner Medal won by Thorncliffe Rec 1946-47

Sheffield and District football local league medals

Sheffield Adult Schools Cup 1923-24

The Dore Challenge Shield Winners Medal 1947

Holbrook Junior Cup Winners Medal 1914-15

Intermediate League Division 2 Champions 1941-42 war time medal

Intermediate League 14-16 Champions 1935-36

S&H CFA Challenge Cup winners 1906-07
won by William Lloyd of The Wednesday

Minor Championship Runners-Up Medal 1951-52

Works Premier League Winners Medal 1945-46 by H. Hopkinson

Sheffield and District football local league medals

Works Leagues, Raleigh League Runners-Up Medal for 1922

Works Leagues, Beatty League Runners-Up Medal for 1924-25

Holbrook & District League Cup-Winners Medal 1924-25 won by H Briggs

Holbrook & District League K.O. Cup
Winners Medal 1928-29 won by H Briggs

Holbrook & District League Cup-Winners Medal 1927-28 won by H Briggs

Sports and Athletic League Senior Division-Runners-Up Medal 1931-32

Works Leagues, Drake League 14-16 Winners Medal 1928-29

Works Leagues, Raleigh League Winners Medal 1925-26

Sheffield and District football local league medals

Works Leagues: Beatty League Runners-Up Medal 1919-20 Laycocks Sports

Totley and District Football League Winners Medal 1904-05

Sports and Athletic League-Senior Division Runners-Up 1950-51

Amateur League Winners Medal 1913-14

Thursday Amateur League Winners 1922-23
Original presentation box

Junior League Winners Medal won for season1902-03 by Sale Memorial
Original presentation box

Sheffield and District football local league medals

Hope Valley Football League Champions in 1933-34 won by Totley Sports

Catholic League Winners Medal 1935

Thursday Challenge Cup Winners Medal 1947-48

Works League: Drake League Winners 1919-20 won by Edgar Allens FC

Hatchard Cup Runners-Up Medal 1906-07

Holbrook Challenge Cup joint holders 1914 won by Clifford Oldfield

S&H CFA Junior Challenge Cup Winners Medal 1931-32

Tinsley Charity Competition-Winners Medal in 1933-34

Sheffield and District football local league medals

Wragg Challenge Cup won in 1905-06 by Clifford Oldfield

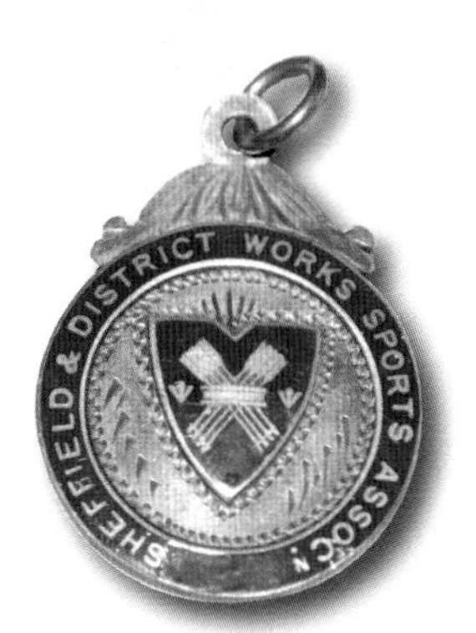

Drake League Knockout Winners Medal in 1919-1920 won by I. Milner of Edgar Allen F.C.

Wragg Challenge Cup won in 1906-07 by Clifford Oldfield

Works Leagues, Beatty League, Winners Medal in 1949-50

Woodhouse Kelley Cup 1937

Hope Valley Football League Winners Medal 1929-30 won by Totley Sports

S&H CFA-Senior Challenge Cup-Runners-Up Medal 1939-1940

S&H CFA-Senior Challenge Cup-Winners Medal 1937-38

Sheffield and District football local league medals

Hatchard League Champions in 1951-52 won by Thorncliffe Rec

S & D W.S.A. League Winners Medal1926-27

Sheffield Churches Football Senior League Runners-Up 1934-35

Sheffield Friends Adult League Winners 1911-12 won by C. Swift

City League Runners-Up Medal - 1948-49

Handsworth Cup Lapel Pin 1938, won by Arthur Eaton

Three Medals all won by Arthur Eaton when playing for Thorncliffe Rec

Sheffield and District football local league medals

Haig League Champions in 1929-30

Works Premier League Winners Medal 1948-49

Atlas & Norfolk Departmental League Winners Medal 1926-27

Premier League: Runners-Up 1919-20 won by Sandersons Sports

Atlas & Norfolk Departmental League Runners-Up Medal 1927-28

Atlas & Norfolk Boys Departmental League Winners Medal 1928-29

Wednesday Shield Winners Medal 1901-02

Intermediate League 14-16 Winners Medal in 1937-38

Sheffield and District football local league medals

Wednesday Shield won by G. H. Mellar in 1912

Clegg Shield also won by G. H. Mellar who was the captain in 1912-13

Wragg League Cup, Runners-Up 1927-28

Thursday Amateur League, Runners-Up 1947-48

Hope Valley Amateur Football League Badge/Pin

Wednesday Shield won by T. French in 1928-29

Wednesday Shield won by W. Hakes in 1913-14

Wednesday Shield won by H. Webster in 1918-19

Sheffield and District football local league medals

Sheffield & Hallamshire County Football Association
Invitation Challenge Cup Medal 1936-37
Won by Doncaster Rover Reserves

Sheffield Junior Challenge Cup
Winners Medal 1911-12
Won by Eckington Red Rose

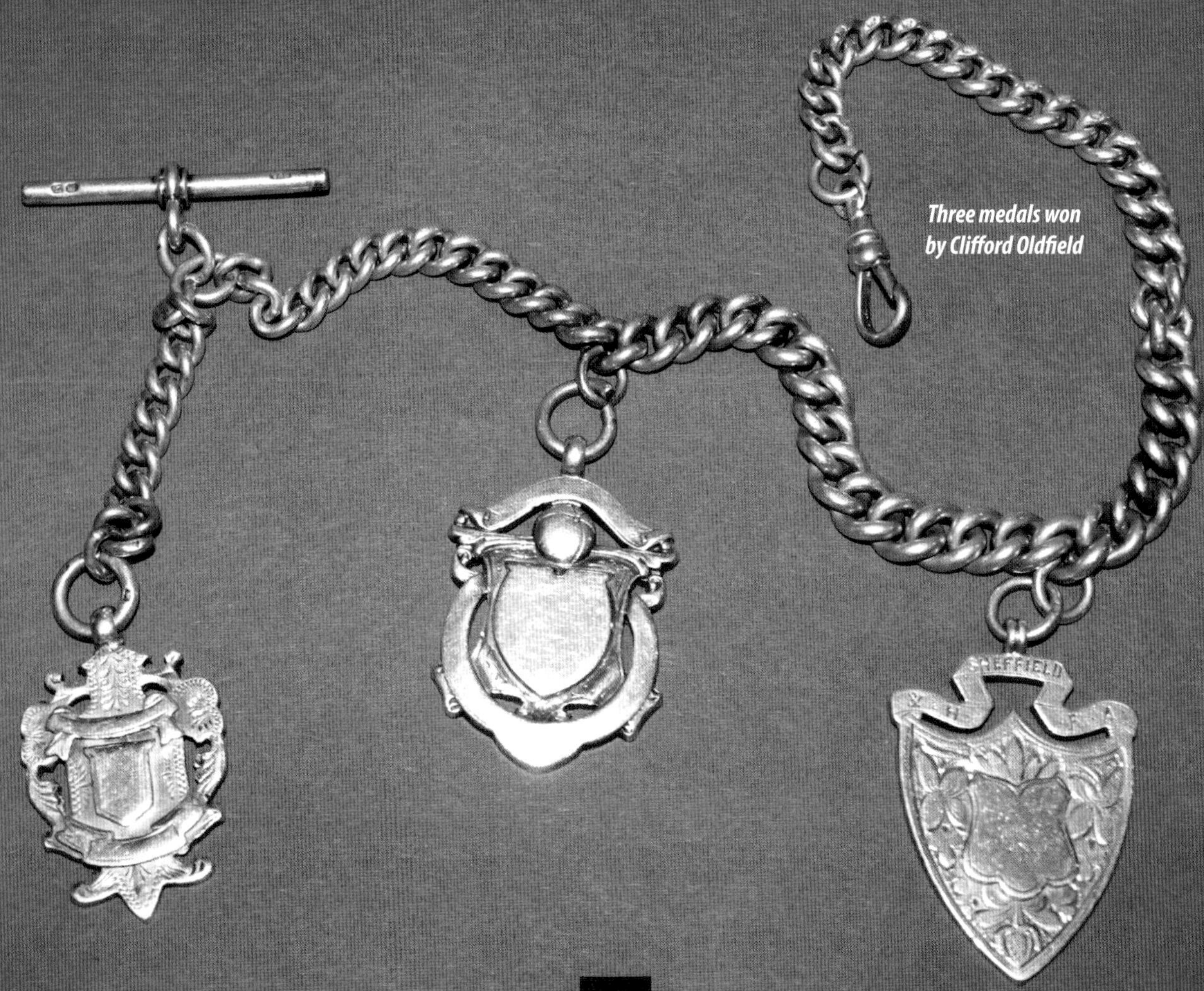

Three medals won
by Clifford Oldfield

Sheffield and District football local league trophies

The Youdan Cup, first ever football trophy

Cromwell Cup - 1868

Aston cum Aughton Hospital Charity Cup

The Wragg League Sid Butterfield Shield

The Wragg League Knock-out Cups

Ecclesfield Red Rose winning the Tinsley Charity Football Shield. This shield was a gift from Mr. G. Vickers in 1922.

Sports and Athletic League Division One

Sports and Athletic League Division Two

Sports and Athletic League - Ben Cup Runner-up

Sheffield and District football local league trophies

Amateur League Knockout Cup

Wragg League

Wharncliffe Charity Cup

South Yorkshire Amateur Div. II

Tinsley Charity Cup

Steel Peech and Tozer Inter Departmental Cup

Sports and Athletic League Kenning Cup

Sports and Athletic League Inter League Runner up

Sports and Athletic League Ben Cup Winners

Sheffield and District football local league trophies

South Yorkshire Amateur League Shield

South Yorkshire Amateur League Division One

South Yorkshire Amateur Premier Division League

Sheffield Works Sports Association
Haig League-Division One

Sheffield Works Sports Ass. Beatty Shield

Sheffield Works Sports Ass. Premier Division

Sheffield & Hallamshire Youth Cup Under 16

Sheffield & Hallamshire Junior League

Sheffield & Hallamshire Senior Cup

Sheffield and District football local league trophies

County Senior League Cup 1877
Former Hallamshire FA Challenge Cup

South Yorkshire Amateur League Cup

Sheffield Works Sports Association
Haig League Division One

Sheffield Licensed Victuallers League Cup

Sheffield Licensed Victuallers League Shield

Sheffield and District League 1889 Shield
First Football League in Sheffield

Sheffield Licensed Victuallers
Intermediate Challenge Cup

Sheffield & Hallamshire Early CLosing League
aka Thursday League

Sheffield & Hallamshire County Cup

Sheffield and District football local league trophies

Sheffield & Hallamshire Midweek League

Sheffield & Hallamshire Association Cup

Sheffield & Hallamshire Challenge Cup

Friendlies League Sporting Award

AJ Sanders Trophy, Friendlies League

Nomads Sunday League

Hatchard Cup

Hallamshire Sunday League Division Three

Amateur League Sporting Award

Sheffield and District football local league medals

Chapter Four
Local Leagues & Winners

FOREWORD BY CHRIS EYRE

The league and cup winners in the following section are as a result of many years spent by myself going through local newspapers in the Sheffield and Rotherham Archives. Also various league handbooks have been found with winner's details in them and some of the cups and trophies illustrated in this book have proved a great source of information. The Sheffield Telegraph football guides, which were produced from 1908 to 1960, and the Sheffield Independent Football guide which was produced for several years until 1939, have proved a valuable source of information.

Also the Secretaries of the various competitions still running have been of great help as have other like-minded football historians in the area. I'd like to thank you all for your help.

Whilst trying to cover the first 150 years, I have had to restrict the Competitions listed to those that ran for a realistic time. In the 1880s and 1890s there were many local knock out competitions, often run by pub landlords on a spare piece of land at the side of his establishment. The winners would receive medals or jerseys and the landlord would hopefully have increased trade. Numerous pubs had pitches at the side of them, some like the Ball Inn at Heeley being in operation until quite recently. This ground and the Sheaf Hotel ground on Bramall Lane were used by many of the early Competitions to host their finals

However, The Sheffield Sunday School Football Union Competition, which started in 1887, had a rule that teams could not change or play on a public house ground. This rule was eventually dropped when they started to play their own finals on the Ball Inn or Sheaf grounds.

The actual first league in Sheffield was the Sheffield & District League, being formed in 1889. The first league in England was the Football League which was formed a year earlier. The S&D league included the Reserve teams from Barnsley, Chesterfield (Chesterfield Town), Rotherham Town (Rotherham United), Sheffield United (Sheffield Strollers) and Sheffield Wednesday (Wednesday Wanderers). This league caused other adult leagues to start up, more details of which you will find in the "Football in the 1890s" section.

Other areas, especially the Attercliffe area, ran various competitions such as the Carbrook Challenge Cup and the Lewis Cup. By the 1890s various adult leagues were being set up in the Sheffield and District area. Quite a few were also geared at the under 16 year olds. Some of note were the All Saints League (Attercliffe area), Abbeydale & District League, Heeley & District League, High Hazel League, Hillsborough & District League and the Sheffield East End League. However, reporting on these leagues in the press was very spasmodic and so it is impossible to work out a full list of winners. However, photos of medals for the Carbrook Challenge Cup, the Lewis Cup and the All Saints League are included in the book.

In compiling the list of competition winners, I have used my best endeavour to get all the winners, but you will notice that there are a few gaps. The problem is that in the early days of football, the team at the top of the division was not always the Leagues winner. The leagues divided the teams that entered into divisions. This was the meaning of the division in those days. There was no promotion or relegation, so teams stayed in the same division each season. However, they only had one cup to play for. Because of this, the practice was for the top teams in each division to play a knock-out competition to decide the overall League winners. These winners are not always easy to find. The press did not help as they had a cut-off date for football in their papers. Often you would find details of a final to be played on a certain Saturday, but in the following week's issue there was no report because it was now the cricket season, and only cricket was reported on.

Also the press worked on the principle that they did not report on old news, so if the competition was late forwarding their report, then it was not used. Some leagues at times just appeared to not report their results all season for some reason. Some cup competition's reported right up to the semi-final stage and gave a date for the final, obviously to attract a crowd, but then did not forward a report on their final. You will come across years when I have put team A or team B were in the final, but I have no idea who won. You will find this in the Darnall Medical Aid and Tinsley Charity Cup Competitions.

I am always on the lookout for old team photos, league handbooks or forgotten about cups and trophies gathering dust in somebody's attic or garage. These items will help to expand my data records.

These are often in various states of disrepair. There is a photo in the book of the first Darnall Medical Aid Cup which was used for the winners until 1933. This was found in a garage recently. It has a dent on the lip of the cup and woodworm in the base. I now intend to have this cup repaired to "as new" condition. Also in the book is a photo of the Tinsley Charity Challenge Cup which operated in the 1950's. Unfortunately, this now appears to be beyond repair.

Information on lost items or some of the missing winners would be appreciated and I can be contacted on 01709 541619 or through the printers of the book.

Chris Eyre

THE BEGINNING OF ORGANISED FOOTBALL IN SHEFFIELD

By CHRIS EYRE (S&HCFA Area Historian)

It is accepted that Sheffield FC, who were formed in 1857, were the first football club. However several other clubs set up shortly afterwards including Hallam FC in 1860.

These clubs generally played against other members in the club. Eventually, they started to play in friendly inter-club games against each other on a Saturday afternoon.

In February 1867, local theatre owner Tomas Youdan, put up a cup (actually it was a claret jug) for a football competitions for local teams. 12 prominent teams from the Sheffield area took part in The Youdan Cup competition, which is now accepted as being the first ever football cup competition in the World. The final was between Hallam FC, the winners and Norfolk on 5 March 1867 at Bramall Lane with the second/third play off between Norfolk and Mackenzie on the 9 March 1867.

The 12 teams from the Sheffield area who took part in The Youdan Cup competition, were Broomhall, Fir Vale, Garrick, Hallam, Heeley, Mackenzie, Milton, Norfolk, Norton, Pitsmoor, Wellington and the United Mechanics.

A report appeared in the Sheffield Independent newspaper on 11 March 1867 about a match to be played by players from Sheffield FA against London under the 1867/68 rules of the Sheffield FA later that week. Press reports in respect of football or foot-ball as they often referred to it, was very limited, hence the formation date of the Sheffield Football Association has never been found. However, because of this report, I believe that the Sheffield Football Association was formed by the 12 clubs who took part in The Youdan Cup competition, possibly during the Competition. This reference in the press is the first reference about the Sheffield FA that I have found.

The idea of the Sheffield Football Association was to properly organise local football and players as well as place block adverts in the press on a Saturday in respect of that day's football matches, something that had successfully been done during the Youdan Cup. Previously each club had placed their own adverts, which had become costly.

The Association also set up a players accident society, the first ever one for footballers, to which players paid 1/- on the pretext that they would receive 12/- per week if a football accident prevented them from working. This was a sensible thing to do as many players suffered injuries such as broken collar bones due to the rough nature of the game in those day.

A press report has been found in respect of the first Annual General meeting which took place on Wednesday 9 October 1867 at the Adelphi Hotel, when various alterations to the 1867/68 rules previously published were discussed. However only one rule was amended. H W Chambers (Sheffield FC) was re-elected President, T Clarke (Pitsmoor) Vice-President, J Tomlinson (United Mechanics) Treasurer and W Skinner (Norfolk FC) as Secretary. There were 13 Committee members elected, which was one from each club in membership, Exchange now having joined the original 12 clubs.

A number of new teams had started up, including The Wednesday, all wanting to join the Sheffield FA. However, Sheffield FA would only accept teams into membership that had been running for 2 seasons, and then only on condition that 2 years back subs were paid. Because of this rule, and with the number of new teams increasing, in 1877 a rival organisation was set up under the name of The New Football Association to cater for these teams. This soon became the Hallamshire Football Association. After 10 years of operating in opposition to each other, the two Associations amalgamated at a meeting of the local area clubs in the Lower Room at the Albert Hall on Tuesday 17 May 1887, thus forming the Sheffield & Hallamshire FA. The word County was incorporated into the title many years later. This organisation still controls the running of football today within a radius of 20 miles of Sheffield Cathedral.

The year following the Youdan Cup, another theatre manager, Oliver Cromwell, put up a cup for competition for clubs that had been running for less than two seasons, which was won by The Wednesday. The next major competition was in 1876/77 when the Sheffield FA started the Sheffield Challenge Cup. This competition and cup are still being played for today. The New FA started their own cup competition in 1877/78.

Earl Fitzwilliam gave the Wharncliffe Cup in 1878 to the Sheffield FA for them to run a competition which would help raise money for the local hospitals.

Various other local football cup competitions started, including The Sheffield Sunday School Football Union (1887) which eventually became a league and ran until the Second World War.

However, the first local league was the Sheffield & District League. A full report and photo of the winners shield is included in this book which was formed in 1889, a season after the formation of The Football League. This league ran for 6 seasons and was the inspiration for the many local Sheffield leagues that followed, most of which are included in the pages of this book.

Two of these leagues, the Sheffield (Association) County Senior League (1896) and the Wragg League (1892) are still in operation today.

ALPHABETICAL INDEX to the LOCAL SHEFFIELD AND DISTRICT LEAGUES

SHEFFIELD AMATEUR LEAGUE

1904/05	CLIFTON MISSION
1905/06	SHARROW ST ANDREWS
1906/07	HATHERSAGE
1907/08	MIDLAND JUNIORS
1908/09	PENISTONE CHURCH
1909/10	TINSLEY CHURCH
1910/11	PENISTONE CHURCH
1911/12	ATLAS & NORFOLK WORKS
1912/13	HALLAM
1913/14	HALLAM
1914/15	BLACKBURN
1915-1919	NO COMP WAR
1919/20	HATHERSAGE
1920/21	MALIN BRIDGE OLD BOYS
1921/22	DARNALL OLD BOYS
1922/23	HALLAM
1923/24	NORTON WOODSEATS
1924/25	MALIN BRIDGE OLD BOYS
1925/26	ATTERCLIFFE VICTORY
1926/27	HALLAM
1927/28	DRONFIELD WOODHOUSE
1928/29	STOCKSBRIDGE CHURCH
1929/30	STOCKSBRIDGE CHURCH
1930/31	LOPHAM STREET METHS
1931/32	FULWOOD FC
1932/33	ATLAS & NORFOLK
1933/34	CARBROOK HALL SPORTS
1934/35	NEW STUBBIN COLLIERY
1935/36	DORE FC
1936/37	MALTBY MAIN
1937/38	ECCLESFIELD RED ROSE
1938/39	ST PHILIPS C & I
1939/40	STOCKSBRIDGE WORKS SS

AMALGAMATED WITH CITY LEAGUE AS CITY AMATEUR LEAGUE

1940/41	GRENOSIDE CHURCH SPORTS
1941/42	SWALLOWNEST
1942/43	ATTERCLIFFE RADICALS
1943/44	SHEFFIELD FC
1944/45	NORMANTON SPRINGS

BACK AS AMATEUR LEAGUE

1945/46	TINSLEY PARK WMC
1946/47	TINSLEY PARK COLLIERY WMC
1947/48	HAMPTONS SPORTS
1948/49	AUGHTON JUNIORS
1949/50	OAK STREET
1950/51	AUGHTON JUNIORS
1951/52	TRAVELLERS SPORTS
1952/53	CROOKES WMC
1953/54	WOODHOUSE MILL WMC
1954/55	WOODHOUSE MILL WMC
1955/56	ECCLESFIELD COLLEY ROVERS
1956/57	TRAVELLERS SPORTS
1957/58	PARSON CROSS
1958/59	ECCLESFIELD RED ROSE
1959/60	ECCLESFIELD RED ROSE
1960/61	ECCLESFIELD RED ROSE
1961/62	ECCLESFIELD RED ROSE
1962/63	ECCLESFIELD RR/TRAVELLERS SPORTS (JT) (Note 1)
1963/64	ECCLESFIELD RED ROSE
1964/65	ECCLESFIELD RED ROSE
1965/66	ECCLESFIELD RED ROSE
1966/67	DARNALL LIBERALS
1967/68	ECCLESFIELD RED ROSE
1968/69	ECCLESFIELD RED ROSE
1969/70	ECCLESFIELD RED ROSE
1970/71	ECCLESFIELD RED ROSE
1971/72	ECCLESFIELD RED ROSE
1972/73	WINDSOR
1973/74	WOODHOUSE ASHBERRY
1974/75	WINDSOR
1975/76	WOODHOUSE ASHBERRY
1976/77	MOSBOROUGH TRINITY
1977/78	WINDSOR
1978/79	BELLHOUSE ROAD WMC (Note 2)
1979/80	BELLHOUSE ROAD WMC
1980/81	ARTHUR LEE & SON
1981/82	BRADLEY WELL
1982/83	BRADLEY WELL
1983/84	MOSBOROUGH TRINITY
1984/85	BRADLEY WELL
1985/86	MOSBOROUGH TRINITY
1986/87	MOSBOROUGH TRINITY

DIVISION 2

1961/62	BRINSWORTH ATH
1962/63	(See Note 1)
1963/64	CROOKES WMC
1964/65	MOSBOROUGH TRINITY
1965/66	INTAKE F & SC
1966/67	DARNALL HORTICULTUAL
1967/68	NEW CROSS
1968/69	ST PATRICKS
1969/70	SHEFFIELD LOCO WMC
1970/71	MIDHILL WMC
1971/72	WINDSOR FC
1972/73	DIAL HOUSE SOCIAL
1973/74	BRINSWORTH WMC
1974/75	CROOKES WMC
1975/76	STANIFORTH ARMS
1976/77	WYBOURN HOTEL
1977/78	MANCHESTER VILLA
1978/79	TINSLEY WMC (See Note 2)

DIVISION 3

1962/63	(See Note 1)
1963/64	NO COMP
1964/65	NO COMP
1965/66	HUNTSMAN
1966/67	LOXLEY VILLAGE
1967/68	WOODHOUSE ASHBERRY
1968/69	GRENOSIDE SPORTS
1969/70	MIDHILL WMC

AMATEUR LEAGUE (continued)

LEAGUE KO CUP

The Cup is engraved Amateur League – Knock Out Cup founded 1981/82

1981/82	BRINSWORTH ATHLETIC
1982/83	SHEFFIELD TRADES & LABOUR
1983/84	FORTY FOOT
1984/85	BRADLEY WELL
1985/86	MOSBOROUGH TRINITY
1986/87	NEW STUBBIN COLLIERY

Amateur League Knockout Cup

AMATEUR LEAGUE SPORTING AWARD

This award (Shield) was presented by Boynton Sports in 1976 in memory of P Bramhall

1976/77	TINSLEY WIRE
1977/78	INTAKE S & SC
1978/79	BELLHOUSE ROAD WMC
1979/80	ST PATRICKS
1980/81	WOODHOUSE JUNCTION
1981/82	FORTY FOOT
1982/83	HORTICULTURAL
1983/84	BOYNTON SPORTS
1984/85	ST PATRICKS "B"
1985/86	HANDSWORTH NEW CROWN
1986/87	ST PATRICKS

NOTES

1. Due to bad weather, all leagues abandoned and one cup competition for main trophy played
2. Due to bad weather league competition abandoned and ancillary competitions played instead

Amateur League Runners-Up Medal won by F Couldwell of Hathersage

Amateur League Sporting Award

ASTON – CUM – AUGHTON HOSPITAL CHARITY FOOTBALL CUP

The Cup appears to have first been played for in the 1902/03 season. The Cup has no markings on it, but appears to be silver plate. The Cup was found several years ago and after renovation it now resides in the William Layne reading rooms at Aston (formerly the Aston Reading Room). The competition was previously known as the Aston Hospital Charity Cup. A request was made to Sheffield & Hallamshire FA in 1927 for a new competition, The–Aston–cum-Aughton Nursing Cup, to use the old cup, which was granted. Because of this, it appears that the old competition did not run between 1924 and 1927.

Aston cum Aughton Hospital Charity Cup

1903	KIVETON PARK
1904	KIVETON PARK
1905	KIVETON PARK
1906	CATCLIFFE
1907	KIVETON PARK
1908	KIVETON PARK
1909	DINNINGTON MAIN
1910	DINNINGTON MAIN
1911	BEIGHTON REC
1912	TREETON WESLEYANS
1913	ASTON COLLIERY
1914	ECKINGTON ATH
1915	TREETON READING ROOM
1916	TREETON READING ROOM
1917	TREETON READING ROOM
1918	NO COMPETITION
1919	SWALLOWNEST
1920	SWALLOWNEST
1921	DINNINGTON MAIN
1922	INTAKE WMC
1923	WOODHOUSE FC
1924-1927	NO COMPETITION
1928	ASTON MW
1929	DINNINGTON ATH
1930	WOODHOUSE BRUNSWICK
1931	WOODHOUSE BRUNSWICK
1932	SWALLOWNEST BAPTIST
1933	DINNINGTON LORDENS HOTEL
1934	ANSTON UTD
1935	SWALLOWNEST
1936	DINNINGTON ATH
1937	ECKINGTON UTD
1938	SWALLOWNEST **(Not On Plinth)**
1939	SWALLOWNEST
1946	KIVETON PARK COLLIERY (awarded as Mosboro Trinity failed to turn up)
1947	NO COMPETITION (due to bad weather)
1948	WOODHOUSE WEST END
1949	AUGHTON JUNIORS

ATTERCLIFFE AREA FOOTBALL

The Attercliffe area of Sheffield was a hotbed in the early days of football hosting various football competitions. The first recorded club in the area was Attercliffe FC who were formed in 1870. According to the 1882/83 Sheffield FA handbook, their ground was on Brightside Lane, with the teams getting changed at the Forge Inn at Newhall. In 1882 it was recorded that they had 200 members and that they played in blue and black.
With that number of members, and obvious interest in football in the area, it was no surprise that various competitions started to appear, the first being the Carbrook Challenge Cup which started in 1883.

CARBROOK CHALLENGE CUP

This Competition ran in the Attercliffe area between 1883 and 1891. Teams winning the competition three times in succession or four times in all were awarded the cup to keep. This happened in 1891 with Carbrook Church. This appears to be the reason that the competition finished with Carbrook Church winning the cup outright.
The cup in 1888 was valued at £30. The Secretary at that time was J T Parker of 77, Broughton Lane.

1883/84				
CARBROOK BETHEL- won		v		CARBROOK REFORM
1884/85				
ECCLESFIELD	5	v	1	PHILADELPHIA
1885/86				
BETHEL REDS	4	v	1	SHIREGREEN
1886/87				
BETHEL REDS	4	v	0	BEIGHTON
1887/88				
GRIMESTHORPE		v		RAWMARSH (see note 1)
1888/89				
CARBROOK CHURCH	7	v	2	BRIGHTSIDE ROVERS
1889/90				
CARBROOK CHURCH	2	v	1	WALKLEY
1890/91				
CARBROOK CHURCH	5	v	0	WORKSOP TOWN RES

Note 1. The first game finished 1-1. The Competition ordered the teams to complete the game the following week, with the 3 players missing. It appears that Rawmarsh sent a telegraph at kick off time stating Rawmarsh is not coming today. The press report states that the Competition Committee instructed the Grimesthorpe players to kick off and score a goal, which they did. The match and cup was then awarded to them.

Carbrook Challenge Cup Runners-Up Medal presented to Worksop Town in 1891

LEWIS CUP

With the Carbrook Challenge Cup appearing to have finished, it is possible that the competition re-started again but under the name of the Lewis Cup in 1892. No connection has been found at the moment other than it was run from the same area of Attercliffe. It is quite possible that the name Lewis was from a sponsor. There was a bookmakers in Attercliffe by the name Lewis, and it is suspected that he could have been the sponsor. There was also a Lewis Attercliffe cricket league in existence at around this period, whose secretary was Walter Wragg.

Baldwin Street Sunday School won the first two finals, and were awarded the cup to keep, so a new cup was obtained, possibly from the same sponsor.

Obviously the rules were changed because Nelson who won the cup three times in a row had to do so before they could keep the cup. However the competition carried on under the new name of the Wragg Challenge Cup, a competition that is still being played for today. The Secretary of the competition was Walter Wragg of 555, Attercliffe Road who provided the new cup which is still in use today, having taken his name

1893	BALDWIN STREET SUNDAY SCHOOL
1894	BALDWIN STREET SUNDAY SCHOOL
1895	?
1896	?
1897	?
1898	?
1899	?
1900	TINSLEY
1901	NELSON
1902	NELSON
1903	NELSON

ATTERCLIFFE & DISTRICT LEAGUE

With league football starting in the Sheffield area in1889 and expanding throughout the S&H FA area, it was no surprise that a league was set up in the Attercliffe area.

1894/95				
BALDWIN STREET	5	v	1	ATTERCLIFFE ALBION
1895/96				
NORTHFIELDS	3	v	1	GRIMESTHORPE FREE CHURCH (after 2-2)
1896/97				
HOLMES	3	v	1	ATTERCLIFFE ALBION
1897/98				
HOLMES	4	v	1	DARNALL
1898/99				
DARNALL CONGS	2	v	1	TINSLEY CONG

ATTERCLIFFE & DISTRICT CHALLENGE CUP

This competition started in 1902. The first cup was kept by the 1904 winners and a better, new cup used afterwards. It is possible that the cup from the former league competition was used, hence the new cup being provided in 1904

Great Britain Winners Medal

1902/03
WASHFORD - winners (below right)

1903/04
WOODBOURNE ATH 3 v 2 PARKWOOD SPRINGS

1904/05
GREAT BRITAIN 3 v 1 BALTIC

1905/06
GREAT BRITAIN 5 v 0 FORGE FC

ATTERCLIFFE CHARITY CUP

This competition was affiliated to S&H FA during 1917/18. With the war over, various Charity Cup competitions came into being. Locally there was the Darnall Medical Aid Cup and the Tinsley Charity Cup. Various areas of the city started their own competitions and Attercliffe followed the trend

1917/18	HOLMWOOD RED ROSE
1918/19	BOLTON ROVERS
1919/20	WASHFORD SPORTS
1920/21	KINGS HEAD
1921/22	WOODGROVE
1922/23	KINGS HEAD
1923/24	PHILADELPHIA AMATEURS
1924/25	ATTERCLIFFE WMC
1925/26	INDUSTRY SPORTS
1926/27	LOPHAM STREET PM
1927/28	OWLERTON ATHLETIC
1928/29	TINSLEY PARK STEELS
1929/30	NETHER EDGE AMATEURS
1930/31	INTAKE SPORTS
1931/32	FULWOOD FC
1932/33	ST PHILIPS C&I
1933/34	TINSLEY PARK SPORTS
1934/35	FULWOOD
1935/36	CROOKES WMC
1936/37	PITSMOOR WMC
1937/38	PITSMOOR WMC
1938/39	ST PHILIPS C&I
1939/40	
1940/41	ATTERCLIFFE RADICALS

ATTERCLIFFE ALLIANCE LEAGUE

This competition was previously the Fowler League (Started 1917/18) which had 2 divisions. Mr A Fowler was to continue the League & Cup competition in 1918/19, but for some reason the name changed and it became the Attercliffe Alliance League

FOWLER LEAGUE 1917/18

Division 1 Winners - DARNALL OB
Division 2 Winners - ATTERCLIFFE ALBION

ATTERCLIFFE ALLIANCE LEAGUE

1918/19	HOPE & ANCHOR
1919/20	OXFORD HOTEL
1920/21	KINGS HEAD
1921/22	KINGS HEAD
1922/23	KINGS HEAD

ATTERCLIFFE LICENSED VICTUALLERS LEAGUE

This competition appears to start in 1903 and may have lasted for only two seasons. However a couple of references have been found in the press giving scores from games in 1908/09 season. There are no other references found in respect of this league.

Drinking and football was something of a no go with the religious people running football in those days. Because of this, the local press possibly did not show reports or results of the games, however for some reason reports were available for the Sheffield Licensed Victuallers League.

In 1904, W Salt of the Lodge Inn at Attercliffe, tried to affiliate the league with S&H FA, who rejected it on the grounds that it had run the previous season as an unaffiliated competition. W Salt was actually the treasurer of Attercliffe football club at the time, and was the licensee of the house where the meetings were held. He had provided medals for the previous season's competition.

Image supplied by The David Richardson Collection

Washford Arms public house, Attercliffe Road. First winners of The Attercliffe & District Challenge Cup in 1902-03 and also the first winners of The Sheffield Licensed Victuallers League 1903-04.

THE CROMWELL CUP

After the success of the Youdan Cup, a local theatre manager, Oliver Cromwell, offered a cup to be played for by teams under two years old. Only four teams fitted this criteria, so a draw took place and two semi-finals were arranged to be played on Saturdays 1st and 8th February 1868 at the Mackenzie Ground, which was on Myrtle Road, Sheffield.

The first game was between The Wednesday and Exchange which was played on a very windy day. The game was played 14 a-side, with The Wednesday having the better of the game and easily winning by 4 goals and 3 rouges to nil.

The second game featured Garrick and Wellington and was a close affair with Garrick winning by scoring the only rouge of the game.

The final between The Wednesday and Garrick took place on Saturday 15th February at Bramall Lane cricket ground before 400 spectators on another very windy day. Garrick were expected to win easily as they incorporated 7 of the best Hallam players. Hallam had won the Youdan Cup the year before.

The game was closer than expected with Garrick coming closest to scoring when The Wednesday keeper tried to kick the ball rather than just stopping it, but fortunately it hit the post and rebounded back into play. After 90 minutes there was no score, so the captains agree to continue to play on until a goal was scored. After 10 minutes of play one of the Garrick players, making a kick, got too much under it and the ball went up almost perpendicularly and in dropping, cannoned off someone through the goal to make The Wednesday the winners.

Cromwell Cup - 1868

The Cup presentation took place on 16th March at the Theatre Royal. Oliver Cromwell had been a very well respected manager at this theatre, but was soon to leave the area to take up another appointment. Because of this, he used the presentation night as his benefit night. Players from all the local football teams were invited to a performance of Whitefriar Street, or The days of Claude Duval as it was also known, which was a historical drama. This was followed by the screaming ballet The Dancing Scotchman and then the side-splitting farce The Artful Dodge.

The Cup is still in the ownership of Sheffield Wednesday, but is often out on loan to various museums etc.

DARNALL MEDICAL AID CHARITY CUP

1917/18	CRAVENS SPORTS
1918/19	ATTERCLIFFE UNITARIANS
1919/20	CRAVENS SPORTS
1920/21	ATTERCLIFFE UNITARIANS
1921/22	DARNALL OLD BOYS
1922/23	ATTERCLIFFE UTD
1923/24	GREENLAND WMC
1924/25	DARNALL CONGREGATION
1925/26	GREENLAND WMC
1926/27	DARNALL FC
1927/28	GREENLAND WMC
1928/29	GREENLAND WMC
1929/30	LOPHAM ST UM
1930/31	NUNNERY SPORTS
1931/32	ROUNDEL STREET PM
1932/33	THE HALL SPORTS
1933/34	HAMPTON SPORTS
1934/35	THE HALL SPORTS
1935/36	CATCLIFFE JUNIORS
1936/37	DAVY BROTHER SPORTS
1937/38	DAVY UTD
1938/39	STOVIN ATHLETIC
1939/40	HAMPTONS SPORTS
1940 to 1946	NO COMPETITION
1946/47	
1947/48	
1948/49	
1949/50	
1950/51	TRAVELLERS SPORTS or WOODHOUSE MILL
1951/52	EFFINGHAM SPORTS
1952/53	
1953/54	MANOR SOCIAL
1954/55	
1955/56	CATCLIFFE RED ROSE
1956/57	BELLHOUSE RD WMC
1957/58	CATCLIFFE RED ROSE or MANOR SPORTS
1958/59	BELLHOUSE RD WMC
1959/60	BELLHOUSE RD WMC or PARSON CROSS
1960/61	GRENOSIDE SPORTS
1961/62	
1962/63	ASTON FC
1963/64	PITSMOOR WMC
1964/65	OUGHTIBRIDGE WMC
1965/66	LOXLEY VILLAGE
1966/67	SHEFFIELD LOCO WMC
1967/68	BATCHELORS NEW CROSS
1968/69	BELLHOUSE RD WMC
1969/70	WOODHOUSE ASHBERRY
1970/71	ST PATRICKS FC
1971/72	MOSBORO TRINITY
1972/73	MOSBORO TRINITY
1973/74	WOODHOUSE ASHBERRY
1974/75	WOODHOUSE ASHBERRY
1975/76	MOSBORO TRINITY
1976/77	
1977/78	MOSBORO TRINITY or ST PATRICKS
1978/79	BELLHOUSE RD WMC
1979/80	BELLHOUSE RD WMC
1980/81	BRINSWORTH ALBION
1981/82	INDUSTRY INN
1982/83	MOSBORO TRINITY or BRADLEY WELL
1983/84	ROYAL HOTEL
1984/85	NEW STUBBIN COLLIERY
1985/86	MOSBORO TRINITY or HANDSWORTH NEW CROWN
1986/87	HANDSWORTH NEW CROWN
1987/88	NEW STUBBIN COLLIERY
1988/89	NEW STUBBIN COLLIERY
1989/90	BRINSWORTH WMC
1990/91	BRINSWORTH ALBION
1991/92	WOMBWELL TOWN
1992/93	BLACK BULL OVER 35s
1993/94	HALLAM RESERVES
1994/95	PINEGROVE COUNTRY CLUB

A float advertising the Easter Monday final of the cup between Darnall FC and Darnall WMC, probably 1927

The Original Darnall Medical Aid Cup found in distressed disrepair

ECCLESFIELD CHALLENGE CUP

Trophy presented by Frank Bungay

1994 ECCLESFIELD RED ROSE
1995 HIGH GREEN VILLA
1996 OUGHTIBRIDGE WMC
1997 SICEY BEEFEATER
1998 PARK LANE
1999 SHEFFIELD FC (County Senior side)
2000 GRAPES ROY HANCOCK
2001 WOMBWELL MAIN WMC
2002 HALLAM
2003
2004 WOMBWELL MAIN WMC
2005 DOMINO FC

ECCLESFIELD CHARITY CUP

Appears to start 1920

1920/21 SHEFFIELD TRAMWAY
1921/22 ECCLESFIELD WMC
1922/23 ECCLESFIELD WMC
1923/24 HOWELLS SPORTS
1924/25 NO COMPETITION

Ecclesfield Challenge Cup

HALLAMSHIRE FA – CHALLENGE CUP

In 1877 a new Football Association was formed in Sheffield to cater for the clubs that the Sheffield FA would not take. To join the Sheffield FA you had to have been going for two seasons, which stopped any newly formed clubs from entering. The new association was originally called the New FA in the press, but it soon took the title Hallamshire FA

This Challenge Cup appears to be the only Competition run by the Hallamshire (New) FA.

The Cup for this Competition was engraved with Hallamshire FA, Est. 2 April 1877 and the Motto – "The good of football and those that play it". It later had 'Sheffield &' added when the two Associations amalgamated in 1887.

The Cup was then used from 1887/88 for the newly formed Sheffield & Hallamshire FA as the Runners up Cup for the Association Challenge Cup (Senior Cup) and from 1895/96 as the winners of the S&H Junior League. In 1899/1900 it was awarded to the Association League winners up.

1879 RISING STAR
1880 BURTON STAR
1881 INTAKE
1882 INTAKE
1883 SPITAL
1884 ECKINGTON WORKS
1885 STAVELEY
1886 STAVELEY
1887 ECKINGTON WORKS

*County Senior League Cup 1877
Former Hallamshire FA
Challenge Cup*

HATCHARD CUP

Presented by Frank S Hatchard (Conservative MP for the Hallamshire Division) in 1894 to S&H FA. The Cup is stamped J D & S with a Crown, Lion and A (1893). The cup was used for the Sheffield & Hallamshire Alliance League (See separate page) for seasons 1893/94 and 1894/95.

With the new set-up for local football for season 1896/97, the Hatchard Competition became a competition for the remainder of the minor clubs in the area who did not play in any other cup competition. The teams were divided into divisions with the top teams from each division playing off in semi-finals etc. to decide the overall Competition Champion.

.

1896 KIVETON PARK

1897 KIMBERWORTH

1898 MONTROSE WORKS

1899 TREETON/DONCASTER RES - JT

1900 ROUNDEL

1901 DONCASTER ROVERS (See note 1)

1902 ROUNDEL

1903 HALLAM

1904 ROTHERHAM MAIN

1905 DONCASTER ST JAMES

1906 PARKGATE ATHLETIC

1907 WORKSOP TOWN

1908 THORPE HESLEY

1909 THORPE HESLEY

1910 DINNINGTON

1911 DINNINGTON

1912 CAMMELL LAIRD

1913 RETFORD TOWN

1914 BIRD IN HAND

1915 BIRD IN HAND

1916–1919 NO COMPETITION - WAR

1920 TREETON READING ROOM/BEIGHTON REC - JT

1921 BEIGHTON REC

1922 TREETON READING ROOM

1923 TREETON READING ROOM

1924–1939 NO COMPETITION

Hatchard Cup Medal 1919-20

Note 1

Doncaster awarded match abandoned at half time. A large section of Ecclesfield fans invaded the pitch at half time and subjected the Referee (Mr Morton) to gross insults and abuse, resulting in him needing a police escort. Spectators then refused to leave the pitch despite requests by police and officials, so game abandoned

Hatchard Cup

HATCHARD LEAGUE

No competition ran from 1923 until 1948 when it was decided to form a new league to fill the gap between the Association League (now the County Senior League) and the Amateur League.

1949 HALLAM

1950 THORNCLIFFE WELFARE

1951 PENISTONE CHURCH

1952 THORNCLIFFE REC

1953 THORNCLIFFE REC

1954 WICKERSLEY INSTITUTE

1955 ATLAS & NORFOLK

1956 ATLAS & NORFOLK

1957 E S C (ENGLISH STEEL CORP)

1958 DEARNE COMMUNITY MW

1959 DEARNE COMMUNITY MW

1960 YMCA (SHEFFIELD)

1961 PENISTONE CHURCH

1962 YMCA (SHEFFIELD)

1963 SHEFFIELD UNITED

1964 DAVY UNITED

1965 SHEFFIELD UNITED

1966 FRECHEVILLE CA

1967 SHEFFIELD WATERWORKS

1968 SHEFFIELD UNITED

1969 CITY SURVEYORS

1970 WOSBROUGH BRIDGE MWA

1971 CHARLTON UNITED

1972 BSC PARKGATE

1973 OLD EDWARDIANS

1974 OLD EDWARDIANS

1975 ECCLESFIELD

1976 SHEFFIELD WATERWORKS

1977 OLD EDWARDIANS

1978 WOODHOUSE ASHBERRY

1979 ECCLESFIELD ESCA

1980 OUGHTIBRIDGE WMSC

1981 STANNINGTON VILLAGE

1982 WINDSOR FC

1983 CROOKES WMC

Hatchard Cup Runners-Up Medal 1906-07

DIVISION 2

1971/72 OLD EDWARDIANS

1972/73 ECCLESFIELD RED ROSE

1973/74 FIRTH BROWN SPORTS

1974/75 SHEFFIELD WATERWORKS

1975/76 TWIL

1976/77 WOODHOUSE ASHBERRY

1977/78 CROSSPOOL SPORTS

1978/79 WINDSOR

1979/80 MIDDLEWOOD HOSPITAL

1980/81 DORMER SPORTS

1981/82 JAMES FAIRLEY STEELS SFC

1982/83 WOODSETTS WELFARE SPORTS

LEAGUE KO CUP

1981/82 WINDSOR

1982/83 JAMES FAIRLEY STEELS

The Hatchard League ceased to exist at the end of the 1982/83 season when S&H CFA stopped running it. The teams from this league then joined forces with the County Senior.

HEELEY FOOTBALL

Despite the presence of so many hills in Heeley, it is surprising how many local men and boys found flat spaces to play their football. Part of the land on which Lowfield School now stands was the ground for the old Heeley Football Club. The players used a room at the old Earl of Arundel and Surrey public house as a changing room. Eventually the team, which had by now acquired a higher reputation, used a pitch on Meersbrook Park for all their home games.

Many people do not realise that Heeley was the original home of Sheffield Wednesday. It was started at the Olive Grove Ground in1866 by amateur players and did not turn professional until 1887.

Sheffield United were also just an amateur club, playing on the Ball Inn Ground, Myrtle Road, until 1885 when they also turned professional and looked to enter the Football League.

One of the players who turned out for Heeley FC was John Hunter who played and captained England in the 1880s. He moved to Blackburn and won an FA Cup winners medal in 1883. I believe he was the first Sheffield-based player to captain the English side.

In addition to the now famous Wednesday and United there were many amateur teams in Heeley, nearly all the Churches, Chapels, and Sunday Schools had teams who played in the Sunday School League, Free Church Leagues and Bible Class leagues. There were other leagues that had public houses or local clubs who just formed a team of local lads who wished to play together. One such team was Cambridge Villa formed by a group of keen young men who all lived on Cambridge Road.

A sports shop owned by a Mr Fish on Heeley Bottom ran its own football team for 16-years-olds. The field where they played their home games was used by farmers during the week and goalposts were erected and taken down and removed after every match. The Heeley Friends FC played on Black Bank and the Kent Road Mission team played on the field near Cat Lane and Lees Hall FC close to where the Lees Hall Golf Club is now situated. Valley Road played on fields where Newfield School is now sited.

Local schools also had football teams which competed in School football leagues. Heeley Bank School football team was formed in 1884 - it lapsed in the 1890s and happily was reformed in the early part of the 20th Century and stayed strong for many years.

Within the area of Heeley at Olive Grove, The Wednesday played their first match against Blackburn Rovers on Monday, September 12th in 1887.

Heeley area had its own league and its own Cup trophy the Heeley Charity Cup.

HEELEY CHARITY CUP

1921/22	MEERSBROOK CONGREGATION
1922/23	MEERSBROOK CONGREGATION
1923/24	HEELEY FRIENDS (pictured below)
1924/25	ANNS ROAD PM
1925/26	NORTON WOODSEATS
1926/27	SHEFFIELD TRAMWAY
1927/28	NETHER EDGE AMATEURS
1928/29	HEELEY FRIENDS
1929/30	NETHER EDGE AMATEURS
1930/31	NORTON CHURCH/ANNS ROAD PM (shared after 1-1 draw)
1931/32	NORTON WOODSEATS v TRAMWAYS or CITY WORKS
1932/33	PARK LABOUR
1933/34	HEELEY FRIENDS
1934/35	UPPER HEELEY WMC
1935/36	NETHER EDGE AMATEURS
1936/37	UPPER HEELEY WMC
1937/38	NETHER EDGE AMATEURS
1938/39	FULWOOD

Heeley Friends 1924, Heeley Charity Cup Winners

Postcard featuring Blackburn Rovers F.C.
Their trainer: John Hunter, far right of picture, played for Heeley FC for many years and also captained the full England International team in February 1881. He also won an English FA Cup Winners Medal in 1883

HOLBROOK & DISTRICT FOOTBALL

This competition started in 1903/04 for teams in the Holbrook area. Holbrook is an area between Mosborough, Eckington and Killamarsh. After one season under the control of Chesterfield FA, they were granted permission to affiliate the competition with S&H FA.

It is a hard competition to work out who won what as they kept changing the names of their competition. However, what is below, appears to be as accurate as I can possibly get.

JUNIOR LEAGUE

1905/06	NORMANTON SPRINGS
1906/07	ASTON UNITED
1907/08	HANDSWORTH ROVERS RES
1908/09	ECKINGTON RED ROSE & ASTON COLLIERY – JT (after 4 Games)
1909/10	HARTHILL UNITED
1910/11	BEIGHTON RECREATION
1911/12	DINNINGTON
1912/13	BEIGHTON RECREATION
1913/14	MOSBOROUGH JUNIORS & BEIGHTON PRIMS - JT

HOLBROOK & DISTRICT FOOTBALL

KO CUP

1927/28	ECKINGTON WORKS
1928/29	ECKINGTON WORKS
1929/30	RENISHAW WORKS
1930/31	WOODHOUSE MILL UNITED
1931/32	ANSTON READING ROOM
1932/33	BEIGHTON MW
1933/34	BEIGHTON MW
1934/35	WOODHOUSE MILL WELFARE
1935/36	WOODHOUSE WEST END
1936/37	KIVETON PARK COLLIERY
1937/38	MOSBOROUGH TRINITY
1938/39	SWALLOWNEST
1939/40	ECKINGTON ST PETERS
1940/45	NO COMPETITION - WAR
1945/46	RENISHAW
1946/47	KILLAMARSH ATHLETIC
1947/48	AUGHTON JUNIORS
1948/49	ECKINGTON MW
1949/50	ECKINGTON MW
1950/51	CATCLIFFE RED ROSE

Holbrook & District League K.O. Cup Winners Medal 1928-29 won by H Briggs

SENIOR LEAGUE

1903/04	HOLBROOK WORKS
1904/05	KILLAMARSH RISING STAR
1905/06	KILLAMARSH RISING STAR
1906/07	HOLBROOK WORKS
1907/08	ANSTON JUNIORS
1908/09	ECKINGTON RED ROSE
1909/10	DINNINGTON MAIN
1910/11	ECKINGTON RED ROSE
1911/12	ECKINGTON RED ROSE
1912/13	MOSBOROUGH WESLEYANS
1913/14	ECKINGTON RED ROSE
1914/15	ECKINGTON ATHLETIC
1915/16	HOLBROOK WORKS
1916/17	NO COMPETITION - WAR
1917/18	HOLLINSEND WESLEYAN
1918/19	ECKINGTON ROVERS
1919/20	ECKINGTON ATHLETIC
1920/21	LAUGHTON COMMON
1921/22	NORMANTON SPRINGS
1922/23	ECKINGTON ATHLETIC
1923/24	HOLBROOK RECREATION
1924/25	KILLAMARSH BL
1925/26	ECKINGTON WORKS RES
1926/27	
1927/28	ECKINGTON WORKS
1928/29	BARLBOROUGH
1929/30	RENISHAW WORKS
1930/31	WOODHOUSE MILL UNITED
1931/32	WOODHOUSE MILL UNITED
1932/33	SPEEDWELL OB
1933/34	MOSBOROUGH TRINITY
1934/35	WOODHOUSE WEST END
1935/36	ECKINGTON UNITED
1936/37	ECKINGTON UNITED
1937/38	WOODHOUSE WEST END
1938/39	MOSBOROUGH BLUE BELL
1939/46	NO COMPETITION - WAR
1946/47	KILLAMARSH ATHLETIC
1947/48	ECKINGTON MW
1948/49	ECKINGTON MW
1949/50	ECKINGTON MW or MOSBOROUGH TRINITY
1950/51	KILLAMARSH JUNIORS

This plinth has all the above nine Junior League winners engraved on the silver plaques which surround the dark wooden base

SHEFFIELD & HALLAMSHIRE CFA ASSOCIATION CHALLENGE CUP

This Competition was started in 2002 for senior Saturday teams who are not invited into the Senior Cup or reserve teams of clubs that are invited into the Senior Cup

2003	ELMTREE	1-0	STOCKSBRIDGE PARK STEELS RES
2004	HSBC	3-2	ATHERSLEY REC
2005	KIVETON PARK	2-2	ATHERSLEY REC (KIVETON 4-2 ON PENS)
2006	KIVETON PARK	5-0	SHEFFIELD LANE TOP
2007	STOCKSBRIDGE PARK STEELS RES	3-1	HEMSWORTH MINERS WELFARE
2008	ATHERSLEY REC	1-0	HOLLINSEND AMATEURS
2009	HALL GREEN UTD	2-1	KIRKBURTON
2010	SHEFFIELD FC	2-1	DEARNE CMW
2011	STOCKSBRIDGE PARK STEELS RES	3-0	KIRKBURTON
2012	AQUAFORCE BARNSLEY FC	3-1	SHEPLEY
2013	SWINTON ATHLETIC	3-0	KIRKBURTON
2014	JUBILEE SPORTS	4-0	WICKERSLEY FC
2015	DENABY MAIN	2-0	AFC EMLEY
2016	HANDSWORTH PARRAMORE RES	5-2	GRIMETHORPE SPORTS

CITY LEAGUE

This league was run by S&H for teams that played within the City boundary. It appears to have started in 1919.

1919/20	ATTERCLIFFE UNITARIANS
1920/21	ATTERCLIFFE UNITARIANS
1921/22	ATTERCLIFFE UTD
1922/23	NORTON WOODSEATS
1923/24	PORTLAND
1924/25	BIRLEY CARR INST
1925/26	NORFOLK
1926/27	LOPHAM ST UM
1927/28	GREENLAND WMC
1928/29	LOPHAM ST UM "B"
1929/30	MEADOW ALLIANCE
1930/31	ST PHILIPS S C & I
1931/32	ST MICHAELS
1932/33	TINSLEY PARK COLLIERY MW
1933/34	PARK GARDENERS
1934/35	PITSMOOR WMC
1935/36	CROOKES WMC
1936/37	CROOKES WMC
1937/38	NETHER EDGE AMATEURS
1938/39	GRENOSIDE SPORTS
1939/40	NORFOLK JUNIORS
1940-1945	Competition amalgamated with the Amateur League for duration of war
1945/46	BALFOUR SPORTS
1946/47	CARLTON ATHLETIC
1947/48	MARSHALLS SPORTS
1948/49	MARSHALLS SPORTS
1949/50	MARSHALLS SPORTS
1950/51	PIMRO SPORTS
1951/52	WESTON PARK ATHLETIC "A"
1952/53	PIMRO SPORTS
1953/54	WESTON PARK ATHLETIC "A"
1954/55	LOWSHIRE A
1955/56	ROAD TRANSPORT
1956/57	PIMRO SPORTS
1957/58	EDUCATION TRANSPORT
1958/59	PIMRO SPORTS A
1959/60	BRAMAHS SPORTS
1960/61	INTAKE F & SC
1961/62	INTAKE F & SC
1962/63	BRINSWORTH ATHLETIC
1963/64	WINDSOR BL
1964/65	HIGHFIELD AMATEURS "A"
1965/66	BRINSWORTH ATHLETIC

League finished as only 4 clubs applied who moved over to Amateur lge

Upper Heeley WMC played in City League in the 1930s

DIVISION 2

1948/49	SHIREGREEN WMC
1954/55	WESTON PARK ATH

SHEFFIELD & HALLAMSHIRE CFA COUNTY CUP

The Cup was presented to Sheffield & Hallamshire CFA by J C Clegg (JP) in May 1921. The cup base, which has the details of who presented it and most of the winners details, is silver, stamped with a crown – lion – C which is for 1921 together with J D & S.

The last winners shown on the base are Sheffield United in 1982, although there have been three winners since.

This Cup was played for annually by the 5 senior clubs in the area from 1920 until 1982 when the clubs were given the opportunity to opt out each year on payment of a levy to Sheffield & Hallamshire CFA. Previously, part of the proceeds from the games was taken by S&H. Because of the advent of more midweek football imposed on the clubs and end of season tours resulting, in the 1970's, in finals often being carried over into the following season, and the fact clubs had to play their first team squad in the games, clubs opted out most years since the 70's, with only the occasional playing of the competition. The full 1974/75 competition was played in the 1975/76 season with the 1975/76 competition also played later that season. By the end of the 1970's clubs were allowed to play their Reserve teams in the competition.

1920/21	SHEFFIELD UNITED	2-1	SHEFFIELD WEDNESDAY
1921/22	BARNSLEY	2-1	SHEFFIELD WEDNESDAY
1922/23	ROTHERHAM COUNTY	2-1	BARNSLEY
1923/24	SHEFFIELD UNITED	2-0	SHEFFIELD WEDNESDAY
1924/25	BARNSLEY	1-0	ROTHERHAM COUNTY
1925/26	SHEFFIELD UNITED	3-1	SHEFFIELD WEDNESDAY
1926/27	SHEFFIELD WEDNESDAY	4-1	BARNSLEY
1927/28	SHEFFIELD WEDNESDAY	5-2	ROTHERHAM UNITED
1928/29	SHEFFIELD WEDNESDAY	2-0	SHEFFIELD UNITED
1929/30	SHEFFIELD UNITED	3-1	SHEFFIELD WEDNESDAY
1930/31	SHEFFIELD UNITED	9-2	BARNSLEY
1931/32	SHEFFIELD WEDNESDAY	3-0	BARNSLEY
1932/33	SHEFFIELD UNITED	4-2	SHEFFIELD WEDNESDAY
1933/34	SHEFFIELD WEDNESDAY	3-0	DONCASTER ROVERS
1934/35	BARNSLEY	1-0	ROTHERHAM UNITED
1935/36	DONCASTER ROVERS	2-1	SHEFFIELD UNITED
1936/37	BARNSLEY	3-2	SHEFFIELD UNITED
1937/38	DONCASTER ROVERS	1-0	BARNSLEY
1938/39	SHEFFIELD UNITED	0-0	SHEFFIELD WEDNESDAY
	(CUP SHARED – 6 MONTHS EACH)		
1939/40	(NO COMPETITION – WAR)		
1940/41	DONCASTER ROVERS	3-2	ROTHERHAM UNITED
1941/42	BARNSLEY	3-2	ROTHERHAM UNITED
	ROTHERHAM UNITED	1-5	BARNSLEY
	(BARNSLEY WON 8-3 ON AGG)		
1942/43	BARNSLEY	7-1	ROTHERHAM UNITED
	ROTHERHAM UNITED	5-3	BARNSLEY
	(BARNSLEY WON 10-6 ON AGG)		
1943/44	ROTHERHAM UNITED	1-0	SHEFFIELD UNITED
	SHEFFIELD UNITED	2-3	ROTHERHAM UNITED
	(ROTHERHAM WON 4-2 ON AGG)		
1944/45	SHEFFIELD UNITED	1-3	SHEFFIELD WEDNESDAY
	SHEFFIELD WEDNESDAY	4-2	SHEFFIELD UNITED
	(WEDNESDAY WON 7-3 ON AGG)		
1945/46	BARNSLEY	1-1	SHEFFIELD WEDNESDAY
	SHEFFIELD WEDNESDAY	1-0	BARNSLEY
	(WEDNESDAY WON 2-1 ON AGG)		
1946/47	BARNSLEY	3-1	ROTHERHAM UNITED
1947/48	BARNSLEY	3-1	SHEFFIELD WEDNESDAY
1948/49	BARNSLEY	1-0	SHEFFIELD UNITED
1949/50	SHEFFIELD WEDNESDAY	2-1	SHEFFIELD UNITED
1950/51	SHEFFIELD WEDNESDAY	2-1	DONCASTER ROVERS

SHEFFIELD & HALLAMSHIRE COUNTY CUP - continued

1951/52	SHEFFIELD UNITED	3-1	ROTHERHAM UNITED	10/5/52
1952/53	SHEFFIELD UNITED	5-0	ROTHERHAM UNITED	26/10/53
1953/54	SHEFFIELD UNITED	4-2	ROTHERHAM UNITED	8/5/54
1954/55	ROTHERHAM UNITED	4-2	SHEFFIELD WEDNESDAY	
1955/56	DONCASTER ROVERS	4-0	SHEFFIELD UNITED	10/5/56
1956/57	SHEFFIELD UNITED	3-1	ROTHERHAM UNITED	6/5/57
1957/58	SHEFFIELD UNITED	3-0	SHEFFIELD WEDNESDAY	30/4/58
1958/59	SHEFFIELD UNITED	4-1	SHEFFIELD WEDNESDAY	4/5/59
1959/60	SHEFFIELD UNITED	2-1	ROTHERHAM UNITED	4/5/60
1960/61	NOT COMPLETED			
1961/62	NOT COMPLETED			
1962/63	NO COMPETITION			
1963/64	SHEFFIELD UNITED	4-3	BARNSLEY	5/5/64
1964/65	SHEFFIELD UNITED	4-0	DONCASTER ROVERS	3/5/65
1965/66	ROTHERHAM UNITED	1-0	SHEFFIELD UNITED	2/1/67
1966/67	SHEFFIELD UNITED	3-2	BARNSLEY	28/11/67
	(AFTER 1-1)			8/5/67
1967/68	DONCASTER ROVERS	1-0	BARNSLEY	29/10/68
1968/69	SHEFFIELD UNITED	2-0	DONCASTER ROVERS	20/4/70
	(AFTER 0-0)			9/5/69
1969/70	ROTHERHAM UNITED	1-0	BARNSLEY	1/3/71
1970/71	BARNSLEY		SHEFFIELD UNITED	
	(NO FINAL PLAYED – SHARED CUP)			
1971/72	NO COMPETITION			
1972/73	SHEFFIELD WEDNESDAY	0-0	SHEFFIELD UNITED	26/1/74
	(WEDNESDAY WON 4-3 ON PENS)			
1973/74	SHEFFIELD UNITED	0-0	ROTHERHAM UNITED	29/10/74
	SHEFFIELD (UNITED WON 4-2 ON PENS)			
1974/75	SHEFFIELD WEDNESDAY	2-1	SHEFFIELD UNITED	14/10/75
1975/76	DONCASTER ROVERS	2-1	SHEFFIELD UNITED	7/5/76
1976/77	ROTHERHAM UNITED	1-0	SHEFFIELD UNITED	19/5/77
1977/78	SHEFFIELD UNITED	4-1	DONCASTER ROVERS	18/9/78
1978/79	NO COMPETITION			
1979/80	SHEFFIELD UNITED	2-1	SHEFFIELD WEDNESDAY	8/5/80
1980/81	ROTHERHAM UNITED	2-1	SHEFFIELD WEDNESDAY	
1981/82	SHEFFIELD UNITED	3-2	SHEFFIELD WEDNESDAY	21/5/82
1982/1985	NO COMPETITION			
1985/86	DONCASTER ROVERS	1-0	ROTHERHAM UNITED	11/8/86
1986/87	NO COMPETITION			
1987/88	ROTHERHAM UNITED	2-1	DONCASTER ROVERS	23/2/88
1988-1992	NO COMPETITION			
1992/93	BARNSLEY	3-2	DONCASTER ROVERS	4/5/93
1993	ONWARDS NO COMPETITION			

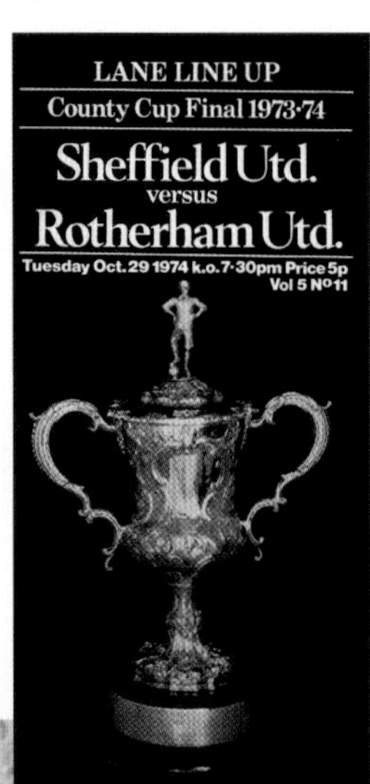

Sheffield County Cup Final 1973-74 Programme

Sheffield County Cup

SHEFFIELD & HALLAMSHIRE CFA INTERMEDIATE CHALLENGE CUP (UNDER 18)

The cup was presented by Councillor A Thompson of Doncaster in 1926. Cup marked C B & S with Lion & Crown which is 1926. Cup was engraved Sheffield & Hallamshire Midweek League and was played for in 1926/27. There are no other inscriptions until 1933/34, when it appears that it was used for the Thursday Challenge Cup, but no inscription to indicate this. Last inscription is 1939/40. The Cup was then re-engraved on the other side and used as the Intermediate Challenge Cup from 1942 until 1975.

The Competition was for under 18 teams. The competition was often referred to as the Youth Cup in the local press

1942/43	OWLER LANE ES
1943/44	ATLAS & NORFOLK JUNIORS
1944/45	WYBOURN & PARK YC
1945/46	MEYNELL ROAD BS
1946/47	OAKS FOLD
1947/48	HILLSBOROUGH BC
1948/49	COLERIDGE ROAD CI
1949/50	HANDSWORTH ROVERS
1950/51	WOODBOURNE YC "B"
1951/52	OAKS FOLD
1952/53	SHEFFIELD UTD JUNIORS
1953/54	SHEFFIELD UTD JUNIORS
1954/55	ST PATRICKS JUNIORS
1955/56	THORNCLIFFE REC
1956/57	HILLSBOROUGH BC
1957/58	HILLSBOROUGH BC
1958/59	THORNCLIFFE REC
1959/60	HILLSBOROUGH BC
1960/61	PENISTONE CHURCH
1961/62	HILLSBOROUGH BC
1962/63	SHEFFIELD UTD JUNIORS
1963/64	THURCROFT WELFARE
1964/65	THURCROFT WELFARE
1965/66	CLUB 92
1966/67	SHEFFIELD UTD JUNIORS
1967/68	HILLSBOROUGH BC
1968/69	STOCKSBRIDGE WORKS
1969/70	SHEFFIELD UTD JUNIORS
1970/71	SHEFFIELD UTD JUNIORS
1971/72	UPPERTHONG SC
1972/73	UPPERTHONG SC
1973/74	UPPERTHONG SC
1974/75	BILL CHAFER YC

Intermediate Cup 16-18 Winners Medal 1942-43 - War Time won by Owler Lane ES

SHEFFIELD & HALLAMSHIRE CFA INTERMEDIATE LEAGUE

In the first season of 1926/27 a competition was run for 14-18 year olds, but this was split into 2 the following season with a 14-16 and 16-18 competitions.

This Competition appears to have taken over from the S&H Minor League which ceased in 1925

14-18 YEAR OLD COMPETITION

1926/27	ALL SAINTS OLD BOYS

14-16 YEAR OLD COMPETITION

1927/28		HADFIELD SPORTS
1928/29		HADFIELD SPORTS
1929/30		WOODBOURNE OLD BOYS
1930/31		HARTSHEAD JUNIORS
1931/32		HARTSHEAD JUNIORS
1932/33		WOODBOURNEALLIANCE
1933/34		WOODBOURNEALLIANCE
1934/35		WOODBOURNEALLIANCE
1935/36		ST VINCENT
1936/37		WOODBOURNEALLIANCE
1937/38		WOODBOURNEALLIANCE
1938/39		ATLAS & NORFOLK JUNIORS
1939/44		NO COMP - WAR
1945/46		OAKS FOLD YC
1946/47		WOODTHORPE C & I
1947/48		ARBOURTHORNE
1948/49	DIV 1	OAKS FOLD YC
	2	ROTHERHAM JUNIORS
1949/50		SHIRECLIFFE
1950/51		OAKS FOLD YC
1951/52		OAKS FOLD YC
1952/53		THORNCLIFFE REC
1953/54		SHEFFIELD UTD JUNIORS
1954/55		SHEFFIELD YMCA
1955/56		SHEFFIELD UTD JUNIORS
1956/57		SHEFFIELD UTD JUNIORS
1957/58		CENTRAL YMCA
1958/59		HARTLEY SPORTS
1959/60	`	MEYNELL ROAD YC

UNDER 16 1/2 LEAGUE

Started 1959 and Finished 1972

1959/60	NEW CROSS
1960/61	NEW CROSS
1961/62	HILLSBOROUGH BC
1962/63	(Competition cancelled due to bad weather)
1963/64	MEYNELL ROAD YC
1964/65	MEYNELL ROAD YC
1965/66	HARBOROUGH AMT
1966/67	TREETONIANS
1967/68	GRANVILLE COLLEGE
1968/69	CITY JUNIORS
1969/70	DRONFIELD YC
1970/71	DRONFIELD YC
1971/72	MEYNELL ROAD YC

16-18 YEAR OLD COMPETITION

1927/28		ATTERCLIFFE OLD BOYS
1928/29		ATLAS & NORFOLK
1929/30		ATLAS & NORFOLK
1930/31		WOODBOURNEALLIANCE
1931/32		ROTHERHAM YMCA
1932/33		ROTHERHAM YMCA
1933/34		HARTSHEAD JUNIORS
1934/35		ECCLESFIELD BC
1935/36		WOODBOURNEALLIANCE
1936/37		WOODBOURNEALLIANCE
1937/38		ROTHERHAM YMCA
1938/39		ROTHERHAM YMCA
1939/45		NO COMP - WAR
1945/46		MEYNELL ROAD YC
1946/47		OAKS FOLD YC
1947/48		HILLSBOROUGH BOYS CLUB
1948/49	DIV 1	OAKS FOLD YC
	2	HILLSBOROUGH BC
	3	COLERIDGE ROAD C & I
	4	YMCA – FIRTH PARK
1949/50	DIV 1	FOXHILL COMMUNITY
	2	WOODBOURNEYC
1950/51		COLERIDGE ROAD C & I
1951/52		SHIREGREEN EVENING SCHOOL
1952/53		SHEFFIELD UTD JUNIORS
1953/54		SHEFFIELD UTD JUNIORS
1954/55		THORNCLIFFE REC
1955/56		THORNCLIFFE REC
1956/57		MEYNELL ROAD CI
1957/58		SHEFFIELD WEDNESDAY JUNIORS
1958/59		THORNCLIFFE REC
1959/60		SHEFFIELD UTD JUNIORS

DIVISION 1

1960/61	SHEFFIELD UTD JUNIORS
1961/62	CENTRAL YMCA
1962/63	(Competition cancelled due to bad weather)
1963/64	BARNSLEY COLTS
1964/65	SHEFFIELD UTD JUNIORS
1965/66	MEYNELL ROAD YC
1966/67	SHEFFIELD UTD JUNIORS
1967/68	HILLSBOROUGH BOYS CLUB
1968/69	SHEFFIELD UTD JUNIORS
1969/70	STOCKSBRIDGE WORKS
1970/71	CITY JUNIORS
1971/72	PENISTONE CHURCH
1972/73	COLLEY ROAD YC

DIVISION 2

1960/61	KILLAMARSH JUNIORS
1961/62	CHARLTON UTD
1962/63	(Competition cancelled due to bad weather)
1963/64	WOODBOURNEYC
1964/65	CLUB 62
1965/66	CLUB 62
1966/67	THORNBRIDGE ATH
1967/68	NO COMPETITION
1968/69	LISTERDALE JUNIORS
1969/70	CITY JUNIORS
1970/71	NO COMPETITION

100 YEARS AGO
By Chris Eyre

In 2010, Sheffield & Hallamshire CFA celebrated the Centenary season of their Junior Challenge Cup Competition which this year is sponsored by Owlerton Stadium, which is appropriate as one of the teams in the first competition was local church team Owlerton UM.

There had been a competition for minor clubs in the area which ran in the 1880's and 1890's, but this stopped in 1895. In 1909 the Sheffield & Hallamshire FA decided that it was time to start a Cup competition again for minor clubs. This would be for clubs that could not enter the Senior Cup, or Challenge Cup as it was known at the time, and also included second teams of the senior clubs, with Hallam FC entering their second team.

The first competition had 64 teams split into 4 divisions of 16 clubs. They tried to make the teams in each division as local to each other as possible to save travelling, which in those days was usually by bus, tram or the train. These teams played games on a knock out basis within the division until just one team from each division remained. These 4 teams then went into the hat and where drawn out to make two semi-finals.

Both the semi-finals were played on the same day, having previously been called off for bad weather. At Vickers ground in Sheffield on a very wet day which nearly made the pitch unplayable, Meadow Hall, (the place name was two words in those days), beat Midland Athletic 4-2 to reach the final. Penistone Church beat Darnall Congregational 2-1 at Bracken Moor, Stocksbridge in conditions that were described as a driving snowstorm.

The first final between Penistone Church and Meadow Hall, both teams playing in the Sheffield Amateur League, took place at the Atlas & Norfolk ground at Pitsmoor, which is now the Sheffield United's Academy ground, on Saturday 12th March 1910 before a good attendance. The press report indicates that Meadow Hall had the better of the play, but tried to walk the ball into the goal with their forwards missing several good chances. Penistone Church took advantage of this and won the game 4-2 with 3 goals being scored by J Clarkson and one by R Walker.

When the Penistone team arrived back at Penistone station at 8.55pm they were greeted by a large crowd who drowned out the full Thurlstone Brass Band that had turned out to greet them. The players were put on a waggonette which followed the band, which was playing "See the conquering hero come", to their headquarters, the Spread Eagle Hotel. A crowd of 2,000 people were waiting to greet them. Their captain J H Wood, who it is reported, played the game of his life in the final, was carried shoulder high into the club room. Surprisingly, it is reported that the Cup was not present at the celebrations. I assume that the Cup was held back by S&H to be awarded later together with the medals at a formal presentation evening as often happened in those days.

The Penistone Church team had only been formed in 1906, but everybody seemed to get involved. If you look at the team photo which was eventually taken with the cup, even the local doctor and village policeman got involved. Penistone Church are still going strong today.

Junior Challenge Cup

SHEFFIELD & HALLAMSHIRE JUNIOR CHALLENGE CUP

This Cup competition started in 1909/10. The Cup is silver and is stamped R&B (Roberts & Belk of Sheffield) with a crown and letter r to show it was made in 1909.

1910	PENISTONE CHURCH
1911	HANDSWORTH ROVERS
1912	ECKINGTON RED ROSE
1913	VALLEY ROAD BC
1914	VALLEY ROAD BC
1915	NETHER EDGE
1916-1918 NO COMPETITION	
1919	KIMBERWORTH OLD BOYS
1920	OUGHTIBRIDGE
1921	GRENOSIDE
1922	GRENOSIDE
1923	NETHER EDGE
1924	ATTERCLIFFE VIC
1925	MALIN BRIDGE OB
1926	PARK LABOUR
1927	LOPHAM STREET UM
1928	TURTON PLATTS SPORTS
1929	LOPHAM STREET UM
1930	TINSLEY PARK SPORTS
1931	TINSLEY PARK SPORTS
1932	TINSLEY PARK SPORTS
1933	TINSLEY PARK SPORTS
1934	LOPHAM STREET METHODISTS
1935	TINSLEY PARK SPORTS
1936	FULWOOD
1937	PENISTONE CHURCH
1938	STOVIN ATHLETIC
1939	CITY SURVEYORS
1940	HOYLAND LAW
1941	GRIMETHORPE ROVERS
1942	ATTERCLIFFE RADICALS
1943	ATTERCLIFFE RADICALS
1944	THORNCLIFFE WELFARE
1945	HEELEY SOCIAL
1946	HOYLAND COMMON H & S
1947	HOYLAND COMMON ATHLETIC
1948	WOODHOUSE MILL SPORTS
1949	TRAVELLERS SPORTS
1950	WOODHOUSE MILL WMC
1951	EFFINGHAM STEEL WORKS
1952	KENDRAY SPORTS
1953	CROOKES WMC
1954	YOTAR SPORTS
1955	ECCLESFIELD COLLEY ROVERS
1956	BELLHOUSE ROAD WMC
1957	DINNINGTON MW
1958	YOTAR SPORTS
1959	ECCLESFIELD RED ROSE
1960	TRAVELLERS SPORTS
1961	LAUGHTON COMMON MW
1962	ECCLESFIELD RED ROSE
1963	BRINSWORTH ATHLETIC
1964	ECCLESFIELD RED ROSE
1965	CROOKES WMC
1966	NORTHERN IDEAL HOMESTEADS S&SC
1967	BENTLEY VICTORIA
1968	LUNDWOOD WMC
1969	BARNSLEY GRAMMAR SCHOOLS OB
1970	CHARLTON UNITED (See Note 1)
1971	MONCKTON COLLIERY
1972	ECCLESFIELD RED ROSE
1973	NO RESULT – (See Note 2)
1974	ELDON YC
1975	WINDSOR
1976	ELDON YC
1977	WARD GREEN WMC
1978	UPPERTHONG SC
1979	WARD GREEN WMC
1980	ELDON YC
1981	CUTTING EDGE
1982	REDFEARN NATIONAL GLASS
1983	UPTON BROOKSIDE WMC
1984	BRODSWORTH MW
1985	WALTON MW
1986	KINSLEY COLTS
1987	NORTHGATE WMC
1988	WHARNCLIFFE ARMS
1989	STORTHES HALL
1990	ATHERSLEY REC
1991	ATHERSLEY REC
1992	ATHERSLEY REC
1993	DARFIELD RD WMC
1994	DARFIELD RD WMC
1995	DARFIELD RD WMC
1996	ATHERSLEY REC
1997	ATHERSLEY REC
1998	HEMSWORTH MW
1999	EDLINGTON WMC
2000	HOUGHTON MAIN
2001	CUTTING EDGE
2002	CUTTING EDGE
2003	WHITE BEAR
2004	RYHILL & HAVERCROFT SPORTS
2005	HALLAM MALIN
2006	KINSLEY BOYS
2007	KINSLEY BOYS
2008	KIRKBURTON
2009	TELECOM SPORTS (Over 35)
2010	SKELMANTHORPE AFC
2011	JUBILEE SPORTS
2012	SHAFTON VILLA
2013	HOLMFIRTH TOWN
2014	SHEFFIELD FC (Over 35)
2015	HANDSWORTH PARRAMORE (U21)
2016	STOCKSBRIDGE PARK STEELS (U21)

Note 1 Bentley won, but dismissed for playing unregistered player

Note 2 Bentley Victoria won final but played ineligible player. The Competition Committee decided to call the Competition void, rather than award it to their opponents Windsor. The player in question was George Mansell who had played for Hatfield Main in the Yorkshire League

S&H County FA.
Junior Challenge Cup Winners Medal won by Stovin Athletic 1937-38

S & H CFA JUNIOR CHALLENGE SHIELD

This Competition was started by S&H CFA in 1959 for the teams who kept opting out of the Junior Challenge Cup Competition as they often felt they had little chance of winning against the more senior teams that entered that cup. With the reduction in Saturday football in the late 1980's, it was decided to terminate the competition.

1959/60	BRODSWORTH MW
1960/61	EMLEY
1961/62	HIGHFIELDS ATHLETIC
1962/63	WHARNCLIFFE WOODMOOR SPORTS
1963/64	DARTON WELFARE
1964/65	WOMBWELL MW
1965/66	GRIMETHORPE EX-SERVICEMENS
1966/67	BRINSWORTH ATHLETIC
1967/68	NORTHCLIFFE WMC
1968/69	BARUGH GREEN SPORTS
1969/70	KIRKBURTON AFC
1970/71	MALTBY YC
1971/72	WALTON COLLIERY
1972/73	MEXBOROUGH M W
1973/74	HEMSWORTH WEST END
1974/75	HEMSWORTH ST PATRICKS
1975/76	UPPERTHONG
1976/77	ROYAL GEORGE
1977/78	STEETLEY SPORTS
1978/79	HALL GREEN SPORTS
1979/80	GRANGE MOOR WMC
1980/81	WORKSOP BOROUGH
1981/82	WOODSETTS WELFARE
1982/83	HEMSWORTH ST PATRICKS
1983/84	STATION HOTEL ROSSINGTON
1984/85	KEXBOROUGH SOCIAL
1985/86	BLACKSTOCK
1986/87	BLACKSTOCK
1987/88	RING O BELLS
1988/89	INDUSTRY INN
1989/90	UNSTONE ATHLETIC

Sheffield and Hallamshire Junior Shield Runners-Up Tankard for season 1971. Presented to Woodhouse West End who lost to Maltby YC.

SHEFFIELD & HALLAMSHIRE PUBLIC PARKS & RECREATION GROUNDS LEAGUE

This competition appears to have been run between 1933 and 1940 by S&H CFA.

As the name suggests, the competition was only for teams that played on Public Parks or Council-owned recreational grounds. These teams were not allowed to enter other leagues at the time as most leagues insisted that member clubs owned their own ground.

It ceased due to the war and does not appear to have restarted.

1933/34	NEW INN
1934/35	ROYAL SPORTS
1935/36	BOUNDARY SOCIAL
1936/37	DONCASTER SPORTS
1937/38	WOODBOURNE ROVERS
1938/39	WOODBOURNE ROVERS
1939/40	ARBOURTHORNE SPORTS

Public Parks League Runners-up medal for season 1933-34.

Woodthorpe Amateurs, played in the Public Parks League in season 1935-36.

SHEFFIELD & HALLAMSHIRE CFA – SENIOR CUP

The Cup is made of silver and is engraved Challenge Cup, Sheffield Football Association. It is hallmarked with a lion, crown, a head with the letter "J" which is for the year 1876. Sheffield FA ran a competition for the design of this cup for which F Fidler of Sheffield School of Art won the £5 prize

Sheffield & Hallamshire Senior Cup

	WINNER		RUNNER-UP
1877	THE WEDNESDAY	4-3	HEELEY
1878	THE WEDNESDAY	2-0	ATTERCLIFFE
1879	THURSDAY WANDERERS (Sheffield FC non-Saturday Team)	3-1	HEELEY
1880	STAVELEY	3-1	HEELEY
1881	THE WEDNESDAY	8-1	ECCLESFIELD
1882	HEELEY	5-0	PYEBANK
1883	THE WEDNESDAY	2-1	LOCKWOOD BROS
1884	LOCKWOOD BROS	2-0	HEELEY
1885	LOCKWOOD BROS	2-0	PARK GRANGE
1886	MEXBOROUGH	2-1	HEELEY
1887	THE WEDNESDAY	2-1	COLLEGIATE
1888	THE WEDNESDAY	3-2	ECCLESFIELD
1889	ROTHERHAM TOWN	2-1	STAVELEY
1890	ROTHERHAM TOWN	2-1	SHEFFIELD UNITED (after draw)
1891	DONCASTER ROVERS	2-1	SHEFFIELD UNITED
1892	SHEFFIELD UNITED	2-1	THE WEDNESDAY
1893	SHEFFIELD STROLLERS (Sheffield Utd Reserve Team)	3-1	WEDNESDAY WANDERERS (Sheffield Wednesday Reserve Team)
1894	MEXBOROUGH	3-1	SHEFFIELD UNITED RES
1895	SHEFFIELD WEDNESDAY RES		League Champions (see Note 1)
1896	MEXBOROUGH		League Champions (see Note 1)
1897	SHEFFIELD UNITED RES	3-0	WATH
1898	SHEFFIELD UNITED RES	3-1	SHEFFIELD WEDNESDAY RES
1899	SHEFFIELD UNITED RES	5-2	ATTERCLIFFE (after 1-1)
1900	SHEFFIELD WEDNESDAY RES	2-0	WORKSOP TOWN
1901	SHEFFIELD UNITED RES	6-1	CHANNING ROVERS
1902	SHEFFIELD WEDNESDAY RES	1-0	ROYSTON
1903	SHEFFIELD WEDNESDAY RES	5-0	ROUNDEL (after 1-1)
1904	BARNSLEY	6-1	HALLAM
1905	SHEFFIELD UNITED RES	3-1	SHEFFIELD WEDNESDAY RES
1906	DENABY UNITED	4-2	SHEFFIELD WEDNESDAY RES
1907	SHEFFIELD WEDNESDAY RES	2-0	SHEFFIELD UNITED RES
1908	SHEFFIELD UNITED RES	1-0	SOUTH KIRKBY COLLIERY
1909	SHEFFIELD UNITED RES	5-1	ROTHERHAM COUNTY
1910	DENABY UNITED	Aband 1-0	BARNSLEY (See Note 2)
1911	SHEFFIELD UNITED RES	4-1	MEXBOROUGH
1912	DONCASTER ROVERS	3-0	SHEFFIELD UNITED RES
1913	ROTHERHAM COUNTY	3-0	WORKSOP TOWN
1914	ROTHERHAM COUNTY	1-0	SHEFFIELD WEDNESDAY RES
1915	BARNSLEY RES	3-0	WORKSOP TOWN
1916 – 1919 NO COMPETITION			
1920	ROTHERHAM TOWN	1-0	SHEFFIELD UNITED RES
1921	SHEFFIELD WEDNESDAY RES	2-0	BARNSLEY RES
1922	SHEFFIELD WEDNESDAY RES	2-0	BARNSLEY RES
1923	WOMBWELL	2-0	MEXBOROUGH
1924	WORKSOP TOWN	3-0	BARNSLEY RES
1925	ROTHERHAM TOWN	5-1	WORKSOP TOWN

SHEFFIELD & HALLAMSHIRE CFA – SENIOR CUP continued

Year	Winner	Score	Runner-up
1926	WATH ATHLETIC	3-0	BARNSLEY RES
1927	DARFIELD	5-0	ECCLESFIELD
1928	FRICKLEY COLLIERY	3-1	ARDSLEY ATHLETIC
1929	ARDSLEY ATHLETIC	6-2	ECCLESFIELD
1930	SOUTH KIRKBY COLLIERY	2-0	CUDWORTH
1931	MEXBOROUGH ATHLETIC	2-0	FRICKLEY COLLIERY
1932	DINNINGTON ATHLETIC	3-0	SOUTH KIRKBY COLLIERY
1933	DENABY UNITED	1-0	RAWMARSH ATHLETIC
1934	MEXBOROUGH ATHLETIC	8-1	WOODHOUSE ALLIANCE
1935	FIRBECK MAIN COLLIERY	3-0	DENABY UNITED
1936	DENABY UNITED	4-2	WORKSOP TOWN
1937	UPTON COLLIERY	4-3	THURNSCOE VICTORIA
1938	NORTON WOODSEATS	2-1	LOPHAM STREET UM
1939	RAWMARSH WELFARE	3-2	WORKSOP TOWN
1940	BEIGHTON MW	2-1	FRICKLEY COLLIERY ATH
1941	SOUTH KIRKBY COLLIERY	2-1	BEIGHTON MINERS WELFARE
1942	MANVERS MAIN	1-0	SHEFFIELD UNITED "A"
1943	ROYAL ARMY SIGNAL CORPS	1-0	SHEFFIELD WEDNESDAY RES
1944	ROYAL ARMY SIGNAL CORPS	5-3	NORTON WOODSEATS
1945	BARNSLEY RES	3-1	BRODSWORTH MW
1946	WOMBWELL ATHLETIC	2-0	HARWORTH COLLIERY
1947	THURCROFT MAIN		DINNINGTON ATH
1948	HARWORTH COLLIERY	1-0	BEIGHTON MINERS WELFARE
1949	ROYSTON SOCIAL	3-2	HARWORTH COLLIERY
1950	UPTON COLLIERY	5-3	BEIGHTON MINERS WELFARE
1951	HALLAM	3-0	STOCKSBRIDGE WORKS
1952	STOCKSBRIDGE WORKS	4-1	DENABY UNITED
1953	WORKSOP TOWN	3-1	BEIGHTON MINERS WELFARE
1954	SHEFFIELD WEDNESDAY "A"	2-1	WORKSOP TOWN
1955	WORKSOP TOWN	2-1	STOCKSBRIDGE WORKS
1956	BEIGHTON MW	4-2	STOCKSBRIDGE WORKS
1957	FRICKLEY COLLIERY	3-2	WORKSOP TOWN
1958	BENTLEY COLLIERY	3-1	STOCKSBRIDGE WORKS
1959	BENTLEY COLLIERY	1-0	YOTAR SPORTS
1960	GRIMETHORPE MW	3-2	DENABY UNITED
1961	FRICKLEY COLLIERY	2-1	WORKSOP TOWN
1962	HALLAM	1-0	SHEFFIELD FC
1963	FRICKLEY COLLIERY	2-1	SHEFFIELD UNITED "A" (WORKSOP ON CUP)
1964	MEXBOROUGH TOWN	0-1	STOCKSBRIDGE WORKS
	(TIE AWARDED TO MEXBOROUGH) - (STOCKSBRIDGE ON CUP)		
1965	HALLAM	3-2	THURCROFT WELFARE
1966	WORKSOP TOWN	3-2	FRICKLEY COLLIERY
1967	FRICKLEY COLLIERY ATH	4-1	NORTON WOODSEATS
1968	HALLAM	1-0	NORTON WOODSEATS
1969	REDFEARNS SPORTS	1-0	FRICKLEY COLLIERY ATH
1970	WORKSOP TOWN	2-1	DINNINGTON ATHLETIC
1971	RAWMARSH WELFARE	3-1	FRICKLEY COLLIERY ATH
1972	KIVETON PARK UNITED	3-0	FRECHEVILLE CA
1973	WORKSOP TOWN	4-1	WORSBOROUGH BRIDGE MW
1974	FRECHEVILLE COMMUNITY	2-1	WORKSOP TOWN

SHEFFIELD & HALLAMSHIRE CFA – SENIOR CUP continued

Year	Winner	Score	Runner-up
1975	MEXBOROUGH TOWN	1-0	DENABY UNITED
1976	EMLEY	2-0	WORKSOP TOWN
1977	MEXBOROUGH TOWN	2-1	WORKSOP TOWN
1978	MALTBY MAIN	2-1	MEXBOROUGH TOWN
1979	FRICKLEY ATHLETIC	3-2	MEXBOROUGH TOWN
1980	EMLEY	2-0	WORKSOP TOWN
1981	EMLEY	2-1	FRICKLEY ATHLETIC
1982	WORKSOP TOWN		FRICKLEY ATHLETIC (see Note 3)
	(TIE AWARDED TO WORKSOP)		
1983	MEXBOROUGH TOWN	2-1	DENABY UNITED
1984	EMLEY	2-0	FRECHEVILLE CA
1985	WORKSOP TOWN	2-1	FRICKLEY ATHLETIC
1986	FRICKLEY ATHLETIC	2-0	CROOKES
1987	DENABY UNITED	3-2	EMLEY
1988	FRICKLEY ATHLETIC	2-1 agg	WORKSOP TOWN
1989	EMLEY	2-0	WOOLLEY MINERS WELFARE
1990	FRICKLEY ATHLETIC	2-1agg	DENABY UNITED
1991	EMLEY (EMLEY WON 4-3 ON PENS)	1-1	WORKSOP TOWN
1992	EMLEY	1-0	FRICKLEY ATHLETIC
1993	STOCKSBRIDGE PARK STEELS	agg 5-3	WORKSOP TOWN (2 LEGS - 3-2 & 2-1)
1994	SHEFFIELD FC (SHEFFIELD WON 6-5 ON PENS)	1-1	WORKSOP TOWN
1995	WORKSOP TOWN	1-0	EMLEY
1996	STOCKSBRIDGE PARK STEELS	1-0	GRIMETHORPE MW
1997	WORKSOP TOWN	7-0	HARWORTH CI
1998	EMLEY	3-0	PARKGATE
1999	STOCKSBRIDGE PARK STEELS	1-0	EMLEY
2000	FRICKLEY ATHLETIC	3-0	EMLEY
2001	DONCASTER ROVERS	2-1	EMLEY
2002	DONCASTER ROVERS	3-0	EMLEY
2003	WORKSOP TOWN	2-1	DONCASTER ROVERS
2004	FRICKLEY COLLIERY	3-2	WORKSOP TOWN
2005	SHEFFIELD FC	1-0	WORKSOP TOWN
2006	SHEFFIELD FC	2-1	PARKGATE FC
2007	STOCKSBRIDGE PARK STEELS	2-1	WORKSOP TOWN
2008	SHEFFIELD FC	2-0	WORKSOP TOWN
2009	STOCKSBRIDGE PARK STEELS	3-0	BRODSWORTH MW
2010	SHEFFIELD FC	4-2	HALLAM FC
2011	STOCKSBRIDGE PARK STEELS	3-0	PARKGATE FC
2012	WORKSOP TOWN	3-2	FRICKLEY ATHLETIC
2013	FRICKLEY ATHLETIC	4-3	SHEFFIELD FC
2014	ATHERSLEY REC	1-0	FRICKLEY ATHLETIC
2015	FRICKLEY ATHLETIC	4-1	NOSTELL WM
2016	FRICKLEY ATHLETIC		SHAW LANE AQUAFORCE (see Note 4)

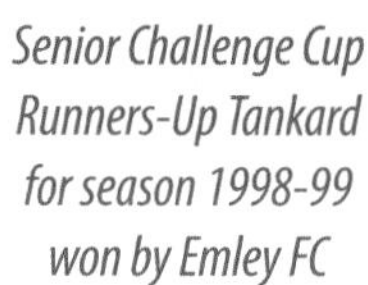

Senior Challenge Cup Runners-Up Tankard for season 1998-99 won by Emley FC

Note 1 For two seasons, 1894/95 and 1895/96 the Competition was played on a league basis rather than a knock out cup.

Note 2 With 75 mins gone, Denaby Utd were awarded a penalty. The Barnsley fans came on the pitch and grabbed the ball, later recovered by a police office. Barnsley by then had left the field, and with only 9 players left, they refused to come back on the field, so the game was abandoned. Game later awarded to Denaby.

Note 3 The final was due to be played after the end of Frickley's league season. By this time all the Frickley players were out of contract, so they could not field a team

Note 4 Tie awarded to Frickley Athletic as Shaw Lane Aquaforce withdrew.

For seasons 1925/26 to 1945/46 the competition was split into 2 groups, invitation and open. The winners of the Invitation Cup were awarded the Senior Cup and their name engraved on the Cup, except for 1945/46 when nothing appears on the cup. The Open Cup winners received another trophy. Between 1939/40 and 1947/48 this was the Hatchard Cup, but at this stage nothing found for other years. The above list includes the winners of the Open Cup, which I consider to be more appropriate as the Invitation Cup appears to be mainly pro teams. The winners for 1948/49 and 1949/50 are not engraved on the Cup even though there was only one competition.

INVITATION CUP WINNERS

	WINNER		RUNNER-UP
1926	SHEFFIELD WEDNESDAY RES	4-2	DONCASTER ROVERS RES
1927	SHEFFIELD UTD RES	2-0	SHEFFIELD WEDNESDAY RES
1928	SHEFFIELD WEDNESDAY RES	4-0	WORKSOP TOWN
1929	SHEFFIELD WEDNESDAY RES	4-1	SHEFFIELD UNITED RES
1930	BARNSLEY RES	1-0	SHEFFIELD UNITED RES
1931	SHEFFIELD WEDNESDAY RES	3-1	SHEFFIELD UNITED RES
1932	SHEFFIELD WEDNESDAY RES	3-1	WOMBWELL
1933	BARNSLEY RES	4-1	DONCASTER ROVERS RES (after 2-2)
1934	BARNSLEY RES	8-0	SHEFFIELD WEDNESDAY RES
1935	NO COMP		
1936	NO COMP		
1937	DONCASTER ROVERS RES	3-1	BARNSLEY RES
1938	DONCASTER ROVERS RES	1-0	ROTHERHAM UNITED RES (After 1-1)
1939	DONCASTER ROVERS RES	1-0	BARNSLEY
1940	BOLSOVER COLLIERY	3-2	BEIGHTON MW
1941	THURCROFT MAIN	2-0	DENABY MAIN
1942	ROYAL ARMY SIGNAL CORP	6-1	ATTERCLIFFE RADICALS
1943	NO COMP		
1944	ROYAL ARMY SIGNAL CORP	4-2	SHEFFIELD UNITED RES
1945	FIRBECK MAIN COLLIERY	3-2	SHEFFIELD WEDNESDAY RES
1946	THURNSCOE VICTORIA	5-3	KIVETON PARK

SHEFFIELD & HALLAMSHIRE SUNDAY JUNIOR CHALLENGE CUP

WINNERS

2004	BATCHELORS FC (WORKSOP)
2005	SWINTON WMC
2006	RING O BELLS AFP
2007	THE POCKET 2003
2008	LANGOLD OLD BOYS
2009	FC BRIMINGTON
2010	DOMINO FC
2011	REDMIRES FC
2012	MEMORIES FC
2013	ROYAL ALBERT
2014	THE PHEASANT FC
2015	FC HANDSWORTH TURF
2016	BAGSHAWE ARMS

SHEFFIELD & HALLAMSHIRE CFA – SUNDAY CHALLENGE CUP (SENIOR)

There was no official football played in the Sheffield & Hallamshire CFA area on a Sunday until 1965, although several leagues did play unofficially earlier. Anybody caught playing could end up being suspended and any private ground used for Sunday football could be closed down to Saturday football by the County FA.

With England hosting and winning the World Cup in 1966, there was a boom in people wanting to play football and so Sheffield & Hallamshire relented and allowed leagues to start up officially on a Sunday. The S&H started and ran the Sunday Under 18 League and the Hallamshire Sunday League for the 1966/67 season. The Under 18 league only ran for a few seasons, but the Hallamshire League ran until 2009 when it joined with the Meadowhall League, originally the Sheffield and District Sunday League which started in 1964.

With two cup competitions in operation for junior clubs on a Saturday (Junior Challenge Cup and Junior Challenge Shield) and more Sunday clubs and Leagues starting each season in was decided for the 1968/69 season that S&H would run a Sunday Competition. It was originally open to all teams.

The winners of the Senior Sunday Cup tended to be teams with players who played in the Northern Premier and Northern Counties East Leagues on a Saturday. These teams tended to be in the top divisions of the local leagues. Because of this, more junior lower division clubs started to pay the opting out fee rather than joining the competition.

As a result of this, the S&H CFA decided that for the 2003/04 season, a separate competition would be set up for the more junior clubs in the area, and so the Sunday Junior Cup was started. As a result more teams started to play in the Sunday Cup competitions again, with S&H deciding, based on league positions, which of the competitions a club would compete in.

Athersley Rec. winners in 2009

WINNERS

1969	ARBOURTHORNE COMMUNITY
1970	RAWMARSH UTD
1971	RAWMARSH UTD
1972	ANGEL
1973	WOODBOURNE
1974	RAWMARSH HORSE & JOCKEY
1975	KIVETON PARK
1976	EARL UTD
1977	BLACK BULL TAVERNERS
1978	ANGEL
1979	FULWOOD AMATEURS
1980	SWINTON WMC
1981	ABOURTHORNE EA
1982	WOODBOURNE
1983	JOKER
1984	OLIVE GROVE
1985	OLIVE GROVE
1986	JOKER
1987	THE GATE
1988	GRASSMOOR
1989	THURCROFT HOTEL
1990	ARBOURTHORNE EA
1991	ROYSTON SOCIAL
1992	ROYAL EARL
1993	MILL 92
1994	NORMAN INN
1995	HOYLAND TOWN JAGS
1996	ROYSTON SHIP
1997	HOYLAND TOWN JAGS
1998	HOYLAND TOWN JAGS
1999	ATHERSLEY REC
2000	BRADWAY
2001	HOYLAND TOWN JAGS
2002	BRADWAY
2003	HOYLAND TOWN JAGS
2004	HOYLAND TOWN JAGS
2005	HOYLAND TOWN JAGS
2006	ATHERSLEY REC
2007	RERESBY ARMS
2008	ROYSTON STEELERS
2009	ATHERSLEY REC
2010	ARBOURTHORNE EA
2011	AFP FC
2012	ATHERSLEY REC
2013	ATHERSLEY REC
2014	RAWSON SPRING
2015	ROYAL EARL
2016	WESTVILLE

SHEFFIELD THURSDAY AMATEUR LEAGUE

This league started in 1911/12, and amalgamated with the Early Closing League in 1913/14.

The cup for this competition is engraved Sheffield & Hallamshire CFA Early Closing League. The cup is silver and marked Crown/Lion/T which is for 1911. It appears the Thursday Amateur League took over the cup from the Early Closing League on amalgamation.

1911/12	POST OFFICE
1912/13	WILD & SONS
1913/14	WHITWORTHS
1914/15	SHEFFIELD TRAMWAY
1915-19	NO COMP – WAR
1919/20	SHEFFIELD TRAMS FC
1920/21	BARNSLEY AMATEURS
1921/22	SHEFFIELD TRAMWAY
1922/23	BARNSLEY AMATEURS
1923/24	EDWARD WILD & SON
1924/25	MEXBOROUGH THURSDAY
1925/26	MEXBOROUGH THURSDAY
1926/27	SHEFFIELD THURSDAY AMATEURS
1927/28	MEXBOROUGH THURSDAY
1928/29	SHEFFIELD TRAMWAY
1929/30	MEXBOROUGH THURSDAY
1930/31	B & C SPORTS
1931/32	YORKSHIRE TRACTION SPORTS
1932/33	CENTRAL THURSDAY
1933/34	ROTHERHAM THURSDAY SPORTS
1934/35	CENTRAL THURSDAY
1935/36	CENTRAL THURSDAY
1936/37	NO COMPETITION
1937/38	ROTHERHAM BUTCHERS
1938/39	THURSDAY ATHLETIC
1939-1946	NO COMP - WAR
1946/47	CENTRAL THURSDAY
1947/48	CENTRAL THURSDAY
1948/49	SHEFFIELD TRANSPORT "A"
1949/50	SHEFFIELD TRANSPORT "A"
1950/51	CENTRAL THURSDAY "B"
1951/52	B&C CO-OP SPORTS
1952/53	CENTRAL THURSDAY
1953/54	B&C CO-OP SPORTS
1954/55	CENTRAL THURSDAY
1955/56	CENTRAL THURSDAY "A"
1956/57	RAF NORTON
1957/58	B & C SPORTS

At this stage the League amalgamated with the Rotherham & District Midweek League clubs to form the Sheffield & Rotherham Mid-week League

SHEFFIELD MIDWEEK LEAGUE & THURSDAY CHALLENGE CUP

Cup presented by Councillor A Thompson of Doncaster in 1926. Cup marked C B & S with Lion & Crown which is 1926. Cup was engraved Sheffield & Hallamshire Midweek League and was played for in 1926/27. There are no other inscriptions until 1933/34, when it appears that it was used for the Thursday Challenge Cup, but no inscription to indicate this. Last inscription is 1939/40. The Cup was then re-engraved on the other side and used as the Intermediate Challenge Cup from 1942 until 1975.

1926/27	DONCASTER ROVERS
1933/34	SHEFFIELD CITY POLICE
1934/35	CENTRAL THURSDAY
1935/36	CENTRAL THURSDAY
1936/37	SHEFFIELD TRANSPORT A
1937/38	ROTHERHAM BUTCHERS
1938/39	ROTHERHAM BUTCHERS
1939/40	B&C CO-OP SPORTS

SHEFFIELD THURSDAY FRIENDLIES LEAGUE

1927/28	JEWISH ATHLETIC SPORTS	
1928/29	ROTHERHAM THURSDAY SPORTS	
1929/30	CENTRAL THURSDAY	
1930/31	SHEFFIELD THURSDAY AMATEURS	
1931/32	WIGFALL SPORTS	
1932/33	WIGFALL SPORTS	
1933/34	DINNINGTON TRADESMEN	
1934/35	SHEFFIELD GPO	
1935/36	THURSDAY ATHLETIC	
1936/37	DIV A	CENTRAL THURSDAY
	DIV B	ROTHERHAM BUTCHERS
1937/38	DIV A	ROTHERHAM BUTCHERS
	DIV B	SHEFFIELD BUTCHERS
1938/39	YORKSHIRE PENNY BANK	
1939/40	SHEFFIELD TRANSPORT	

YOUTH CHALLENGE CUP UNDER 13s

2008	SHEFFIELD WEDNESDAY YOUNG OWLS
2009	HANDLEY WOOD JFC
2010	SHEFFIELD UTD JFC
2011	HANDLEY WOOD JFC
2012	HANDSWORTH BOYS
2013	THORNCLIFFE JUNIORS
2014	HOYLAND TOWN JUNIORS
2015	THORNCLIFFE JUNIORS
2016	YOUNG OWLS

SHEFFIELD & HALLAMSHIRE CFA YOUTH CHALLENGE CUP (UNDER 16s)

2000	SHEFFIELD RANGERS		
2001	SW FC		
2002	UPPERTHONG SCJFC		
2003	HANDSWORTH BOYS		
2004	WICKERSLEY YOUTH FC		
2005	WISEWOOD JUNIORS		
2006	HYDE PARK KNIGHTS JFC	2-0	DODWORTH MW JFC
2007	BRUNSMEER ATH AGC	2-1	DODWORTH MW JFC
2008	WOMBWELL MAIN WARRIORS	3-2	HOYLAND COMMON FALCONS
2009	SHEFFIELD UNITED JUNIOR BLADES (WON ON PENS 6-5)	3-3	REDFEARNS JFC
2010	UPPERTHONG SCJFC	3-2	SILKSTONE UTD JFC
2011	SHEFFIELD WEDNESDAY YOUNG OWLS	3-1	MALTBY JUNIORS
2012	WICKERSLEY YOUTH	5-4	BRAMPTON ROVERS
2013	SHEFFIELD UNITED JUNIOR BLADES	3-0	HEPWORTH UTD JUNIORS
2014	SHEFFIELD WEDNESDAY YOUNG OWLS		(Awarded as Sheff Utd Juniors played ineligible player)
2015	HANDSWORTH BOYS JFC	3-1	SHEFF WEDNESDAY YOUNG OWLS
2016	SHEFFIELD FC (GREENHILL JFC)	2-0	ABBEY LANE

SHEFFIELD & HALLAMSHIRE WOMENS CHALLENGE CUP

2000	SHEFFIELD WEDNESDAY LADIES		
2001	SHEFFIELD WEDNESDAY LADIES		
2002	PARKGATE LADIES		
2003	DONCASTER BELLES		
2004	DONCASTER ROVERS BELLES		
2005	DONCASTER ROVERS BELLES		
2006	DONCASTER ROVERS BELLES	2-1	SHEFFIELD WEDNESDAY
2007	SHEFFIELD WEDNESDAY LADIES	1-0	DONCASTER ROVERS BELLES
2008	DONCASTER ROVERS BELLES	4-0	SHEFFIELD WEDNESDAY LADIES
2009	DONCASTER ROVERS BELLES	5-0	SHEFFIELD WEDNESDAY LADIES
2010	DONCASTER ROVERS BELLES	3-0	ROTHERHAM UNITED LADIES
2011	ROTHERHAM UNITED LADIES	2-0	HUDDERSFIELD TOWN LADIES
2012	SHEFFIELD LADIES	4-0	SHEFFIELD WEDNESDAY LADIES
2013	SHEFFIELD LADIES	6-0	ROTHERHAM UNITED LADIES
2014	SHEFFIELD LADIES	5-1	STEEL CITY LADIES
2015	SHEFFIELD LADIES	4-1	HUDDERSFIELD TOWN LADIES
2016	BARNSLEY LADIES	4-2	HUDDERSFIELD TOWN LADIES

SHEFFIELD & REGIONAL SUNDAY LEAGUE

This League started in 1967 and ceased in 1999 when it amalgamated with the Sheffield Sunday Alliance League

PREMIER DIVISION

1998/99	SMITHYWOOD WMC

DIVISION 1

1967/68	BALL INN (CROOKES)
1968/69	BALL INN (CROOKES)
1969/70	GREENOAK
1970/71	NETHER EDGE
1971/72	WOODSEATS WMC
1972/73	GLEESONS SPORTS
1973/74	GLEESONS SPORTS
1974/75	WOODSEATS WMC
1975/76	PRINCE OF WALES
1976/77	GREENOAK
1977/78	
1978/79	WOODSEATS WMC
1979/80	
1980/81	TIMBERTOP
1981/82	
1982/83	TIMBERTOP
1983/84	NORFOLK PARK TA
1984/85	NORFOLK PARK TA
1985/86	SWALLOWNEST SC
1986/87	BALL INN THORPE
1987/88	GREENHILL PARK
1988/89	
1989/90	
1990/91	NORFOLK PARK TA
1991/92	NORFOLK PARK TA
1992/93	HACKENTHORPE BLUE BELL
1993/94	NORFOLK PARK TA
1994/95	NORFOLK PARK TA
1995/96	
1996/97	BEIGHTON CUMBERLAND
1997/98	BEIGHTON CUMBERLAND
1998/99	RICHMOND

DIVISION 2

1968/69	- A SICEY HOTEL
	B WOODSEATS WMC
1969/70	GLEESONS SPORTS
1970/71	DEERSTALKER
1971/72	ENFIELD AMATEURS
1972/73	PARK GARDENERS WMC
1973/74	PITSMOOR WMC
1974/75	ROWLINSON YC
1975/76	TIMBERTOP
1976/77	DEERSTALKER
1977/78	NORFOLK PARK TA
1978/79	
1979/80	
1980/81	QUEENS SOCIAL
1981/82	
1982/83	SWALLOWNEST SC
1983/84	ROYAL OAK, MOSBOROUGH
1984/85	MASONS CROOKES
1985/86	NU-LIFE PHOENIX
1986/87	SHEAF HOUSE
1987/88	MANOR SPORTS
1988/89	
1989/90	WOODHOUSE
1990/91	BIG TREE 89
1991/92	OLD BLUE BALL
1992/93	MINERS ARMS
1993/94	
1994/95	WHITE ROSE
1995/96	MANOR CASTLE
1996/97	HUNTSMAN
1997/98	ANGEL

Greenhawk F.C. played in the Sunday Regional League in the 1970s

DIVISION 3

1969/70	NAILMAKERS ARMS
1970/71	ENFIELD AMATEURS
1971/72	SEDGELOW
1972/73	BRUNSMEER ATHLETIC
1973/74	BURNCROSS 67
1974/75	TIMBERTOP
1975/76	MEERSBROOK PARK
1976/77	WHITE HORSE
1977/78	THROSTLES
1978/79	
1979/80	
1980/81	HOUSING
1981/82	
1982/83	ROYAL OAK MOSBOROUGH
1983/84	NU-LIFE PHOENIX
1984/85	PORTER PROV. TY-PHOO
1985/86	MAGPIES
1986/87	
1987/88	BAGSHAWE ARMS
1988/89	
1989/90	BIG TREE
1990/91	CUTLERS ARMS
1991/92	MOUNT PLEASANT
1992/93	BATHFIELD
1993/94	
1994/95	MANOR CASTLE

DIVISION 4

1972/73	MOSBOROUGH
1973/74	MOUNT PLEASANT
1974/75	NORTON WANDERERS
1975/76	WHITE HORSE
1976/77	THROSTLES
1977/78	SHARROW SPORTS
1978/79	GREENHILL PARK
1979/80	SHEFFIELD COMPANIONS
1980/81	MASONS ARMS
1981/82	ROYAL OAK MOSBOROUGH
1982/83	PORTER PROVISIONS
1983/84	STRADBROKE COMMUNITY 82
1984/85	DOMINO FC
1985/86	MANOR CASTLE
1986/87	COBDEN FC
1987/88	PARSON CROSS HOTEL
1988/89	ROYAL OAK PITSMOOR
1989/90	CUTLERS ARMS

DIVISION 5

1976/77	SHARROW SPORTS
1977/78	GREENHILL PARK
1978/79	
1979/80	
1980/81	PARK
1981/82	
1982/83	
1983/84	MILLHOUSES
1984/85	NORTON ATH
1985/86	MILLHOUSES
1986/87	BAGSHAWE ARMS
1987/88	STAFFORDSHIRE ARMS

Sheffield Sunday Regional League Handbook for season 1975-76

LEAGUE CHALLENGE CUP

1967/68	THORNHILL
1968/69	BELL GEARS
1969/70	BALL INN
1970/71	BALL INN
1971/72	GREENOAK
1972/73	BALL INN
1973/74	WOODSEATS WMC
1974/75	PRINCE OF WALES ATHLETIC
1975/76	
1976/77	GREENOAK
1977/78	
1978/79	WOODSEATS WMC
1979/80	
1980/81	
1981/82	
1982/83	NORFOLK PARK TA
1983/84	NORFOLK PARK TA
1984/85	GREENHILL PARK
1985/86	SWALLOWNEST SC
1986/87	CUTLERS ARMS
1987/88	
1988/89	
1989/90	
1990/91	NORFOLK PARK TA
1991/92	
1992/93	HACKENTHORPE BLUE BELL
1993/94	
1994/95	
1995/96	MANOR CASTLE
1996/97	BATHFIELD
1997/98	PUNCHBOWL
1998/99	STAR & GARTER

UNDER 18 LEAGUE

1972/73	STOCKSBRIDGE
1973/74	CUTLERS ARMS
1974/75	ROWLINSON YC
1975/76	CUTLERS ARMS

UNDER 18 KO CUP

1972/73	CUTLERS ARMS
1973/74	CUTLERS ARMS
1974/75	CROOKES JUNIORS
1975/76	CUTLERS ARMS

UNDER 16½ LEAGUE

1971/72	STOCKSBRIDGE
1972/73	CROOKES JUNIORS

UNDER 16½ KO CUP

1971/72	RIDGEWAY
1972/73	CUTLERS ARMS

THE GREEN UN CHARITY CUP

This was a charity game in aid of the Telegraph & Star Old Folks Fund. It was played between the previous seasons League Champions and Challenge Cup winners

1969/70	BALL INN
1970/71	BALL INN
1971/72	NETHER EDGE
1972/73	GREENOAK & WOODSEATS (JT)

SHEFFIELD ASSOCIATION MINOR LEAGUE

With the new set up at S&H FA it appears that the Cup used for the original Minor Cup Competition might have been re-used as the cup for this league.

The league appears to have stopped in 1925, but was played for again in 1929/30 for one season. The idea was for clubs from the Junior League to transfer to this Competition, but this did not happen

In Season 1926/27 the S&H Intermediate League started, which was the replacement for this league.

1904/05	ECCLESFIELD TOWN
1905/06	NELSON
1906/07	ECCLESFIELD TOWN
1907/08	NELSON
1908/09	THORNCLIFFE UTD
1909/10	DARNALL CONGS
1910/11	DARNALL CONGS
1911/12	HANDSWORTH ROVERS
1912/13	BIRD IN HAND
1913/14	SILVERWOOD COLLIERY
1914/15	STOCKSBRIDGE CHURCH
1915/16	BEIGHTON REC
1916/17	CRAVENS SPORTS
1917/18	CRAVENS SPORTS
1918/19	CAMMELLS SPORTS
1919/20	OUGHTIBRIDGE
1920/21	PARKGATE CHRIST CHURCH
1921/22	GREASBROUGH WMC
1922/23	ATTERCLIFFE UTD
1923/24	KIVETON PARK
1924/25	RAWMARSH ATHLETIC
1925-1929	NO COMPETITION
1929/30	BEIGHTON MW

SHEFFIELD MINOR CUP

This competition was originally set up and run by Sheffield FA.

It was usually played in various area leagues with the top teams playing off on a knock out basis to determine the overall winners.

The competition was renamed the Sheffield Association Alliance League in 1896. The Minor Cup continued to be used for the new competition.

1882/83	HEELEY
1883/84	ATTERCLIFFE
1884/85	ATTERCLIFFE
1885/86	ATTERCLIFFE
1886/87	ATTERCLIFFE
1887/88	CARBROOK CHURCH
1888/89	ECCLESFIELD
1889/90	ECCLESFIELD
1890/91	WATH
1891/92	KIVETON PARK
1892/93	PYEBANK ROVERS
1893/94	PYEBANK ROVERS
1894/95	WOMBWELL TOWN
1895/96	BIRDWELL

Winners Medal for Minor Cup for season 1891-92

Stocksbridge Church Football Club, winners of the Sheffield Minor League title in 1914-15.

SHEFFIELD LEAGUE FOOTBALL IN THE 1890'S

With the formation of the Football League competition in 1888 and the Midland League in 1889, football clubs started to look at wanting to play in a league format rather than the localised medals and jerseys competition, often run by local pubs to attract custom.

What follows is a brief history of some of the more important league competitions set up, most having a very short life as Sheffield & Hallamshire FA started to promote and run local league and cup football.

G Willey, an active S&H FA Council member who had the vision of league football in the Sheffield area, was at the forefront of starting several of these competitions, acting as either Secretary or Treasurer.

In fact, at the meeting when the Sheffield & District League disbanded in 1895 to allow for the new set up in local football, G Willey was quoted as saying that he had achieved his intention to promote league football in the area.

SHEFFIELD & DISTRICT FOOTBALL LEAGUE

G Willey formed this, the first football league in the area, called The Sheffield & District Football League in 1889. The first season was a bit of a hit and miss affair. A full fixture list had been worked out for the 8 teams entering, but clubs did not keep to it, with 2 teams having played their full 14 games, whilst 2 teams had only played 6 games. Because of this, it was decided to not declare a winner.

For the 1890/91 season, G Willey presented the GW Shield to the winners, with Kilnhurst being the first winners. Appropriately so as they had topped the league the previous season. This shield turned up in a skip in the 1990's, and was on display at the Wath St James squash club for many years.

1890/91	KILNHURST
1891/92	CHESTERFIELD
1892/93	WEDNESDAY WANDERERS (SHEFFIELD WEDNESDAYS RES)
1893/94	MEXBOROUGH
1894/95	ECKINGTON WORKS

The league ceased in 1895 as the Sheffield & Hallamshire FA intended to run their own competition for 1895/96. However due to problems, this did not happen until the 1896/97 season when they started the Association League. This league is still going today under the name of the County Senior League.

SHEFFIELD & DISTRICT MINOR LEAGUE

Season 1891/92 saw the start of a new junior league with 10 clubs. This League ran for four seasons until Sheffield FA decided to take over the running of junior football by creating the Junior League.

1891/92	PYEBANK ROVERS
1892/93	PYEBANK ROVERS
1893/94	TOLEDO
1894/95	ECCLESFIELD CHURCH

HALLAMSHIRE LEAGUE

This league started in 1891, but only ran for two seasons.. The first season was a strong contest with Sheffield Strollers (Sheffield United's reserve team) Wednesday Wanderers (Sheffield Wednesdays reserve team) and Rotherham United (Rotherham Town's reserve team). These teams moved into the stronger Sheffield & District League the following season. Several more junior teams entered for the following season, which was the competition's last as the S&H FA started their Minor Cup Competition, and the clubs moved into that

1891/92	SHEFFIELD STROLLERS
1892/93	ROTHERWOOD ROVERS

Sheffield & District Football League Winners Shield 1889.
First Football League Trophy in Sheffield & Hallamshire area.

SHEFFIELD & DISTRICT ALLIANCE LEAGUE

This competition started in 1892 and was run by/under the control of a sub-section of the Sheffield & District Football League. Two divisions of 8 teams played in it (No 1 and No 2 Divisions). In the early days of football, leagues split their teams into divisions with an equal number of teams in each division. There was no promotion or relegation between the divisions as now. The top teams in each division used to play off to be crowned the overall champion.

1892/93
Elsecar won Division 1 and Parkgate & Rawmarsh Division 2. The teams played off for the championship, and after a 1-1 draw at Parkgate, Elsecar won the replay 2-0. Elsecar players won medals and the club were presented with a League Championship flag to fly at their ground.

1893/94
Again 8 teams in two divisions with Elsecar and Kiveton Park finishing the top two teams. During the season the Sheffield & Hallamshire FA had been given a cup to use by Frank Hatchard the Conservative MP for the Hallamshire Division. This was handed to the Alliance to use. The competition changed its name during the season because of this and became the Sheffield & Hallamshire Alliance League. Elsecar and Kiveton Park played off for the trophy. The first game finished 4-4, but Kiveton Park won the second game 2-1. Sheffield & Hallamshire now took over control of this competition and renamed it the Hatchard Cup Competition. (See separate page)

SHEFFIELD ASSOCIATION ALLIANCE LEAGUE

In the new set up, this league was run by the Sheffield & Hallamshire FA.

For season 1896/97 there were 2 divisions of 12 teams in each. Division one winner were Parkgate *United and division 2 Heeley. However, the top two in each division played off in a semi-final and then final. In the final between the teams that had finished second in the divisions resulted in a win for Swinton by 2-1 after two 1-1 drawn games. They were presented with the cup previously presented for the Minor cup competition

In 1897/98 there were only 12 teams in one division, which Ecclesfield finished top and were crowned champions. The competition then ceased to run.

SHEFFIELD & DISTRICT COMBINATION LEAGUE

This was another offshoot from the Sheffield & District League. So many junior teams had applied to join the Sheffield & District Alliance League that it was decided to form a new league for season 1893/94. The first season saw three divisions with 22 teams in total. The division's top teams were Patrick Thistle, Saville FC and Grimesthorpe Reds. No reports of any play off to decide an overall champion have ever been found.

Season 1894/95 saw two divisions of 10 teams each with the top two teams Rotherwood Rovers and Normanton Springs playing off in a final for the championship. Rotherwood Rovers won 1-0 before a crowd of over 1,000 spectators at Beighton. On their return to Woodhouse Station the local brass band was waiting and accompanied them up the local streets to their headquarters at the Junction Inn playing "See the conquering hero come."

This league finished with the teams joining the teams from the Sheffield & District Minor League in the newly-formed Sheffield & Hallamshire Junior League for season 1895/96.

SHEFFIELD NEW LEAGUE

Due to various problems, Sheffield & Hallamshire FA did not start the senior league that they had intended for season 1895/96. Several of the senior clubs in the area decided to start their own league. They formed two divisions of 4 teams with the top two teams Attercliffe and Kilnhurst playing off for the championship. Attercliffe won the first game 2-1, but for some reason the teams met again 7 days later with Attercliffe winning this game 5-1. Medals were issued by Sheffield & Hallamshire FA to both clubs

DIVISION 1	P	W	D	L	F	A	P
ATTERCLIFFE	6	4	1	1	9	3	9
SHEEPBRIDGE	6	3	0	3	12	7	6
WORKSOP TOWN	6	2	1	3	8	7	5
ROTHERWOOD ROVERS	6	2	0	4	4	10	4

DIVISION 2	P	W	D	L	F	A	P
KILNHURST	6	4	1	1	17	7	9
HOYLAND SILKSTONE	5	3	1	1	14	5	7
ELSECAR	5	2	0	3	8	17	4
WOMBWELL	6	1	0	5	6	15	2

SHEFFIELD & DISTRICT FAIR PLAY LEAGUE

The Sheffield & District Fair Play League was set up in 1998 in order to provide local Churches in the Sheffield district to play football in a safe, friendly, but competitive environment, away from the more physical Saturday/Sunday pub leagues.

DIVISION -1

1998/99	CROWDED HOUSE
1999/00	SWALLOWNEST BETHESDA
2000/01	SWALLOWNEST BETHESDA
2001/02	SWALLOWNEST BETHESDA
2002/03	SWALLOWNEST BETHESDA
2003/04	FC ECCLESIA
2004/05	SWALLOWNEST BETHESDA
2005/06	FC ECCLESIA
2006/07	SWALLOWNEST BETHESDA
2007/08	ECCLESIA
2008/09	BROOMHILL PIRATE
2009/10	ECCLESIA PHOENIX
2010/11	KILLAMARSH ST GILES
2011/12	KILLAMARSH ST GILES
2012/13	AFC DYNAMO
2013/14	AFC DYNAMO
2014/15	BRUNSMEER ATHLETIC
2015/16	TROWAY FC

DIVISION 2

The Division 2 trophy is the original Trophy won by Lopham Street UM for winning Division 1 of the 1906/07 Bible Class League. This was taken by William Wood when he went to become a lay reader at Frinton, Essex in 1916. This was given to the league in 2009 by his family for them to use.

2001/02	CITY MUPPETS
2002/03	CITY MUPPETS
2003/04	ZION NEW BOYS
2004/05	AC SOUTHSIDE
2005/06	MATTERSLEY HALL BIBLE CLASS
2006/07	CITY CENTRAL
2007/08	FC PHILLY
2008/09	FC PHILLY
2009/10	HSBC B
2010/11	HSCB B
2011/12	HSBC ATHLETIC
2012/13	NORTON OAKES
2013/14	TROWAY FC
2014/15	TOTLEY SPORTS
2015/16	MALIN BRIDGE

DIVISION 3

2011/12	ECCLESFIELD PLAYERS LOUNGE
2012/13	TROWAY FC
2013/14	TOTLEY SPORTS
2014/15	A MALIN BRIDGE
	B CITY CENTRAL
2015/16	AC SOUTHSIDE

DIVISION 4

2015/16	NEW BOHEMIANS

FAIR PLAY AWARD

The trophy played for is the original Sheffield Free Church League 1902-1915 which was taken by William Wood when he went to become a lay reader at Frinton, Essex in 1916. This was given to the league in 2009 by his family.

1998/99	ECCLESIA
1999/00	ECCLESIA
2000/01	ECCLESIA
2001/02	ECCLESIA
2002/03	ECCLESIA
2003/04	-
2004/05	CROWDED HOUSE
2005/06	CROWDED HOUSE
2006/07	MATTERSLEY HALL BIBLE CLASS
2007/08	ARBOURTHORNE CC
2008/09	WOODSEATS FC
2009/10	ARBOURTHORNE CC
2010/11	WOODSEATS FC
2011/12	ECCLESIA PHOENIX

The League now award a Fair play Award for each division

CHALLENGE CUP

1998/99	CROWDED HOUSE
1999/00	CROWDED HOUSE
2000/01	SWALLOWNEST BETHESDA
2001/02	SWALLOWNEST BETHESDA
2002/03	SWALLOWNEST BETHESDA
2003/04	SWALLOWNEST BETHESDA
2004/05	SWALLOWNEST BETHESDA
2005/06	KINGS CENTRE
2006/07	ARBOURTHORNE CC
2007/08	ECCLESIA
2008/09	BROOMHILL PIRATE
2009/10	KILLAMARSH ST GILES
2010/11	AFC DYNAMO
2011/12	AFC DYNAMO
2012/13	TROWAY
2013/14	AFC DYNAMO
2014/15	MALIN BRIDGE
2015/16	RANMOOR GALAXY

SHEFFIELD ASSOCIATION LEAGUE – COUNTY SENIOR LEAGUE

The Association League was started in 1896 and ran under that title until 1960 when the competition was renamed the S&H County Senior League. S&H CFA stopped running the County Senior League at the end of the 1982/83 season when it joined forces with the Hatchard League and with new sponsorship it became the Whitbread County Senior League.

Since then there have been various name changes to reflect the competition sponsors. It ran as the Whitbread until 1994 when Beefeater took over sponsorship for 3 seasons. In 1997 British Industrial Reclamation took over sponsorship until 2000. With no sponsors the title reverted to just the County Senior League until Windsor Food Services took over sponsorship in 2003. In 2012/13, Pete's Patisserie took over sponsorship

An Under 21 League was formed for season 2013/14

CUPS

The original winners cup was used from 1896 to 2003. The cup is engraved with Sheffield & Hallamshire FA, Est. 2 April 1877 and the Motto – The good of football and those that play it. The cup was originally played for as the senior KO cup for the Hallamshire FA 1877-1887. It then had Sheffield & added to it and was used for various S&H competitions until being allocated to the then Association League in 1896.

On the amalgamation of the County Senior League and the Hatchard League at the start of the 1983/84 season, the Hatchard Cup was used for the winners of the new Division 1.

Both cups were retired in 2003 when Windsor Food Services supplied new cups for both divisions.

A cup for the Division 2 winners is still being played for, which is believed to have been the original Division 2 winners for the Hatchard League.

There is a KO Cup being played for. Again it is believed that this was previously used by the Hatchard League as their KO Cup.

COUNTY SENIOR LEAGUE KNOCK OUT CUP

A KO Cup was played for 2 seasons in the 1960's. The Competition restarted in 1981. The CS League handbook wrongly shows Windsor & James Fairley Steels as the first 2 winners, but these were Hatchard League clubs at that time

1964 WORKSOP TOWN
1965 SHEFFIELD UNITED

1982 DOUBLE BARREL
1983 YORKSHIRE MAIN
1982 SWINTON ATHLETIC
1983 A LEE SPORTS CLUB
1984 BSC PARKGATE
1985 MALTBY MW
1986 SHEFFIELD FC
1987 AURORA UNITED
1988 MEXBOROUGH NORTHGATE WMC
1989 WOODSETTS WELFARE SPORTS
1990 ASH HOUSE
1991 FRECHEVILLE CA
1992 MEXBOROUGH MAIN STREET
1993 ASH HOUSE
1994 WORSBROUGH BRIDGE MW & ATHLETIC
1995 SWINTON ATHLETIC
1996 ATHERSLEY REC
1997 FRECHEVILLE CA
1998 FRECHEVILLE CA
1999 WORKSOP TOWN
2000 WOMBWELL MAIN
2001 EDLINGTON WMC
2002 AFC BARNSLEY
2003 SPORTSMAN ROY HANCOCK
2004 ATHERSLEY REC
2005 STOCKSBRIDGE PARK STEELS RES
2006 WOMBWELL MAIN
2007 ATHERSLEY REC
2008 STOCKSBRIDGE PARK STEELS RES
2009 ATHERSLEY REC
2010 STOCKSBRIDGE PARK STEELS RES
2011 ATHERSLEY REC
2012 PENISTONE CHURCH
2013 WOMBWELL MAIN
2014 PENISTONE CHURCH
2015 JOKER FC
2016 JUBILEE SPORTS

UNDER 21 LEAGUE

To try and encourage the growth of Saturday football, the League started an Under 21 Competition in 2013

2014 HANDSWORTH
2015 HANDSWORTH PARRAMORE
2016 STOCKSBRIDGE PARK STEELS

SHEFFIELD ASSOCIATION LEAGUE – COUNTY SENIOR LEAGUE

SHEFFIELD ASSOCIATION LEAGUE

1897 SHEFFIELD UTD RES
1898 PARKGATE UTD
1899 PARKGATE UTD & WORKSOP TOWN (Joint) (after 2-2 play off)
1900 WEDNESDAY RES
1901 WEDNESDAY RES
1902 BARNSLEY RES
1903 ROTHERHAM FC
1904 MEXBORO TOWN
1905 THORNHILL UTD
1906 SOUTH KIRKBY
1907 SOUTH KIRKBY
1908 WATH ATH
1909 DENABY UTD
1910 MONCKTON ATH
1911 WATH ATH
1912 WATH ATH
1913 WATH ATH
1914 SOUTH KIRKBY
1915 ROTHERHAM COUNTY
1916 HOYLAND UTD
1917-1919 NO COMPETITION – WAR
1920 BENTLEY COLLIERY
1921 FRICKLEY COLLIERY
1922 GAINSBROUGH TRINITY RES
1923 WORKSOP TOWN
1924 ECKINGTON WORKS
1925 ATTERCLIFFE
1926 MALTBY MAIN
1927 MALTBY MAIN
1928 NORTON WOODSEATS
1929 WORKSOP TOWN RES
1930 SOUTH KIRKBY COLLIERY
1931 SOUTH KIRKBY COLLIERY
1932 WATH ATH
1933 SILVERWOOD COLLIERY
1934 THURNSCOE VICTORIA
1935 DINNINGTON ATH
1936 RAWMARSH WELFARE
1937 THURNSCOE VICTORIA
1938 NORTON WOODSEATS
1939 RAWMARSH WELFARE
1940 BOLSOVER COLLIERY
1941 DENABY UNITED
1942 STEN (D) RASC
1943 THURCROFT MAIN
1944 WEDNESDAY RES
1945 RASC (ROYAL ARMS SIGNAL CORP)
1946 THURNSCOE VICTORIA
1947 KILNHURST COLLIERY
1948 WORKSOP TOWN
1949 WORKSOP TOWN
1950 HALLAM
1951 RAWMARSH WELFARE
1952 BEIGHTON MW
1953 THORNCLIFFE REC
1954 UPTON COLLIERY
1955 DENABY UTD
1956 UPTON COLLIERY
1957 UPTON COLLIERY
1958 GRIMETHORPE ATH
1959 UPTON COLLIERY
1960 THORNCLIFFE REC

NOW SHEFFIELD & HALLAMSHIRE COUNTY SENIOR LGE DIV 1

1961 WORKSOP TOWN
1962 PARKGATE WELFARE
1963 FRICKLEY COLLIERY
1964 BROWN BAYLEY STEELS
1965 HARWORTH CI
1966 WORSBROUGH BRIDGE MW A
1967 MANTON ATH
1968 FRECHEVILLE CA
1969 SHEFFIELD WATERWORKS
1970 WORSBROUGH BRIDGE MW A
1971 WOOLLEY MW
1972 KILNHURST COLLIERY
1973 PILKINGTON REC
1974 KILNHURST COLLIERY
1975 SWINTON ATH
1976 HARWORTH CI
1977 SWINTON ATH
1978 CHARLTON TAVERN
1979 ECCLESFIELD RED ROSE
1980 SWINTON ATH
1981 SWINTON ATH
1982 DOUBLE BARREL
1983 YORKSHIRE MAIN COLLIERY

With the amalgamation with the Hatchard League, the top division was now referred to as the Premier Division

COUNTY SENIOR PREM DIVISION

1984 WINDSOR FC
1985 ECCLESFIELD RED ROSE
1986 BSC PARKGATE
1987 MEXBORO MAIN STREET
1988 ASH HOUSE
1989 ASH HOUSE
1990 ASH HOUSE
1991 ASH HOUSE
1992 PHOENIX
1993 FRECHEVILLE CA
1994 MEXBORO MAIN STREET
1995 FRECHEVILLE CA
1996 HIGH GREEN VILLA
1997 DENABY & CADEBY MW
1998 PHOENIX
1999 WOMBWELL MAIN
2000 ATHERSLEY REC
2001 THE WETHERBY
2002 WOMBWELL MAIN
2003 WOMBWELL MAIN
2004 ATHERSLEY REC
2005 ATHERSLEY REC
2006 MEXBORO MAIN STREET
2007 ATHERSLEY REC
2008 WOMBWELL MAIN
2009 ATHERSLEY REC
2010 SHEFFIELD FC RES
2011 SWALLOWNEST MINERS WELFARE
2012 ATHERSLEY REC
2013 SHAW LANE AQUA FORCE BARNSLEY
2014 HANDSWORTH
2015 SWINTON ATHLETIC
2016 FRECHEVILLE CA

COUNTY SENIOR LEAGUE – DIV 1

COUNTY SENIOR LEAGUE - DIV 1 (PREVIOUSLY DIV 2)

There had previously been at least 2 divisions in the Association league, but it is more than likely that there where play offs between the top teams in the divisions to decide the overall league champions

STARTED IN 1962
1963 PENISTONE CHURCH
1964 HATFIELD MAIN
1965 DEARNE CMW
1966 MALTBY MW
1967 FRECHEVILLE CA
1968 SHEFFIELD WATERWORKS
1969 CENTRALIANS
1970 WORKSOP TOWN
1971 KILNHURST COLLIERY
1972 CHARLTON UNITED
1973 BROWN BAYLEY STEELS
1974 JUBILEE SPORTS
1975 KIVETON PARK
1976 B.S.C PARKGATE
1977 ECCLESFIELD RED ROSE
1978 NORTON WOODSEATS
1979 WOODHOUSE ASHBERRY
1980 DOUBLE BARREL
1981 KIVETON PARK
1982 YORKSHIRE MAIN COLLIERY
1983 WINDSOR FC

On the amalgamation with the Hatchard League at the end of the 1982/83 season when S&H CFA stopped running it, the former Division 2 was renamed Division 1

1984 CROOKES WMC
1985 FIRPARNIANS
1986 OXLEY PARK
1987 MALTBY MAIN
1988 ECCLESFIELD RED ROSE
1989 DENABY & CADEBY MW
1990 CARIBBEAN
1991 WATH SARACENS
1992 FRECHEVILLE CA
1993 HIGH GREEN VILLA
1994 PENISTONE CHURCH
1995 GRIMETHORPE MW
1996 ECCLESFIELD RED ROSE
1997 SWINTON ATH
1998 THE WETHERBY
1999 HARE & HOUNDS
2000 WICKERSLEY FC
2001 PENISTONE CHURCH
2002 WICKERSLEY FC
2003 ELM TREE
2004 HOLLINSEND AMATEURS
2005 EDLINGTON WMC
2006 SHEFFIELD LANE TOP
2007 SPRINGWOOD DAVY
2008 HANDSWORTH FC
2009 SHEFFIELD FC RES
2010 ECCLESFIELD RED ROSE
2011 HANDSWORTH FC RES
2012 HOUGHTON MAIN
2013 OUGHTIBRIDGE WMSC
2014 JUBILEE SPORTS
2015 NORTH GAWBER COLLIERY
2016 DENABY UNITED

COUNTY SENIOR LEAGUE - DIV 2

On the amalgamation with the Hatchard League at the end of the 1982/83 season when S&H CFA stopped running it a new Division 2 & Division 3 were formed..

1984	WOODSETTS WELFARE SPORTS
1985	BRUNSMEER ATH
1986	WORSBROUGH BRIDGE MW & ATHLETIC
1987	PARRAMORE SPORTS
1988	DENABY & CADEBY MW
1989	GOLDTHORPE COLLIERY
1990	WATH SAINT JAMES
1991	THURCROFT IVANHOE
1992	HIGH GREEN VILLA
1993	STAVELEY MW
1994	GRIMETHORPE MW
1995	DAVY
1996	WICKERSLEY OLD BOYS
1997	WOMBWELL MAIN
1998	ATHERSLEY REC
1999	NORTON WOODSEATS
2000	GRAPES ROY HANCOCK
2001	SOUTH KIRKBY COLLIERY
2002	ELM TREE
2003	EDLINGTON WMC
2004	AFC BARNSLEY
2005	DODWORTH MW
2006	PARKGATE RES
2007	WORSBROUGH BRIDGE ATHLETIC RES
2008	MILLMOOR JUNIORS
2009	ASTON FC
2010	FRECHEVILLE CA
2011	HOUGHTON MAIN
2012	ATHERSLEY REC RES
2013	JUBILEE SPORTS
2014	NORTH GAWBER COLLIERY
2015	DENABY MAIN
2016	HEMSWORTH MW RES

COUNTY SENIOR LEAGUE - DIV 3

1984	STELLA
1985	STAVELEY WORKS RES
1986	BRADLEY
1987	DENABY & CADEBY MW
1988	CARIBBEAN SPORTS
1989	WATH SARACENS ATH
1990	TREBLE
1991	HIGH GREEN VILLA
1992	STAVELEY MW

Sheffield County Senior League Cup

Handbooks for County Senior and Hatchard Leagues Covering seasons 1972-76

SHEFFIELD BIBLE CLASS LEAGUE

DIVISION - SENIORS

1904/05 ALL ST MISSION
1905/06 LOPHAM STREET UM
1906/07 Div 1 LOPHAM STREET UM
2 TINSLEY CHURCH
1907/08 Div 1 TINSLEY CHURCH
2 OAK STREET UM
1908/09 Div 1 ATTERCLIFFE CHURCH
2 ALL ST CHURCH
1909/10 ALL ST MISSION or BRIGHTSIDE CONGS
1910/11 BRIGHTSIDE CONGS
1911/12 ATTERCLIFFE CHURCH
1912/13 GRIMESTHORPE UM
1913/14 GRIMESTHORPE UM
1914/15 GRIMESTHORPE UM (Note 1)
1915/16 ST JOHNS WES
1916/17 CARBROOK REFORM
1917/18 CARBROOK REFORM
1918/19 ATTERCLIFFE WES
1919/20 ATTERCLIFFE WES
1920/21 ATTERCLIFFE WES
1921/22 BIRLEY CARR
1922/23 HEELEY ST PETERS
1923/24 HIGH GREEN PM
1924/25 ST MICHAELS
1925/26 ST MICHAELS
1926/27 WESLEY HALL
1927/28 WADSLEY CHURCH
1928/29 WADSLEY BRIDGE
1929/30 ATTERCLIFFE CHURCH
1930/31 BIRLEY CARR INSTITUTE
1931/32
1932/33 HEELEY FRIENDS
1933/34 OWLERTON METHS
1934/35 GLEADLESS METHS
1935/36 BRUNSWICK MISSION
1936/37 BRUNSWICK METHS
1937/38 ST VINCENTS
1938/39 OAK ST METHS BC
1939/40
1940/41 BRUNSWICK MISSION
1941/42
1942/43
1943/44
1944/45
1945/46
1946/47 BRUNSWICK MISSION

Note 1 Grimesthorpe UM awarded cup for winning it three year in a row.

1947/48 WOODHOUSE WES
1948/49 ST PATRICKS
1949/50 MORTOMLEY STREET
1950/51
1951/52
1952/53 LOPHAM STREET METHS
1953/54 ST CHRISTOPHERS RC CHURCH
1954/55 HEELEY FRIENDS
1955/56 WALKLEY CHURCH
1956/57 ST PATRICKS
1957/58 WALKLEY CHURCH
1958/59 LOPHAM STREET METHS
1959/60
1960/61
1961/62 ECCLESFIELD EBENEZER
1962/63
1963/64
1964/65
1965/66
1966/67 WOODHOUSE YC
1967/68 WOODHOUSE YC
1968/69
1969/70
1970/71 WOODHOUSE YC
1971/72 HANDSWORTH "A"
1972/73 OWLERTON ST JOHNS
1973/74 WOODSEATS ST THOMAS
1974/75 Div A - DARNALL BAPTIST
Div B - ST PATRICKS
1975/76 ST JOHN PARK "A"
1976/77 HILLSBORO TRINITY
1977/78 ECCLESALL METHS
1978/79 SACRED HEART
1979/80 SACRED HEART
1980/81 SACRED HEART
1981/82 HANDSWORTH METHS
1982/83 SHEFFIELD CITADEL
1983/84 SHEFFIELD CITADEL
1984/85 SHEFFIELD CITADEL
1985/86 HANDSWORTH METHS
1986/87 Div A - HOUSE CHURCH LIONS
Div – B –LDS "A"
Play off - LDS "A"
1987/88 LDS
1988/89 SHEFFIELD CITADEL
1989/90 HANDSWORTH METHS
1990/91 HANDSWORTH METHS
1991/92
1992/93
1993/94
1994/95 HANDSWORTH METHS

SHEFFIELD BIBLE CLASS LEAGUE continued

DIVISION - JUNIORS

1906/07	TINSLEY CHURCH
1907/08	OAK STREET UM
1908/09	ALL ST CHURCH
1909/10	WOODBOURNE RES
1910/11	ATTERCLIFFE ZION
1911/12	OAK STREET UM
1912/13	ATTERCLIFFE BAPS
1913/14	GRENOSIDE CHURCH
1914/15	CHRIST CHURCH
1915/19	NO COMPETITION
1919/20	ECKINGTON UM
1920/21	ST JOHNS INST
1921/22	BLACKBURN WESLEYANS
1922/23	WYCLIFFE BC
1923/24	GRIMESTHORPE WES
1924/25	GRIMESTHORPE WES
1925/26	GRIMESTHORPE WES
1926/27	WADSLEY BRIDGE
1927/28	CARVER STREET
1928/29	ATTERCLIFFE CHURCH
1929/30	CARVER STREET
1930/31	ST MARIES OB
1931/38	NO COMPETITION
1938/39	DARNALL METHS

DIVISION - YOUTH

1924/25	OWLERTON UMC
1925/26	CARVER STREET
1926/27	WOODHOUSE WES

Grenoside Church 1913-14, Bible Class team with Junior Cup and an unknown trophy-possibly Bible Class Winners trophy

SHEFFIELD BLADES SUPER DRAW SUNDAY SPORTS LEAGUE

This League was originally called the Sheffield Sunday Sports League. Several short lived name changes until it took its present name in 2004. The league was set up to cater for the growing number of teams in the Sheffield area who wanted to play organised league football. The other leagues in operation at that time had reach the capacity numbers allowed by their mandate, and so they could not take further teams into membership.

PREMIER DIVISION (was Div 1 until 1988/89)

1969/70 TELSTAR
1970/71 BAIGENT & BIRD
1971/72 DELTA SPORTS
1972/73 VULCAN UTD
1973/74 VULCAN UTD
1974/75 GENEFAX
1975/76 CROWS NEST
1976/77 DELTA SPORTS
1977/78 CROWS NEST
1978/79 CROWS NEST
1979/80 WILLINGTON PHEASANT
1980/81 PARKHILL
1981/82 STANNINGTON COMMUNITY
1982/83 SPRINGWOOD
1983/84 HEELEY WHITE LION
1984/85 BARTONS RESTAURANT
1985/86 STANNINGTON COMMUNITY
1986/87 DEEPCAR PEN NOOK
1987/88 YORKSHIREMAN
1988/89 SHEFFIELD TRADES & LABOUR
1989/90 SHEFFIELD TRADES & LABOUR
1990/91 SHEFFIELD TRADES & LABOUR
1991/92 SHEFFIELD TRADES & LABOUR
1992/93 PARK 89
1993/94 BASS STONES
1994/95 WOODHOUSE GEORGE
1995/96 PARK LANE
1996/97 PARK LANE
1997/98 RISING SUN
1998/99 GOODFELLOWS
1999/00 CROSSPOOL 96
2000/01 HOLMESFIELD
2001/02 LAYCOCK SPORTS
2002/03 LAYCOCK SPORTS
2003/04 STANNINGTON VILLAGE
2004/05 WOODHOUSE GEORGE
2005/06 WOODHOUSE GEORGE
2006/07 WOODHOUSE WEST END
2007/08 WOODHOUSE WEST END
2008/09 WOODHOUSE WEST END
2009/10 WOODHOUSE WEST END
2010/11 STOCKSBRIDGE PARK STEELS
2011/12 SHEFFIELD CIVIL SERVICE
2012/13 STANNINGTON VILLAGE
2013/14 STANNINGTON VILLAGE
2014/15 STANNINGTON VILLAGE
2015/16 WADSLEY BRIDGE PHEASANT

DIVISION 1 (was Div 2 until 1988/89)

1970/71 BOOMERANG
1971/72 FELLBRIGG
1972/73 STOCKSBRIDGE
1973/74 EAST END ATH
1974/75 PARKWAY HOTEL
1975/76 QUEENS
1976/77 STOCKSBRIDGE D
1977/78 CELTIC TRAVELLERS
1978/79 SPRINGWOOD
1979/80 OXSPRING
1980/81 BRUNSMEER A
1981/82 DEEPCAR
1982/83 SHEFFIELD AMATEURS
1983/84 WOODSEATS SOCIAL
1984/85 SHELDON
1985/86 STANNINGTON VILLAGE
1986/87 PRINCE OF WALES
1987/88 WEST BAR UTD
1988/89 HILLSBOROUGH FC
1989/90 AFC TIMBERTOP
1990/91 BATH 78
1991/92 PARK LANE
1992/93 TELECOM SPORTS
1993/94 WESTFIELD
1994/95 BATEMOOR HARWOOD
1995/96 ECCLESFIELD WHITE BEAR
1996/97 KING & MILLER
1997/98 CROSSPOOL 96
1998/99 NIAGARA
1999/00 OLD BLUE BALL
2000/01 LAYCOCKS SPORTS
2001/02 DEEP END
2002/03 STANNINGTON VILLAGE
2003/04 WOODHOUSE STAG
2004/05 WOODHOUSE WEST END
2005/06 LAYCOCK SPORTS
2006/07 TELECOM SPORTS
2007/08 MILLHOUSES ABACROMBIE
2008/09 LAYCOCK SPORTS
2009/10 WOODHOUSE ANGEL
2010/11 THE VINE
2011/12 BULLS HEAD
2012/13. WOODHOUSE ANGEL
2013/14 OUGHTIBRIDGE WM
2014/15 HANDSWORTH TURF
2015-16 BRINSWORTH PHOENIX

DIVISION 2 (was Div 3 until 1988/89)

1971/72	STOCKSBRIDGE D
1972/73	EAST DENE ATH
1973/74	CRICKETERS
1974/75	QUEENS
1975/76	STEEL INN
1976/77	CELTIC TRAVELLERS
1977/78	WILLINGTON PHEASANT
1978/79	THROSTLES
1979/80	BASS NORTH
1980/81	CROWN INN
1981/82	SHEFFIELD AMATEURS
1982/83	HILLSBOROUGH BOYS CLUB
1983/84	SHELDON
1984/85	FIGHTING COCK
1985/86	BATH HOTEL
1986/87	BASS ATH
1987/88	SBS
1988/89	BRINCLIFFE OAKS
1989/90	MASONS
1990/91	NEW BARRACK TAVERN
1991/92	RED GROUSE
1992/93	HOOD GREEN
1993/94	NORTON HARWOOD
1994/95	ACORN ACADEMICALS
1995/96	MINERS ARMS
1996/97	MIDDLEWOOD TAVERN
1997/98	HEMSWORTH VILLA
1998/99	GEORGE IV
1999/00	LOWOOD
2000/01	REDMIRES
2001/02	STANNINGTON VILLAGE
2002/03	WOODHOUSE STAG
2003/04	WOODHOUSE WEST END
2004/05	JORDANTHORPE HOTEL
2005/06	ECCLESFIELD TRAVELLERS
2006/07	HANDSWORTH OLD BOYS
2007/08	SHEFFIELD CIVIL SERVICE
2008/09	RANCH
2009/10	SOUTHEY SOCIAL
2010/11	BULLS HEAD
2011/12	THE PARK
2012/13	LOXLEY
2013/14	THE PHEASANT
2014/15	PHOENIX
2015-16	PENISTONE CHURCH

LEAGUE KNOCK OUT CUP

	WINNERS	RUNNERS UP
1969/70	BAIGENT & BIRD	DELTA SPORTS
1970/71	SHEFFIELD CITY AMB.	SIMM
1971/72	DEEPCAR	SIMM
1972/73	VULCAN UTD	PLIMSOLL
1973/74	VULCAN UTD	PLIMSOLL
1974/75	STEEL INN	REVENUE
1975/76	QUEENS	KENNINGS
1976/77	CROWS NEST	NORTON AMATEURS
1977/78	CROWS NEST	DEEPCAR
1978/79	CROWS NEST	CELTIC TRAVELLERS
1979/80	ROSE HOUSE	VINERS
1980/81	WILLINGTON PHEASANT	CAPTIVE QUEEN MINSTRELS
1981/82	STANNINGTON COMMUNITY	HARWOOD
1982/83	SPRINGWOOD	NORTON AMATEURS
1983/84	DEEPCAR PEN NOOK	HEELEY WHITE LION
1984/85	STANNINGTON COMMUNITY	SHELDON
1985/86	STANNINGTON COMMUNITY	BASS NORTH SPORTS
1986/87	DEEPCAR PEN NOOK	HILLSBOROUGH OB
1987/88	SHEFFIELD TRADES & LABOUR	WADSLEY VILLAGE
1988/89	DEEPCAR PEN NOOK	HILLSBOROUGH FC
1989/90	SHEFFIELD TRADES & LABOUR	BASS ATH
1990/91	YORKSHIRE WATER AUTH.	STANNINGTON UTD
1991/92	FREEMASONS	PARK 89
1992/93	BASS REGENCY	PARK LANE
1993/94	BASS STONES	WESTFIELD
1994/95	BASS STONES	ECCLESFIELD WHITE BEAR
1995/96	BASS STONES	ACORN ACADEMICALS
1996/97	KING & MILLER	THE CASTLE
1997/98	RISING SUN	KING & MILLER
1998/99	HOLMESFIELD	GOODFELLOWS
1999/00	HOLMESFIELD	THE KESTRELS
2000/01	PEN NOOK	BOUNDRY SPORTS
2001/02	BOUNDARY SPORTS	HOLMESFIELD
2002/03	HEMSWORTH VILLA	LAYCOCK SPORTS
2003/04	STANNINGTON VILLAGE	FREEDOM HOUSE
2004/05	HEMSWORTH VILLA	WOODHOUSE WEST END
2005/06	HEMSWORTH VILLA	STANNINGTON VILLAGE
2006/07	ECCLESFIELD TRAVELLERS	PITSMOOR HOTEL
2007/08	HANDSWORTH WMC	WOODHOUSE WEST END
2008/09	STANNINGTON VILLAGE	WOODHOUSE WEST END
2009/10	YEW TREE	WOODHOUSE WEST END
2010/11	SHEFFIELD CIVIL SERVICE	STOCKSBRIDGE PARK STEELS
2011/12	SHEFFIELD CIVIL SERVICE	THE PARK
2012/13	STANNINGTON VILLAGE	ECCLESFIELD PLAYERS LNGE
2013/14	REDMIRES	THE PARK
2014/15	OUGHTIBRIDGE WM	STANNINGTON VILLAGE
2015/16	WADSLEY BRIDGE PHEASANT	THE VINE

SHEFFIELD CHURCH LEAGUE

This league appears to start in 1921/22 and finish in 1940. Did not appear to start again after the war, even though the league registered with S&H FA in 1945/46 and 1946/47

This league appears to be the restart of the Sheffield Free Church League 1902-1915, which amalgamated with the Sheffield Sunday School League at the start of the First World War. The amalgamation appears to have stopped after the war and the Free Church title dropped.

A cup was purchased in 1924 for the championship winners. This could be as a result of the trophy played for in the Sheffield Free Church League 1902-1915 being taken by William Wood (possible Lge Secretary) when he went to become a lay reader at Frinton, Essex in 1916.

Medal in its original presentation box from Vaughtons Ltd, Goldsmiths & Silversmiths, Birmingham presented to E. Skinner who played for Brunswick Methodist in season 1933-1934

DIVISION - 1

1921/22	ENDCLIFFE
1922/23	BUTTON LANE FRIENDS
1923/24	POND HILL
1924/25	BRIGHTSIDE WES
1925/26	MOUNT VIEW
1926/27	WOODHOUSE WES
1927/28	WOODHOUSE WES
1928/29	VICTORIA WES
1929/30	UPPER CHAPEL & GRIMESTHORPE WES (JT)
1930/31	ABBEYDALE ST PETERS
1931/32	NORTON CHURCH
1932/33	HANDSWORTH CHURCH
1933/34	BRUNSWICK METHS
1934/35	UPPER CHAPEL
1935/36	BIRLEY CARR
1936/37	RANMOOR ST JOHNS
1937/38	ALLEN STREET METHS
1938/39	ST JAMES MISSION (WOODHOUSE)
1939/40	UNITY CHURCH

2nd TEAM DIVISION

1924/25	ST MARGARETS
1925/26	GRIMESTHORPE WES
1926/27	BETHESDA PSA
1927/28	MALIN BRIDGE UM
1928/29	VICTORIA WES
1929/30	NORTON CHURCH
1930/31	WINCOBANK PM
1931/32	WINCOBANK PM
1932/33	WOODHOUSE AS
1933/34	DOVER MISSION
1934/35	DOVER MISSION
1935/36	BRUNSWICK MISSION
1936/37	WESLEY HALL
1937/38	ST JAMES MISSION (WOODHOUSE)

Abbeydale St Peter's - Members of the Sheffield Adult League & Sheffield Church League.

SHEFFIELD FREE CHURCH LEAGUE

This league appears to start in 1902 and finish in 1915 when the league amalgamated with the Sunday Schools League. It appears that the league may have restarted again after the war in 1921/22 dropping the word FREE

The original trophy played for in the Sheffield Free Church League was taken by William Wood (possible League Secretary) when he went to become a lay reader at Frinton, Essex in 1916. This was given to the Sheffield & District Fair Play League in 2009 by his family, and is now used as their Sporting Award Trophy.

The trophy has the All Saints Mission engraved on it as the winner for the first 3 seasons. Because of this feat, All Saints Missions were given the trophy to keep.

Original League Trophy 1903-1905 won outright by All Saints Mission

DIVISION

1902/03	ALL SAINTS MISSION
1903/04	ALL SAINTS MISSION
1904/05	ALL SAINTS MISSION
1905/06	DARNALL CONGS
1906/07	MILLHOUSE WES
1907/08	MARTIN STREET UM
1908/09	SHREWSBURY ROAD UM
1909/10	CROFT HOUSE
1910/11	CROFT HOUSE
1911/12	MALIN BRIDGE
1912/13	VALLEY ROAD
1913/14	VALLEY ROAD
1914/15	HARTSHEAD 2nd

2ND TEAM DIVISION

1907/08	WOODLAND VIEW PM
1908/09	FITZMAURICE RD WR
1909/10	OAK STREET
1910/11	UPPERTHORPE UNITARIANS
1911/12	MALIN BRIDGE
1912/13	VALLEY ROAD
1913/14	VALLEY ROAD
1914/15	NO COMP

Croft House

SHEFFIELD FRIENDLIES FOOTBALL LEAGUE

The competition started in 1908 with the idea of organising games between teams who, at that time, only played friendlies, which would promote friendly rivalry, with no incentive to rough play because there was no trophy or medals to be won. The competition was to be known as The Sheffield Friendlies Football Association. The word "league" was entered in the minute book, but was crossed out and "Association" inserted over the top of it. Some time later the competition did drop the Association bit and become classed as a league.

The no trophy ruling was ridiculed in the local press when the league started, but everybody accepted this ruling. In fact until the start of the A J Sanders Memorial Competition in 1929 there were no trophies or medals awarded to the winners of any division, only shirt badges for the overall league champions. This ruling survived until the 1977/78 season when trophies and medals started to be awarded.

In fact, to its credit with this rule in place, the league became possibly the largest Sheffield Saturday League, when a record 78 teams joined for the 1967/68 season.

The first meeting was called by A J Sanders, who at the time was President of Hillsborough & Wadsley Athletic football club. The meeting took place on 14th May 1908 at the Wadsley National School with 8 clubs in attendance. These being Mr Sanders' club plus Broad Oaks, (who shortly after changed their name to Ecclesall Church), Sandford Grove, Burngreave Congregational, Heeley Church, Attercliffe Wesleyan Reform, Pitsmoor Church, Ravenswood.

Mr Sanders was elected the first Chairman, the post he held until his death in 1928, and A Dean, also from A J Sanders club, was elected Secretary.

A list of 11 rules was drawn up by the clubs at the meeting, some being unusual and of interest. All clubs had to have a private ground and the home team was expected to provide a Referee who could be an official from any club in the league. The winning team had to report the results to the League Secretary by Wednesday otherwise they would forfeit 2 points. However it was the home club's responsibility to report the result if the match had been a draw. No games were to be played on Good Friday or Christmas Day. The Committee had the power to add to or amend the rules at any time it wished.

The league quickly expanded to more than one division so, up to and including 1945/46, the top teams in each division would play off in semi finals and then a final game to decide the overall league champions. This appears to have stopped the following season with each top team being recognised as the appropriate division champion, but still no trophy or medals.

With the reduction of Saturday football because most players now wanted to play on a Sunday rather than a Saturday, the league folded at the end of the 1986/87 season, with the 8 remaining clubs entering the other Saturday leagues that were still operating..

TROPHIES FROM 1977/78 SEASON

DIVISION 1 LANCASTER TROPHY
DIVISION 2 CURTIS POWER TROPHY
DIVISION 3 HENRY SWIFT TROPHY
DIVISION 4 GEORGE BROOKS TROPHY
DIVISION 5 MANAGEMENT COMMITTEE TROPHY

AJS WINNERS v DIVISION 1 WINNERS
STAN GLOVER CHALLENGE TROPHY

SPORTING TEAM AWARD
ALPHA SPORTS (HALLAM) LTD TROPHY

DIVISION - 1

1908/09	BRINCLIFFE
1909/10	WADSLEY CHURCH
1910/11	SHARROW OLD BOYS
1911/12	NORTON LEES CHURCH
1912/13	HILLSBORO & WADSLEY AMT
1913/14	ST JOHNS AMT
1914/15	KAYSER ELLISON
1915/16	HILLSBORO & WADSLEY AMT
1916/17	NORFOLK AMT
1917/18	WYCLIFFE BIBLE CLASS
1918/19	ATTERCLIFFE UNITARIANS
1919/20	BIRLEY CARR INSTITUTE
1920/21	COMMERCIALS
1921/22	ELLESMERE WESLEYANS
1922/23	ELLESMERE WESLEYANS
1923/24	ELLESMERE WESLEYANS
1924/25	ARUNDEL FC
1925/26	ARUNDEL FC
1926/27	ARUNDEL FC
1927/28	ARUNDEL FC
1928/29	ARUNDEL FC
1929/30	YMCA
1930/31	MUNICIPAL OFFICERS
1931/32	CITY WORKS
1932/33	WARD & PAYNE FC
1933/34	CITY WORKS
1934/35	NETHERTHORPE INSTITUTE
1935/36	OUGHTIBRIDGE WMSC
1936/37	GLEADLESS ROAD CO-OP GUILD
1937/38	DARNALL CHURCH
1938/39	STANNINGTON SPORTS
1939 – 1945	NO COMPETITION DUE TO WAR
1945/46	GRIMESTHORPE OB
1946/47	GRIMESTHORPE OB
1947/48	THOMPSON SPORTS
1948/49	HILLSBORO FRIENDS
1949/50	MOORHEAD FC
1950/51	ST PETERS FC
1951/52	GRIMESTHORPE OB

DIVISION 1 continued

1952/53 HOLLINSEND SPORTS
1953/54 BELLHOUSE ROAD WMC
1954/55 GLEADLESS TE
1955/56 HOLLINSEND SPORTS
1956/57 ST PATRICKS
1957/58 BRUNSWICK
1958/59 SHARROW
1959/60 BRUNSWICK TRINITY
1960/61 BRUNSWICK TRINITY
1961/62 SHARROW LABOUR
1962/63 CARTERKNOWLE YC "A"
1963/64 DYSON "A"
1964/65 CARTERKNOWLE YC
1965/66 ST PATRICKS
1966/67 WADSLEY CHURCH
1967/68 ST PATRICKS "A"
1968/69 BECKFORD
1969/70 BECKFORD
1970/71 MOLLOY SPORTS
1971/72 WYBOURN ROVERS
1972/73 BROOMHILL SPORTS
1973/74 BROOMHILL SPORTS
1974/75 HEELEY SOCIAL
1975/76 ST PETERS
1976/77 HOLLINSEND NEW INN
1977/78 HOLLINSEND NEW INN
1978/79 HURLFIELD YC
1979/80 RICHMOND HOTEL
1980/81 J FAIRLEY STEELS
1981/82 GLEADLESS AMATEURS
1982/83 MIDLAND HOTEL
1983/84 ST NATHANEALS "A"
1984/85 ECKINGTON ACTIVITY CENTRE
1985/86 GRIMESTHORPE
1986/87 SILAS FC

DIVISION - 2

1947/48 HILLSBORO FRIENDS
1948/49 ST PETERS FC
1949/50 ST SILAS IMPS
1950/51 ENGLISH STEEL CORP
1951/52 WORRALL UTD
1952/53 STANDARD AMT
1953/54 MANSFIELD ROVERS "A"
1954/55 ALGOMA SPORTS
1955/56 ST PATRICKS
1956/57 ALGOMA SPORTS
1957/58 DEVONSHIRE ROVERS
1958/59 TOTLEY SPORTS
1959/60 CARTERKNOWLE YC
1960/61 BIRLEY AMT
1961/62 DYSON SPORTS
1962/63 CYCLOPS AMT "A"
1963/64 KISMET SPORTS
1964/65 SHEFFIELD ROVERS
1965/66 GREAVES PARK
1966/67 HEELEY SOCIAL
1967/68 WYBOURN ROVERS
1968/69 MOLLOY SPORTS
1969/70 WADSLEY CHURCH
1970/71 ALGOMA
1971/72 MANOR PARK
1972/73 ESCALOPIANS "A"
1973/74 KIRKS ATHLETIC
1974/75 WORRALL "A"
1975/76 HOLLINSEND NEW INN
1976/77 HURLFIELD YC
1977/78 RICHMOND HOTEL
1978/79 BRIDGE ATHLETIC
1979/80 LITTLEDALE JUNIORS
1980/81 GREENHILL FC
1981/82 CARIBBEAN YC
1982/83 FULWOOD ATHLETIC
1983/84 SHIREGREEN HOTEL

DIVISION - 3

1947/48 CROOKES FC
1948/49 MOORHEAD FC
1949/50 TENANTS SPORTS
1950/51 WORRALL UTD
1951/52 ALGOMA SPORTS
1952/53 HOLLOW DRILL
1953/54 WOODSEATS FRIENDS
1954/55 HELEN WILSON SETTLEMENT
1955/56 MALTBY ST C & I
1956/57 WYBOURN & PARK
1957/58 SHEFFIELD PARKS
1958/59 CARTERKNOWLE YC "A"
1959/60 BIRLEY AMT
1960/61 UNITED COKE
1961/62 600 SPORTS
1962/63 CARTERKNOWLE YC "B"
1963/64 WYBOURN & PARK YC
1964/65 WADSLEY CHURCH
1965/66 WHITELEY WOOD
1966/67 WYBOURN ROVERS
1967/68 NEW GREENHILL
1968/69 WADSLEY CHURCH
1969/70 HEELEY MILLS
1970/71 ST THOMAS MORE "A"
1971/72 STANNINGTON BC
1972/73 PARK YC
1973/74 ST NATHANEALS
1974/75 RICHMOND HOTEL
1975/76 HURLFIELD YC
1976/77 DARNALL FC
1977/78 HANDSWORTH WHITE ROSE
1978/79 NORTHERN CELTIC
1979/80 CROWS NEST
1980/81 MELANIC FC
1981/82 HANDSWORTH WHITE ROSE
1982/83 ECKINGTON ACTIVITY CENTRE

DIVISION - 4

1948/49 ELECTRICITY SPORTS
1949/50 GLEADLESS H I M W

1957/58 ESC "B"
1958/59 COOPERS FC
1959/60 ATTERCLIFFE UTD
1960/61 B.I.S.R.A
1961/62 TUFFNELLS SPORTS
1962/63 SPARTANS
1963/64 HEELEY SOCIAL
1964/65 HALLIWELL ALBION
1965/66 MEERSBROOK
1966/67 OXLEY PARK
1967/68 WOODTHORPE YC
1968/69 HYDE PARK
1969/70 WORRALL UTD "A"
1970/71 MIDDLEWOOD HOSPITAL
1971/72 STANNINGTON COLLEGE
1972/73 HORSESHOES
1973/74 STOCKSBRIDGE TOWN
1974/75 MANSELL YC
1975/76 ARTHUR LEE & SONS LTD
1976/77 DE LA SALLE
1977/78 PARK YC
1978/79 GREENHILL FC
1979/80 MELANIC FC
1980/81 BLACKSTOCK FC
1981/82 ECCLESFIELD RED ROSE

DIVISION - 5

1957/58 STRADBROKE COMMUNITY
1958/59 BLUE BELL "A"
1959/60 ECLIPSE SPORTS
1960/61 MARSHALL SPORTS
1961/62 OUGHTIBRIDGE SPORTS
1962/63 GLEADLESS H.I.M.W
1963/64 DYSON "B"
1964/65 PETRE STREET
1965/66 SUMMERFIELD
1966/67 ROBIN HOOD "A"
1967/68 ST STEPHENS
1968/69 HACKENTHORPE
1969/70 GLEADLESS AMT
1970/71 WADSLEY BRIDGE SPORTS
1971/72 ECCLESFIELD ALBION
1972/73 DARNALL SHOT BLASTING
1973/74 MANSELL YC
1974/75 ARTHUR LEE & SONS LTD
1975/76 VULCAN ATHLETIC
1976/77 JONAS WOODHEAD
1977/78 BSC (TINSLEY)
1978/79 MELANIC FC
1979/80 BLACKSTOCK FC

DIVISION - 6

1957/58 LONGLEY BC
1958/59 WYBOURN & PARK YC
1959/60 HEELEY BC
1960/61 -
1961/62 GLEADLESS H.I.M.W
1962/63 HEELEY SOCIAL
1963/64 HALF MOON FC
1964/65 POMONA STREET YC
1965/66 OXLEY PARK
1966/67 HYDE PARK
1967/68 UPPER HEELEY WMC
1968/69 VINERS
1969/70 KIRKDALE FC

DIVISION - 7

1967/68 SCOTT DURIDE
1968/69 SOUTHEY SOCIAL

DIVISION - ASSOCIATION DIV 1

1950/51 ST GEORGES
1951/52 SHIREGREEN COMMUNITY
1952/53 STANNINGTON METHS
1953/54 WORRALL UTD
1954/55 ELECTRICITY SPORTS
1955/56 BIRLEY AMT
1956/57 KAYSER & PARK

DIVISION - ASSOCIATION – DIV 2

1951/52 BLOOD TRANSFUSION
1952/53 INSURANCE INSTITUTE
1953/54 PARK YC
1954/55 MALTBY ST C&I
1955/56 REGENTS WORKS
1956/57 FINNEGANS

DIVISION – ASSOCIATION DIV 3

1956/57 PADLEY & VENABLES

ALPHA SPORTS (HALLAM) TROPHY

This was the sporting team award

1979/80 CROWS NEST
1980/81 GAFLAC FC
1981/82 CARIBBEAN
1982/83 DETROITS LTD
1983/84 ST PATRICKS
1984/85 WINCOBANK & BLACKBURN
1985/86 TRENT RHA
1986/87 RONNIE'S BAR FC

STAN GLOVER CHALLENGE TROPHY

This was for the winners of a game between the AJS Trophy and Division one winners

1979/80 RICHMOND HOTEL
1980/81 JAMES FAIRLEY STEELS SPORTING
1981/82 NOT PLAYED
1982/83 NOT PLAYED
1983/84 ST NATHANEALS A
1984/85 NOT PLAYED

A J SANDERS MEMORIAL COMPETITION

This appears to have been the only competition run by the League which actually had a trophy for the winner up to 1977/78. It was set up in memory of the league founder in 1908 who died in 1928. The proceeds from the competition were originally donated to the Sheffield Royal Infirmary, but in later years the Committee decided annually where the money raised went.

1929/30 MUNICIPAL OFFICERS
1930/31 SHEFFIELD SPARTANS
1931/32 INDUSTRY FC
1932/33 K.O.Y.L.I
1933/34 CITY WORKS
1934/35 NETHERTHORPE INSTITUTE
1935/36 WOODHOUSE METHODISTS
1936/37 WOODHOUSE METHODISTS
1937/38 WOODHOUSE METHODISTS
1938/39 NORFOLK JUNIORS
1939/40 HOLLY GUILD
1940–1946 NO COMPETITION - WAR
1946/47 GRIMESTHORPE OB
1947/48 HILLSBORO FRIENDS
1948/49 HILLSBORO FRIENDS
1949/50 WOODSEATS METHODIST
1950/51 ST SILAS IMPS
1951/52 WORRALL UTD
1952/53 HILLSBORO ATHLETIC
1953/54 HOLLINSEND SPORTS
1954/55 WADSLEY AMT
1955/56 MALTBY ST C & I
1956/57 WYBOURN & PARK
1957/58 HOLLINSEND SPORTS
1958/59 ST PATRICKS
1959/60 ST PETERS
1960/61 ST PETERS
1961/62 HILLSBORO ATHLETIC
1962/63 DYSONS SPORTS
1963/64 GRAVES PARK "A"
1964/65 CARTERKNOWLE YC
1965/66 WADSLEY BRIDGE SPORTS
1966/67 OXLEY PARK
1967/68 ST STEPHENS
1968/69 WADSLEY CHURCH
1969/70 WYBOURN ROVERS
1970/71 NEWBOULDS FC
1971/72 WYBOURN ROVERS
1972/73 DARNALL S B
1973/74 BROOMHILL SPORTS
1974/75 MANSELL YC
1975/76 HURLFIELD YC
1976/77 FORUM FC
1977/78 RED GROUSE
1978/79 RICHMOND HOTEL
1979/80 RICHMOND HOTEL
1980/81 JAMES FAIRLEY STEELS SPORTING
1981/82 BLACKSTOCK FC
1982/83 MIDLAND HOTEL
1983/84 ECKINGTON AC
1984/85 ST PETERS
1985/86 OLD CROWN
1986/87 SILAS FC

Friendlies League Sporting Award

*Heeley Mining played in the Friendlies League in the 1960s
Chris Eyre second from right on back row*

A J SANDERS

A J Sanders or AJS as he was affectionately known was born at Alderney in the Channel Islands on 13 May 1867. He moved to Gibraltar with his parents at the age of 3 when his father who was a member of HM Forces was posted there. Shortly afterwards the family moved again to Curragh Camp, Ireland where he spent all of his school days.

On leaving school he became a bugler in the Royal Scots Greys. However this was a short stay as he was bought out of the army by his father who on being transferred to Dublin did not want to leave his son behind.

He started out in business life as a photographer in Sackville Street Dublin. His claim to fame being that he took photographs of the site of the Phoenix Park murders, actually claiming to have been the first civilian on the spot. These were stirring times and he vividly remembered the terrible baton charges of the police during the Fenian riots.

At the age of 15 he came to Sheffield, where he was an apprentice tailor to Furnivall & Ibbotson, Merchant Tailors of Fitzalan Square. After 7 years service he moved to become sales manager for Hoyland & Sons of Surrey Street. He remained there until his death on 16 June 1928.

During his teens he was a keen footballer playing for Heeley FC and later transferring to Sheffield Wednesday as a right half-back as they were called in those days. Eventually his employer told him he must decide between football or work. He decided to give his fullest attention to the business. However, not caring to be denied of his love for the game he took up refereeing and was on the list for 15 seasons.

He continued to be actively involved with football being appointed Chairman of Hillsborough & Wadsley Athletic and when they folded he became Chairman of the Wadsley Church club, where because of a special request by the Vicar of Wadsley he remained a club official until his death.

On 14 May 1908, a special meeting of 8 amateur clubs was held at the Wadsley National School with a view to forming a football league. As AJS had been instrumental in calling the meeting, he was elected Chairman of the now newly formed Sheffield Friendlies League. He proved himself a capable official and legislator and he held the post of Chairman right up to his death. During that time the league had grown from the initial 8 clubs up to 72 at one period, possibly making it the largest ever Saturday League in Sheffield. It took until 1967/68 to beat this number when 78 clubs joined for that season, this being the rush to play football following England winning the World Cup the previous season.

During his Chairmanship he had been the Leagues representative to S&H CFA where he served at various times on the Competitions, Referees and County Cup Committees as well as being the S&H CFA representative to the Holbrook and District League and the Wragg League.

It was stated on his death that AJS had been in all respects an admirable administrator, wise and prudent in his judgement, careful and cautious where caution was needed. He had been kindly and patient to the wrong-doer, he carried out the duties of his difficult and exacting office that elicited praise from all.

On his death, the league started the A J Sanders Memorial Competition, the proceeds from which was to go to the Sheffield Royal Infirmary Hospital. In later years the proceeds went to other charitable concerns selected by the Committee. Strangely the winners of this Competition won a shield, which until 1977/78 was the only trophy awarded to any team that won a Friendlies League Competition.

. . SHEFFIELD . .

FRIENDLIES
Football League.

SEASON 1951-52.

Secretary—
F. HORNBY,
166, MARLCLIFFE ROAD, SHEFFIELD, 6.
(Tel. 48116).

Treasurer—
F. C. DORLING,
41, RIDGEWAY ROAD, SHEFFIELD, 12.

A. MACDOUGALL & SON (PRINTERS, SHEFFIELD) LTD.

Friendlies League Handbook

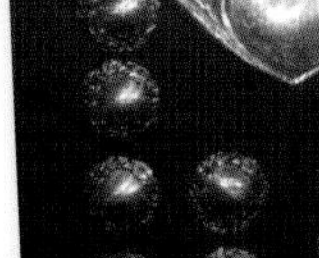

AJ Sanders Trophy, Friendlies League

SHEFFIELD FRIENDS ADULT SCHOOLS LEAGUE

This started as the Sheffield Friends Adults League in 1909/10, dropping the word Friends after the First World War and adding the word Schools. It appears the Competition stopped at the Second World War and never restarted.

LEAGUE

1909/10	PRINCES STREET
1910/11	HEELEY ST PETERS
1911/12	HILLSBRO FRIENDS
1912/13	HEELEY FRIENDS
1913/14	CROFT HOUSE
1914/20	NO COMPETITION - WAR
1920/21	HEELEY FRIENDS
1921/22	HARTSHEAD (2nd team)
1922/23	HARTSHEAD (2nd team)
1923/24	WOODSEATS FRIENDS
1924/25	WOODSEATS FRIENDS
1925/26	CROFT HOUSE
1926/27	ST MICHAELS
1927/28	ST MICHAELS
1928/29	CROFT HOUSE
1929/30	ST MICHAELS
1930/31	ST MICHAELS
1931/32	HAWKSLEY PM
1932/33	HAWKSLEY PM
1933/34	WARREN METHS
1934/35	HARTSHEAD FRIENDS
1935/36	HARTSHEAD FRIENDS
1936/37	BIRLEY CARR INST
1937/38	BIRLEY CARR INST
1938/39	BIRLEY CARR INST

KO CUP

1920/21	HEELEY FRIENDS
1921/22	MEERSBROOK CONGS
1922/23	BUTTON LANE FRIENDS
1923/24	CROFT HOUSE
1924/25	BLACKBURN WES
1925/26	HOLLINSEND WES
1926/27	CROFT HOUSE
1927/28	BETHESDA PSA
1928/29	CROFT HOUSE
1929/30	ST MICHAELS
1930/31	ST MICHAELS
1931/32	HAWKSLEY PM
1932/33	ATTERCLIFFE FRIENDS
1933/34	WARREN METHS
1934/35	ST VINCENTS
1935/36	ST VINCENTS
1936/37	ST VINCENTS
1937/38	WADSLEY CHURCH
1938/39	BIRLEY CARR INST

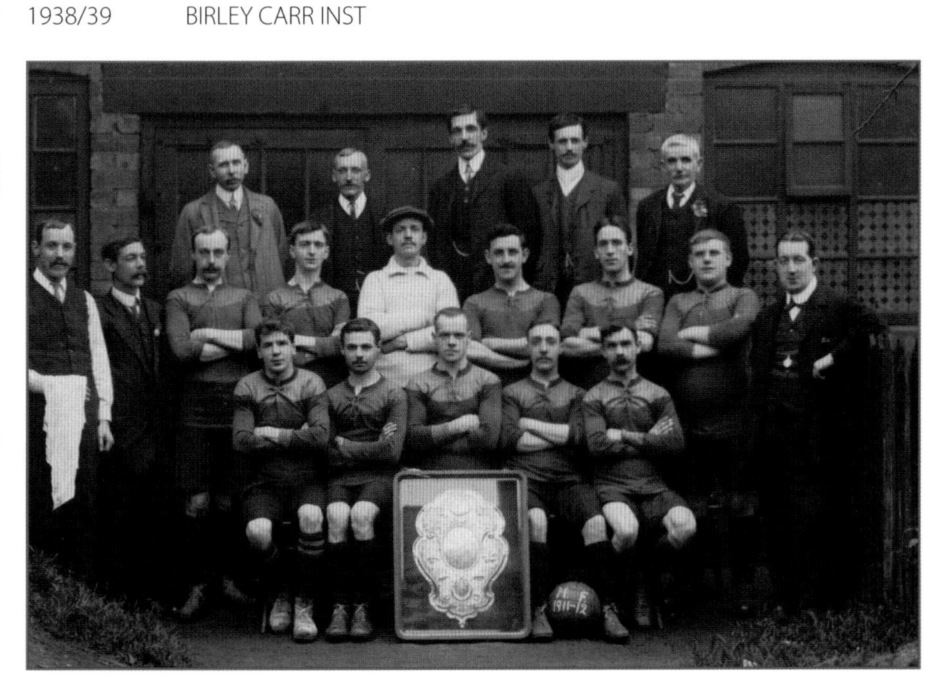

Hillsborough Friends, winners of the Sheffield Friends Adult Schools League in 1911-12

SHEFFIELD HALLAMSHIRE NOMADS SUNDAY LEAGUE

This league started in the 2002/03 season when the Hallamshire Sunday League and the Nomads Sunday League amalgamated. It ran until the end of the 2008/09 season when most of the remaining clubs joined the Meadowhall Sunday League.

PREMIER DIVISION

2002/03 NOAH'S ARK
2003/04 ECCLESFIELD TRAVELLERS
2004/05 ECCLESFIELD GREYHOUND
2005/06 PACK HORSE
2006/07 FOXWOOD EMBASSY
2007/08 FOXWOOD EMBASSY
2008/09 MOSBOROUGH

DIVISION 1

2002/03 NOAH'S ARK
2003/04 PACK HORSE
2004/05 INTAKE ROYAL OAK
2005/06 SHEFFIELD ARMS
2006/07 NORTHERN AVENUE
2007/08 TAVERN TIGERS

DIVISION 2

2003/04 SHEFFIELD TRADES & LABOUR

KO CUP

2002/03 NOAH'S ARK
2003/04 VINE
2004/05 ECCLESFIELD TRAVELLERS
2005/06 ECCLESFIELD GREYHOUND
2006/07 FOXWOOD EMBASSY
2007/08 ECCLESFIELD WMC
2008/09 NORTHERN AVENUE

HALLAMSHIRE SUNDAY LEAGUE

The competition was formed on 27 July 1966. It was originally run by S&H CFA, but like other leagues it was left to run itself from 1984. It ceased at the end of 2001/02 when it amalgamated with the Nomads League

DIVISION 1

1966/67	OLD NEW INN
1967/68	LYCEUM
1968/69	LYCEUM
1969/70	QUEEN HOTEL (MOSB)
1970/71	QUEEN HOTEL (MOSB)
1971/72	QUEEN HOTEL (MOSB)
1972/73	BLUE BALL (WHARNCLIFFE)
1973/74	BLACK SWAN
1974/75	ST JOSEPHS
1975/76	WINN GARDENS
1976/77	STANNINGTON VILLAGE
1977/78	WINN GARDENS
1978/79	SPA CLUB
1979/80	ROYAL OAK (COAL ASTON)
1980/81	WINN GARDENS
1981/82	WINN GARDENS
1982/83	FRECHEVILLE HOTEL
1983/84	ECCLESFIELD WMC
1984/85	ECCLESFIELD WMC
1985/86	SOTHALL
1986/87	SOTHALL
1987/88	NETHER EDGE
1988/89	RAILWAY 88
1989/90	ECCLESALL NP
1990/91	HANDSWORTH NEW CROWN
1991/92	VINE FC
1992/93	FIRTH PARK WMC
1993/94	SPORTSMAN
1994/95	SPORTSMAN
1995/96	SPORTSMAN
1996/97	TAVERN PIRATES
1997/98	HANDSWORTH CC
1998/99	AC BALL
1999/00	WOODHOUSE WEST END
2000/01	STANNINGTON VILLAGE
2001/02	CROWN INN

DIVISION 2

1966/67	RAMS
1967/68	SOUTHEY ACADEMICALS
1968/69	QUEEN HOTEL (MOSB)
1969/70	WINN GARDENS
1970/71	KESTRELS
1971/72	COLLEY ATH
1972/73	OLD BLUE BALL
1973/74	BURNGREAVE LIBERAL CLUB
1974/75	WINN GARDENS
1975/76	BOWLING GREEN
1976/77	PARK UTD
1977/78	HEELEY RED LION
1978/79	WESTFIELD MILL
1979/80	FRECHEVILLE HOTEL
1980/81	CREMORNE FC
1981/82	ECCLESFIELD OLD BOYS
1982/83	GOLDEN PLOVER
1983/84	THE MILL
1984/85	BRUNSMEER ATHLETIC
1985/86	SHEAF ATHLETIC
1986/87	NETHER EDGE
1987/88	GOLDEN PLOVER
1988/89	ANDERSON STRATHCLYDE
1989/90	BOWLING GREEN
1990/91	PRINCESS ROYAL (CROOKES)
1991/92	DEERSTALKER
1992/93	ROSE INN
1993/94	VINE TAVERN
1994/95	TAVERN PIRATES
1995/96	HANDSWORTH WMC
1996/97	HARE & HOUND
1997/98	JACK- IN-A- BOX
1998/99	WOODHOUSE WEST END
1999/00	HANDSWORTH NEW CROWN
2000/01	SICEY FC
2001/02	WOODHOUSE STAG 2001

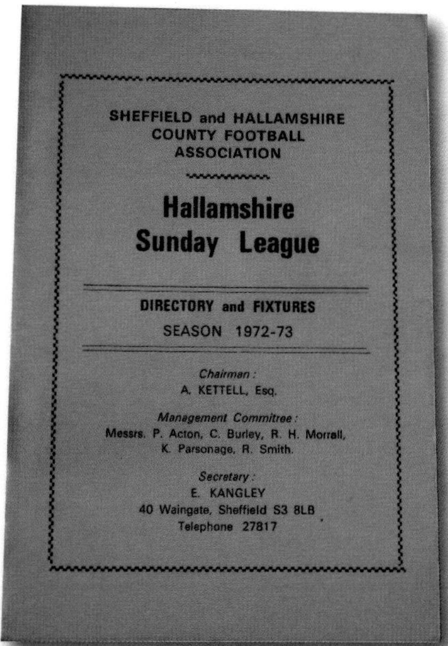
SHEFFIELD and HALLAMSHIRE COUNTY FOOTBALL ASSOCIATION

Hallamshire Sunday League

DIRECTORY and FIXTURES
SEASON 1972-73

Chairman:
A. KETTELL, Esq.

Management Committee:
Messrs. P. Acton, C. Burley, R. H. Morrall, K. Parsonage, R. Smith.

Secretary:
E. KANGLEY
40 Waingate, Sheffield S3 8LB
Telephone 27817

Hallamshire Sunday League Handbook for season 1972-73

DIVISION 3

The cup is engraved Sheffield & Hallamshire County Football Association Hallamshire Sunday League – Division 3.

1967/68	QUEEN HOTEL (MOSB)
1968/69	BRICKLAYERS ARMS
1969/70	KESTRELS
1970/71	CONCORD ROVERS
1971/72	OLD BLUE BALL
1972/73	BARWORTH UTD
1973/74	BOOMERANG
1974/75	BOWLING GREEN
1975/76	RIVELIN VALLEY
1976/77	FULWOOD AMT
1977/78	FRECHEVILLE HOTEL
1978/79	MIDLAND BANK (SHEFFIELD)
1979/80	SACRED HEART
1980/81	ECCLESFIELD OLD BOYS
1981/82	JOHN O GAUNT
1982/83	BRUNSMEER ATH
1983/84	DIXONS SPORTS
1984/85	YORKSHIRE GREY
1985/86	NETHER EDGE
1986/87	BIG TREE
1987/88	ECKINGTON YC
1988/89	PHEASANT ATHLETIC
1989/90	PRINCESS ROYAL (CROOKES)
1990/91	DEERSTALKER
1991/92	ROSE INN
1992/93	QUEENS HOTEL
1993/94	TAVERN PIRATES
1994/95	ECCLESFIELD WMC
1995/96	ECHO SPORTS
1996/97	RAILWAY HOTEL
1997/98	WOODHOUSE WEST END
1998/99	ROYAL HOTEL
1999/00	HORSESHOE
2000/01	ECCLESFIELD GREYHOUND

With the contraction of Sunday football in Sheffield this division ceased to run in 2001.

KO CUP

1969/70	BURNCROSS 67
1970/71	KESTRELS
1971/72	QUEEN HOTEL (MOSB)
1972/73	MINERS ARMS "A"
1973/74	OAKS FOLD YC
1974/75	OAKS FOLD YC
1975/76	OLD BLUE BALL
1976/77	STANNINGTON VILLAGE
1977/78	WINN GARDENS
1978/79	FRECHEVILLE HOTEL
1979/80	HALFWAY HOUSE
1980/81	SACRED HEART
1981/82	WINN GARDENS
1982/83	ECCLESFIELD WMC
1983/84	S.A.D.A.C.A
1984/85	ECCLESFIELD WMC
1985/86	SOTHALL
1986/87	SOTHALL
1987/88	TAVERN FC
1988/89	RAILWAY 88
1989/90	HANDSWORTH NEW CROWN
1990/91	HANDSWORTH NEW CROWN
1991/92	STANNINGTON VILLAGE
1992/93	HANDSWORTH OLD CROWN
1993/94	SPORTSMAN
1994/95	TAVERN PIRATES
1995/96	BIRLEY FC
1996/97	HANDSWORTH WMC
1997/98	HARE & HOUND
1998/99	AC BALL
1999/00	WOODHOUSE WEST END
2000/01	SHERWOOD FC
2001/02	WOODHOUSE STAG 2001

Hallamshire Sunday League Division Three Cup

SHEFFIELD IMPERIAL SUNDAY LEAGUE

PREMIER DIVISION

OLD CUP

1970/71	OLIVE GROVE
1971/72	BURNABY ST WMC
1972/73	HIGH NOON
1973/74	WOODBOURNE
1974/75	ECCLESFIELD Ex S.C
1975/76	WHITE HART
1976/77	ASTON
1977/78	HOLLIN BUSH
1978/79	WHITE HART WANDERERS
1979/80	PRINCESS ROYAL
1980/81	ASTON
1981/82	ASTON
1982/83	NOAH'S ARK
1983/84	NOAH'S ARK
1984/85	HIGH NOON
1985/86	NEW INN ESTATES
1986/87	GREENHILL
1987/88	GREENHILL
1988/89	GREENHILL
1989/90	GREENHILL
1990/91	GREENHILL WHITE HART
1991/92	DARNALL WELLINGTON
1992/93	PARKWAY
1993/94	EARL GEORGE
1994/95	HOLMESFIELD TOWN
1995/96	HOLMESFIELD TOWN
1996/97	HOLLIN BUSH

NEW CUP

1997/98	WINCOBANK BARROW
1998/99	YORK HOTEL ATH
1999/00	HSBC BANK
2000/01	YORK HOTEL ATH
2001/02	BRADKIRK
2002/03	CROOKES WMC
2003/04	VULCAN
2004/05	ECCLESFIELD BALL INN
2005/06	ANVIL
2006/07	ANVIL
2007/08	BAGSHAWE ARMS
2008/09	BOUNDARY 09
2009/10	WARMINSTER WANDERERS
2010/11	CASTLE FC
2011/12	NORTON
2012/13	WOODHOUSE JUNCTION
2013/14	WOODHOUSE JUNCTION
2014/15	BAGSHAWE ARMS
2015/16	STERLING FC

DIVISION 1

1968/69	ENFIELD
1969/70	OLIVE GROVE
1970/71	BURNABY ST WMC
1971/72	MIDWAY
1972/73	ROTARY SPORTS
1973/74	OLD BLUE BALL
1974/75	BURNABY ST WMC
1975/76	PARSON CROSS HOTEL
1976/77	THREE TUNS TAVERNERS
1977/78	CUTLERS ARMS
1978/79	PRINCESS ROYAL
1979/80	YORK HOTEL ATH
1980/81	SHEAF SNAKEBITES
1981/82	OUGHTIBRIDGE COCK INN
1982/83	DARNALL DYNAMOES
1983/84	NEW INN ESTATES
1984/85	BRUNSMEER ATH
1985/86	ST CECILIAS
1986/87	OLD HARROW
1987/88	SHEFFIELD GAS
1988/89	GREENHILL WHITE HART
1989/90	LORD NELSON
1990/91	CROSSPOOL HALLAMSHIRE
1991/92	GRENOSIDE OLD HARROW
1992/93	ECCLESFIELD 147
1993/94	FOXWOOD ROVERS
1994/95	LORD NELSON
1995/96	WADSLEY JACK
1996/97	HAMMER & PINCERS
1997/98	YORK HOTEL ATH
1998/99	STEEL INN
1999/00	BALL INN CROOKES
2000/01	MALIN BRIDGE ATH
2001/02	MOSBOROUGH BRITISH OAK
2002/03	HIGH NOON
2003/04	ECCLESFIELD BALL INN
2004/05	BIG TREE
2005/06	THE ARMS
2006/07	BAGSHAWE ARMS
2007/08	SPORTSMAN 2007
2008/09	MANOR SOCIAL
2009/10	AFC SPORTSMAN
2010/11	HILLSBOROUGH HOTEL
2011/12	BRIDGE INN
2012/13	WINCOBANK FORUM
2013/14	NEW BOHEMIANS VILLA
2014/15	SHIREGREEN WMC

NOW CHAMPIONSHIP

2015/16	BRACKEN MOOR

DIVISION 2

1969/70	ARBOURTHORNE COMM
1970/71	ECCLESFIELD Ex S.C
1971/72	SHEFFIELD POLYTECHNIC
1972/73	BEIGHTON UTD
1973/74	GRIFFIN INN
1974/75	PARSON CROSS HOTEL
1975/76	PARK WANDERERS
1976/77	CUTLERS ARMS
1977/78	ROWLINSON YC
1978/79	HIGH NOON
1979/80	NOAH'S ARK
1980/81	WALKLEY WMC
1981/82	PARSON CROSS HOTEL
1982/83	NEW INN ESTATES
1983/84	BRUNSMEER ATH
1984/85	INTAKE VIDEOS
1985/86	ROBIN HOOD UTD
1986/87	AFC JORDANTHORPE
1987/88	GREENHILL WHITE HART
1988/89	LORD NELSON
1989/90	FAR LEES
1990/91	MIDLAND BANK
1991/92	SOUTH YORKSHIRE TILES
1992/93	HILLSBOROUGH
1993/94	LORD NELSON
1994/95	VULCAN 94
1995/96	FOUNDRY ARMS
1996/97	HOGSHEAD
1997/98	STEEL INN 97
1998/99	BLUE BELL 98
1999-2002	NO COMPETITION
2002/03	ECCLESFIELD BALL INN
2003/04	JORDANTHORPE HOTEL
2004/05	SHEPLEY SPITFIRE
2005/06	BLUE BELL 2005
2006/07	FIRTH PARK WMC
2007/08	GOLF CLUB RANGERS
2008/09	AFC SPORTSMAN
2009/10	WHARNCLIFFE ARMS
2010/11	ROSE INN
2011/12	CROWN INN
2012/13	MANOR SOCIAL
2013/14	TOP CLUB
2014/15	RED LION BOMBERS

NOW DIVISION 1

2015/16	KNOWHOW CC FC

DIVISION 3

OLD CUP

1973/74	WOODTHORPE ARMS
1974/75	BRITISH RELAY
1975/76	ROSE HOUSE VILLA
1976/77	ENFIELD
1977/78	HIGH NOON
1978/79	NOAH'S ARK
1979/80	PARSON CROSS HOTEL
1980/81	TRAMWAY SPORTS
1981/82	DARNALL ROVERS
1982/83	BRUNSMEER ATH
1983/84	INTAKE VIDEOS
1984/85	GLEADLESS VALLEY
1985/86	AFC JORDANTHORPE
1986/87	GREENHILL WHITE HART
1987/88	VULCAN DYNAMOES
1988/89	ROSE & CROWN
1989/90	OSBOURNES
1990/91	WHITE HART ATH
1991/92	HILLSBOROUGH
1992/93	EARL MARSHALL
1993-2009	NO COMPETITION

NEW CUP

2009/10	EARL MARSHALL
2010/11	CENTRE SPOT
2011/12	COSY WARM
2012/13	CROSS KEYS
2013/14	RED LION BOMBERS
2014/15	FDL TOTLEY

NOW DIVISION 2

2015/16	TERMINUS TAVERN

DIVISION 4

2010/11	FORUM 2010
2011/12	WINCOBANK FORUM
2012/13	WHEEL ATHLETIC
2013/14	WISEWOOD WADSLEY
2014/15	THE ROYAL OAK

Sheffield Sunday Imperial League Division Two Champion Trophy, won by Park Wanderers FC

INVITATION CUP

	WINNERS	RUNNERS UP
2002/03	HIGH NOON	ECCLESFIELD BALL INN
2003/04	BANNER CROSS	BLAKE
2004/05	PHEASANT INN	VULCAN
2005/06	PHEASANT INN	ANVIL
2006/07	POMONA	CART AND HORSES
2007/08	MARKHAM	TRICKSHOTS
2008/09	S12 INTAKE BALL INN	GOLDEN PLOVER
2009/10	ANGLERS REST	HILLSBOROUGH HOTEL
2010/11	CENTRE SPOT	EARL MARSHALL
2011/12	NO COMPETITION	
2012/13	HOLLY BUSH	BRACKEN MOOR
2013/14	STERLING COMMODITIES	SHIREGREEN WMC
2014/15	CADBURY CHAUCER	HINDE HOUSE
2015/16	WOODHOUSE VILLAGE	STAFFORDSHIRE ARMS

LEAGUE KO

OLD CUP	WINNERS	RUNNERS UP
1968/69	ENFIELD	BURNABY ST WMC
1969/70	FOX & DUCK	BAGSHAWE ARMS
1970/71	WOODBOURNE	OLIVE GROVE
1971/72	BURNABY ST WMC	WHEATSHEAF
1972/73	HIGH NOON	ROLAND ARMS
1973/74	WOODBOURNE	MIDWAY
1974/75	WOODTHORPE ARMS	SHEFFIELD VILLA
1975/76	WHITE HART	PARK WANDERERS
1976/77	PARSON CROSS HOTEL	CUTLERS ARMS
1977/78	HOLLIN BUSH	PRINCESS ROYAL
1978/79	SHEFFIELD TAXI DRIVERS	BRADKIRK
1979/80	SHEFFIELD TAXI DRIVERS	WHITE HART WANDERERS
1980/81	SHEAF SNAKEBITES	WOODHOUSE JUNCTION
1981/82	NOAHS ARK	DARNALL DYNAMOES
1982/83	ASTON	DARNALL DYNAMOES
1983/84	NEW INN ESTATES	BRUNSMEER ATH
1984/85	BRUNSMEER ATH	ROSE INN
1985/86	DARNALL WELLINGTON	S Y C C
1986/87	WOODHOUSE STAG	WOODSEATS HOTEL
1987/88	GREENHILL	BRADKIRK
1988/89	GREENHILL WHITE HART	INTAKE VIDEOS
1989/90	ROWLINSON	SWAN ATH
1990/91	GREENHILL WHITE HART	DARNALL WELLINGTON

NEW CUP	WINNERS	RUNNERS UP
1991/92	ST CECILIA'S	VULCAN DYNAMOES
1992/93	SWAN ATH	GRENOSIDE OLD HARROW
1993/94	EARL GEORGE	TRADES & LABOUR
1994/95	HILLSBOROUGH	STRAD 93
1995/96	HOLMESFIELD TOWN	LORD NELSON
1996/97	HAMMER & PINCERS	WADSLEY JACK
1997/98	MARKHAM	BRADKIRK YEW TREE
1998/99	RICHMOND VILLA	DARNALL WELLINGTON
1999/00	BALL INN (CROOKES)	DARNALL WELLINGTON
2000/01	BALL INN (CROOKES)	YORK HOTEL ATH
2001/02	BANNER CROSS	ANVIL FC
2002/03	ECCLESALL RANGERS	CROOKES WMC
2003/04	JORDANTHORPE HOTEL	PHEASANT INN
2004/05	ECCLESFIELD BALL INN	PHEASANT INN
2005/06	BIG TREE	MALIN RANGERS
2006/07	ANVIL	STANNINGTON WARRIORS
2007/08	BAGSHAWE ARMS	MALIN RANGERS
2008/09	BOUNDARY 08	FIRTH BROWN WMC
2009/10	1861 LEISURE	NORTON FC
2010/11	HACKENTHORPE VILLA	FC FALCONS
2011/12	WINCOBANK FORUM	EARL MARSHALL
2012/13	BYRON HOUSE	FC SPARTAK
2013/14	WHEEL ATHLETIC	COSYWARM
2014/15	STERLING BOYS	SHIREGREEN WMC
2015/16	THE FRIENDSHIP FC	AFC CROWN

S & H - JUNIOR LEAGUE

This competition was initially for under 18 teams, and ran between 1895 and 1946. With the setting up of the 16-18 league in 1927, this competition then became for 18-21 year old players

The competition took over from the Sheffield & District Combination League for season 1895/96. Originally, the 1877 Cup (Old Hallamshire FA Challenge Cup) was used for the winners for the first four seasons.

The Competition was restarted in 1962 for under 21 teams and ran until 1973. In its later days it was always referred to by the players as the Under 21 League. There were under 16 and a half and under 18 leagues being run by Sheffield & Hallamshire at this time

The Cup is silver, stamped with a Crown, Lion and V which indicates the year 1913. The manufacturers were Walker & Hall of Sheffield. It is stamped as a 3 pint Cup. The original base, if there was one has been lost over the years.

After retirement the Cup was used for two seasons 1976/77 and 1977/78 for the Sheffield & Hallamshire CFA Senior Clubs Youth Competition. Sheffield United won the first Competition and Barnsley the second. Barnsley held onto the Cup until 2008 before returning it to S&H. A new base with a silver band was purchased for the Youth Competition in 1976

Junior League: Winners Medal 1902-03 won by Sale Memorial

1895/96	SWALLOWNEST
1896/97	ROTHERWOOD ROVERS
1897/98	BRUNSWICK MISSION
1898/99	BRUNSWICK MISSION
1899/1900	EASTWOOD ALBION
1900/01	SWALLOWNEST
1901/02	MANGHAM UTD
1902/03	SALE MEMORIAL
1903/04	ST CATHERINES (PITSMOOR)
1904/05	CENTRAL ALBION
1905/06	ICKLES UTD
1906/07	OAK STREET BC
1907/08	OUGHTIBRIDGE INST
1908/09	TINSLEY CHURCH
1909/10	GRENOSIDE CHURCH
1910/11	BRIGHTSIDE CONGS
1911/12	BRIGHTSIDE CONGS
1912/13	FIRS HILL OB
1913/14	INTAKE PM
1914/15	INTAKE PM
1915/16	INTAKE PM
1916/17	TINSLEY PARK
1917/18	KIMBERWORTH OB
1918/19	BRADGATE
1919/20	STOCKSBRIDGE CHURCH
1920/21	INTAKE WMC
1921/22	ATTERCLIFFE VICTORY
1922/23	ATTERCLIFFE VICTORY
1923/24	GREENLAND WMC
1924/25	GREENLAND WMC
1925/26	GREENLAND WMC
1926/27	HORSE & TIGER SWIFTS
1927/28	HATHERSAGE
1928/29	WOODHOUSE WMC
1929/30	ARCHER ROVERS
1930/31	WOODHOUSE MILL UTD
1931/32	CHAPELTOWN
1932/33	ECCLESFIELD RED ROSE
1933/34	KIVETON PARK COLLIERY
1934/35	WOODHOUSE MILL MW
1935/36	WOODHOUSE MILL MW
1936-1941`	NO COMP – WAR
1941/42	HIGHFIELD AMATEURS
1942/43	HADFIELD SPORTS
1943/44	HADFIELD SPORTS
1944/45	SHEFFIELD YMCA
1945/46	JENKINS SPORTS

There then appears to be a break because under 16 & 18 league competitions started 1946/47

1962/63	LITTLEDALE CA
1963/64	LINDSAY RD YC
1964/65	LONGLEY BC
1965/66	MANSEL YC
1966/67	CLUB 62
1967/68	HACKENTHORPE SOCIAL CLUB
1968/69	HACKENTHORPE YC
1969/70	COLLEY YC
1970/71	CLUB DOUBLE SIX
1971/72	CLUB DOUBLE SIX
1972/73	MANSEL YC

SHEFFIELD LICENSED VICTUALLERS LEAGUE

The competition started in 1903/04.

The winners and runners up of the first final in which Washford Arms beat New Inn 2-0 at the Sheaf Ground on Bramall Lane both received shields.

It is possible that the shields were used each year after that for the winners and runners up.

The Cup competition appears to have started in 1905/06. The last entry on the Cup appears to be for season 1912/13 – so I assume the competition finished then as no other results ever found.

Found report/letter in 1905/06 which stated that S&H FA would not sanction the competition – so this might have resulted in the early finishing of the league. It would have been allowed to run unsanctioned until 1913 when football became more regulated

What happened to the cup afterwards is not sure, but both the Cup and one of the Shields were sold at auction by Sotheby's in May 2002 for £7600. Both items were referred to as silver plated.

Sheffield Licensed Victuallers League Cup

Sheffield Licensed Victuallers League Shield

LEAGUE

Season	Winner	Score	Runner-up
1903/04	WASHFORD ARMS	2 – 0	NEW INN
1904/05	TARGET	1 – 0	HALF WAY
1905/06	GREAT BRITAIN HOTEL	2 - 0	HALF WAY
1906/07	GREAT BRITAIN HOTEL	3 – 2	BELLFIELD INN
1907/08	BELLFIELD INN	2 – 1	GREAT BRITAIN HT
1908/09	CRICKET INN	3 – 0	BELLFIELD INN
1909/10	INDUSTRY INN	3 – 2	DOUGLAS HOTEL
1910/11	INDUSTRY INN	1 - 0	DOUGLAS HOTEL
1911/12	BIRD IN HAND	2 – 1	GUARDS REST (after 1-1)
1912/13	INDUSTRY INN		

CUP

Season	Winner	Score	Runner-up
1905/06	GREAT BRITAIN HOTEL	1 – 0	CROWN & ANCHOR
1906/07	BELLFIELD INN	2 – 0	GREAT BRITAIN HT
1907/08	BELLFIELD INN	2 – 0	SAW MILL
1908/09	BELLFIELD INN	1 – 0	GREAT BRITAIN HT
1909/10	PROSPECT VIEW	3 - 2	INDUSTRY INN
1910/11	INDUSTRY INN	4 - 2	DOUGLAS HOTEL
1911/12	INDUSTRY INN	2 - 1	BIRD IN HAND
1912/13	BIRD IN HAND	5 – 1	BEEHIVE

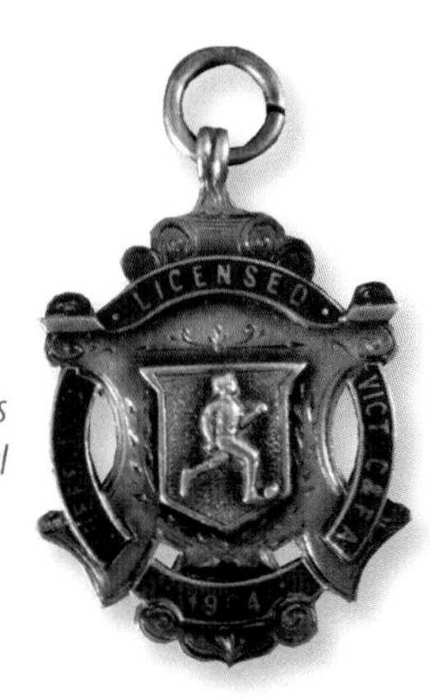

Sheffield Licensed Victuallers Medal

MEADOWHALL SUNDAY LEAGUE

Division 1	Division 2	Division 3
1964/65 Arbourthorne EA & New Inn joint champions		
1965/66 Arbourthorne EA	Dronfield Sports Club	Angel
1966/67 Arbourthorne EA	Angel	Hoyland Town Jaguars
1967/68 Waggon & Horses	Hoyland Town Jaguars	Firvale
1968/69 Black Bull Taverners	Firvale	Tavern Athletic
1969/70 Black Bull Taverners	Tavern Athletic	Arbourthorne EA

Premier Division	Division 1	Division 2	Division 3
1970/71 Arbourthorne EA	Angel	Enfield Amateurs	Woodbourne
1971/72 Waggon & Horses	Hoyland Town Jaguars	Olive Grove	
1972/73 Waggon & Horses	Hoyland Town Jaguars	Woodbourne	
1973/74 Angel	Tavern Athletic	Handsworth Social	
1974/75 Angel	Woodbourne	East House Athletic	
1975/76 Hartley House	Woodbourne	Woodhouse Central	
1976/77 Earl United	Hoyland Town Jaguars	Todwick	
1977/78 Earl United	Hoyland Town Jaguars	Sportsman Trophy 78	
1978/79 Earl United	Brunsmeer Athletic	Burncross 67	
1979/80 Olive Grove	Rowlinson YC	Throstles	
1980/81 Hoyland Town Jaguars	Throstles	Tollgate	
1981/82 Arbourthorne EA	Ball Albion	Rose House	
1982/83 Arbourthorne EA	Rose House	Winn Gardens	
1983/84 Arbourthorne EA	Rowlinson YC	Springwood	
1984/85Arbourthorne EA	Springwood	Woodseats	
1985/86 Arbourthorne EA	Winn Gardens Tavern	Ecclesfield Stocks	
1986/87 Arbourthorne EA	Brunsmeer Athletic	Centre Spot	
1987/88 Arbourthorne EA	Ecclesfield Stocks	Rose House	Sothall
1988/89 Arbourthorne EA	Winn Gardens	Anglers Rest	New Inn Estates
1989/90 Hoyland Town Jaguars	Double Top	Union Services	Nursery Tavern
1990/91 Hoyland Town Jaguars	Ecclesfield Stocks	High Green Club	Norfolk 90
1991/92 Half Moon	Royal Earl	Yew Tree	Greenhill White Hart
1992/93 Half Moon	Brunsmeer Athletic	Centre Spot	Shakespeare Hotel
1993/94 Hoyland Town Jaguars	Rose House	Three Feathers	Deerstalker
1994/95 Hoyland Town Jaguars	Centre Spot	Deerstalker	
1995/96 Hoyland Town Jaguars	Bradway	Swallownest Social	
1996/97 Hoyland Town Jaguars	Norfolk 90	Treddlehoyle	
1997/98 Hoyland Town Jaguars	Treddlehoyle	Denby Sportsman	
1998/99 Bradway	Bradkirk	Holmesfield Town	
1999/00 Bradway	Holmesfield Town	Ridgeway Athletic	
2000/01 Bradway	Brunsmeer Athletic	Handsworth Old Crown	
2001/02 Royal Earl	Chapeltown WMC	Crosspool '96	
2002/03 Royal Earl	Handsworth Old Crown	York Athletic	
2003/04 Hoyland Town Jaguars	Arundel	Hillsborough Phoenix	
2004/05 Bradway	Hillsborough Phoenix	Banner Cross	
2005/06 Crosspool '96	Mosborough	High Noon	
2006/07 Handsworth Old Crown	Chapeltown Royal Oak	Packhorse Celtic	
2007/08 Royal Earl	Arbourthorne EA	Denby Sportsman	African Dream Team
2008/09 Chapeltown Royal Oak	High Noon	Greenhill White Hart	Beighton Magpies
2009/10 AFC Celtic	Arundel ESC	Pheasant Inn	Arbourthorne EA B
2010/11 Royal Earl	High Noon	Jack in a Box	Heeley
2011/12 Hackenthorpe 'A'	Brunsmeer Abbey AJW	Rawson Spring	Woodhouse JFC
2012/13 Handsworth Turf Tav	Arbourthorne EA	City Taxis	
2013/14 Hackenthorpe 'A'	High Noon	SWD	
2014/15 Crookes	Sharrow United	Players Lounge	
2015/16 High Noon	Bagshawe Arms		

Meadowhall Sunday League Cup Winners

League Cup

1964/65	Ellin Street
1965/66	Ellin Street
1966/67	Hoyland Town Jaguars
1967/68	Hollinsend Amateurs
1968/69	Arbourthorne Community
1969/70	Waggon & Horses
1970/71	Angel
1971/72	Olive Grove
1972/73	Olive Grove
1973/74	Angel
1974/75	Olive Grove
1975/76	Fulwood Amateurs
1976/77	Burnaby Street WMC
1977/78	Tavern Athletic
1978/79	Hoyland Town Jaguars
1979/80	Throstles
1980/81	Olive Grove
1981/82	Norfolk Arms 81
1982/83	Half Moon
1983/84	Norfolk Arms
1984/85	Ball Albion
1985/86	Hoyland Town Jaguars
1986/87	Ecclesfield Stocks
1987/88	Arbourthorne EA
1988/89	Earl 86
1989/90	Half Moon
1990/91	Royal Earl
1991/92	Hoyland Town Jaguars
1992/93	Olive Grove 90
1993/94	Royal Earl
1994/95	Royal Earl
1995/96	Centre Spot
1996/97	Hoyland Town Jaguars
1997/98	Treddlehoyle
1998/99	Bradway
1999/00	Bradway
2000/01	Royal Earl
2001/02	Hoyland Town Jaguars
2002/03	Royal Earl
2003/04	Hoyland Town Jaguars
2004/05	Ridgeway Athletic
2005/06	Bradway
2006/07	Handsworth Old Crown
2007/08	Sharrow United
2008/09	Packhorse Celtic
2009/10	Royal Earl
2010/11	Royal Earl
2011/12	Royal Earl
2012/13	Rawson Spring
2013/14	Handsworth Turf Tavern
2014/15	Handsworth Turf Tavern
2015/16	Royal Earl

UNDER 21 COMPETITION LEAGUE

2011/12	DRONFIELD TOWN U21
2012/13	DRONFIELD TOWN U21
2013/14	SHEFFIELD UTD JUNIOR BLADES U21
2014/15	BRUNSMEER BRADWAY U21
2015/16	BRINSWORTH WHITEHILL U21

CUP

2011/12	DRONFIELD TOWN U21
2012/13	SHEFFIELD U21 FC
2013/14	SHEFFIELD UTD JUNIOR BLADES U21
2014/15	MILLMOOR JUNIORS U21
2015/16	BRUNSMEER BRADWAY U21

Handbooks for the Sheffield Sunday Meadowhall League covering some of the years between 2001 and 2014

Programmes for the Meadowhall Sunday League Cup finals played at Bramall Lane, covering the years 2008-2013

NOMADS SUNDAY LEAGUE (SHEFFIELD)

This league started in 1981/82 and ceased when it amalgamated with the Hallamshire League at end of season 2001/02.

PREMIER DIVISION

1996/97 CHAPELTOWN WMC
1997/98 RIDGEWAY ATHLETIC
1998/99 PITSMOOR WMC
1999/2000 PITSMOOR WMC
2000/01 TOLLGATE
2001/02 BRITISH OAK

DIVISION 1

1981/82 ARBOURTHORNE PHOENIX
1982/83 SUNDOWNERS
1983/84 SEPA CONSTRUCTION
1984/85 NETHER EDGE
1985/86 MANCHESTER HOTEL
1986/87 DEERSTALKER
1987/88 DEERSTALKER
1988/89 NORTON OAKES
1989/90 DEERSTALKER
1990/91 PENGUIN
1991/92 PENGUIN
1992/93 TAVERN PIRATES
1993/94 COACH & HORSES
1994/95 DENBY SPORTSMAN
1995/96 CHAPELTOWN WMC
1996/97 WHEEL
1997/98 FOXWOOD EMBASSY
1998/99 OWLERTON OLD CROWN
1999/00 HOGSHEAD
2000/01 PINEGROVE 98
2001/02 J & E

DIVISION 2

1982/83 SEPA CONSTRUCTION
1983/84 CROSS HALL
1984/85 NORTON OAKES
1985/86 NOAHS ARK (INTAKE)
1986/87 PINEGROVE
1987/88 FAIRWAYS
1988/89 EARL GEORGE
1989/90 TAVERN PIRATES
1990/91 DEVONSHIRE ARMS
1991/92 CAROUSEL
1992/93 SHIREGREEN HOTEL
1993/94 KINGS HEAD
1994/95 GOWER ARMS
1995/96 SHIREGREEN VILLA
1996/97 HUNTSMAN
1997/98 RANCH
1998/99 SHEFFIELD TRADES & LABOUR
1999/00 PINEGROVE 98
2000/01 LYNTHORPE

DIVISION 3

1984/85 NOAH'S ARK
1985/86 SHAKESPEARE INN
1986/87 QUEENS HEAD
1987/88 RAILWAY
1988/89 HORSE & GROOM
1989/90 REDHOUSE
1990/91 HIGH GREEN
1991/92 HORSE & JOCKEY
1992/93 BROWN COW
1993/94 ROMAN RIDGE
1994/95 GOLDEN LION
1995/96 MARKET RANGERS

DIVISION 4

1988/89 RED HOUSE
1989/90 HIGH GREEN
1990/91 MARSHALL
1991/92 WHEATSHEAF
1992/93 WHEEL
1993/94 GOLDEN LION
1994/95 JACOBS
1995/96 RAILWAY

KO CUP

1982/83 SEPA CONSTRUCTION
1983/84 MANCHESTER HOTEL
1984/85 DEERSTALKER
1985/86 MANCHESTER HOTEL
1986/87 DEERSTALKER
1987/88 DEERSTALKER
1988/89 NORTON OAKES
1989/90 DEERSTALKER
1990/91 PENGUIN FC
1991/92 PENGUIN FC
1992/93 WHEATSHEAF
1993/94 KINGS HEAD FC
1994/95 MANCHESTER HOTEL
1995/96 MANCHESTER HOTEL
1996/97 CHAPELTOWN WMC
1997/98 RIDGEWAY ATH
998/99 BLACKBURN CROWN
1999/00 REDCAP
2000/01 WHEEL FC
2001/02 BRITISH OAK

REGIONAL ALLIANCE SUNDAY LEAGUE

This Competition started in 1999 when the Sheffield Regional League and the Sheffield Alliance leagues amalgamated. The league ceased around 2007 when clubs joined the other Sunday Leagues that where running.

1999/2000 DIVISION

1A	HEELEY & SHEFFIELD
1B	HARTLEY HOUSE
2A	LANGSETT
2B	HALLCARR TAVERN

PREMIER DIVISION

2000/01	HEELEY & SHEFFIELD
2001/02	FAIRLEIGH MANOR
2002/03	OLD HARROW
2003/04	BATHFIELD
2004/05	SHELDON
2005/06	PARK
2006/07	SHIREGREEN ROVERS

DIVISION 1

2000/01	LANGSETT
2001/02	JACK-IN-A-BOX
2002/03	SHIREGREEN PARK RANGERS
2003/04	RED LION
2004/05	PARK & ARBOURTHORNE
2005/06	SHEFFIELD ARMS

DIVISION 2

2000/01	GLEADLESS RED LION
2001/02	WOODHOUSE WEST END
2002/03	WINCOBANK RANGERS
2003/04	GLEADLESS PUNCHBOWL

LEAGUE CHALLENGE CUP

1999/2000	HARTLEY HOUSE
2000/01	LANGSETT
2001/02	JACK-IN-A-BOX
2002/03	SHIREGREEN ROVERS
2003/04	SHARROW UNITED
2004/05	SHELDON
2005/06	SHELDON
2006/07	SHIREGREEN ROVERS

DON CRITCHLEY MEMORIAL TROPHY

1999/2000	RICHMOND
2000/01	RED GROUSE
2001/02	BRUNSMEER ATHLETIC
2002/03	SPORTSMAN LODGE MOOR
2003/04	HORSE & LION BAR
2004/05	BRADFIELD
2005/06	SWD
2006/07	HANDSWORTH NEW CROWN

EARLY SHEFFIELD THURSDAY FOOTBALL LEAGUES

SHEFFIELD THURSDAY FOOTBALL LEAGUE

The Sheffield Thursday League (started 1892/93), on a league basis with the top team being crowned Champions

1892/93 WHITWORTHS
1893/94 WHITWORTHS
1894/95 CASTLEFOLDS

Whitworth medal for winning the Sheffield Thurday Football League in Season 1892-93

S S A A THURSDAY LEAGUE

The (Sheffield Shop Assistants Association) Thursday League ran between 1893/94 to 1897/98.

1893/94 WHITWORTHS
1894/95 CASTLEFOLDS
1895/96 CASTLEFOLDS
1896/97 MOOR THURSDAY
1897/98 MOOR THURSDAY

S & H THURSDAY FOOTBALL LEAGUE

Due to requests from clubs, S&H set up and ran a Thursday football League in 1897/98.The winners were decided on a play off system between the top teams in each division. This league appears to have ceased in 1907/08

1897/98 BARNSLEY SHOP ASSISTANTS /SHEFFIELD MARKETS - JT
1898/99 ROTHERHAM THURSDAY
1899/00 MEXBORO THURSDAY
1900/01 MEXBORO THURSDAY
1901/02 CASTLEFOLDS
1902/03 CASTLEFOLDS
1903/04 WHITWORTHS
1904/05 WHITWORTHS
1905/06 WHITWORTHS
1906/07 WALKLEY
1907/08 WHITWORTHS

EARLY CLOSING LEAGUE

This League appeared to start in 1909/10, amalgamating with the Thursday Amateur League in 1913/14.

The cup for this is engraved Sheffield & Hallamshire CFA Early Closing League. It appears that in 1913 the competition amalgamated with the Thursday Amateur League. The cup is silver and marked Crown/Lion/T which is for 1911.The Cup was then used by the Thursday Amateur League.

1909/10 WHITWORTHS
1910/11 WHITWORTHS
1911/12 BARNSLEY THURSDAY AMATEURS
1912/13 BARNSLEY THURSDAY AMATEURS

Early Closing Cup

SHEFFIELD SUNDAY ALLIANCE LEAGUE

This competition started in 1967 and finished at the end of season 1998/99 when it amalgamated with the Regional Sunday League

PREMIER DIVISION

1988/89 THORNECLIFFE FC
1989/90 SHAKESPEARE HOTEL
1990/91 JACK-IN-A-BOX
1991/92 JACK-IN-A-BOX
1992/93 SHEAF HOUSE
1993/94 BAGSHAWE ARMS
1994/95
1995/96 SOUTHEY SOCIAL
1996/97
1997/98
1998/99 HORSESHOE

DIVISION 1

1967/68 HANDSWORTH SOCIAL
1968/69 DEERSTALKER "A"
1969/70 MOTEHALL
1970/71 LOWSDALE
1971/72
1972/73 STEEL INN
1973/74 STEEL INN
1974/75 THREE FEATHERS
1975/76 THREE FEATHERS
1976/77 BALL ALBION
1977/78
1978/79
1979/80 BALL ALBION
1980/81
1981/82
1982/83 JOSEPHINES
1983/84
1984/85 RED LION
1985/86
1986/87 WHITE RAILS
1987/88 WHITE RAILS
1988/89 GEORGE & DRAGON
1989/90 MANOR HOTEL
1990/91 KELVIN & CROOKESMOOR
1991/92 WINCOBANK HOTEL
1992/93 JOHN O'GAUNT
1993/94 BESTPLATE
1994/95 HAMMER & PINCERS
1995/96 DALE FARM
1996/97 WOODHOUSE ROYAL
1997/98
1998/99 RED GROUSE

DIVISION 2

1968/69 MOTEHALL
1969/70 FORUM ATH
1970/71 HANDSWORTH
1971/72 STEEL INN
1972/73 BRYON HOUSE
1974/75 SANDERSON KAYSER
1975/76 HACKENTHORPE WOODHOUSE WE
1976/77 WHITE RAILS
1977/78
1978/79
1979/80 HARROW UTD
1980/81
1981/82
1982/83 ROYAL OAK
1983/84
1984/85 YORKSHIRE GREYHOUND
1985/86 MIDLAND VILLA
1986/87 MARKET INN
1987/88 ROYAL STANDARD
1988/89 EARL GEORGE
1989/90 QUEENS UTD
1990/91 GATEFIELD
1991/92 BAGSHAWE ARMS
1992/93 NOAHS ARK RANGERS
1993/94 ANVIL
1994/95
1995/96 SICEY B
1996/97 WOODHOUSE WEST END
1997/98 BELLHOUSE ROAD WMC

DIVISION 3

1970/71 SHEAF "B"
1971/72
1972/73
1973/74 HILLSBOROUGH WMC
1974/75 NEW INN "A"
1975/76 ORGREAVE "B"
1976/77 MANOR HOTEL
1977/78
1978/79
1979/80 MOORFOOT
1980/81
1981/82
1982/83 BELLHOUSE RD WMC
1983/84
1984/85 MIDLAND VILLA
1985/86 MARKET INN
1986/87 ANGLERS REST
1987/88 FREEMASONS
1988/89 ST CUTHBERTS
1989/90 KELVIN & CROOKESMOOR
1990/91 WHEEL
1991/92 NOAHS ARK
1992/93 OWLERTON OLD BOYS
1993/94 ANVIL
1994/95
1995/96 ALEXANDER

DIVISION 4

1982/83	LANDSDOWNE
1983/84	MASONS ARMS
1984/85	ST VINCENTS
1985/86	ANGLERS REST
1986/87	HOOD GREEN
1987/88	ROMAN RIDGE
1988/89	NORMANTON SPRINGS
1989/90	BELLE VUE
1990/91	BAGSHAWE ARMS
1991/92	METRO
1992/93	YEW TREE (COAL ASTON)
1993/94	
1994/95	ALEXANDRA

DIVISION 5

1982/83	MIDLAND VILLA
1983/84	
1984/85	ST VINCENTS
1985/86	HOOD GREEN
1986/87	ROSE & CROWN
1987/88	LE METRO
1988/89	KELVIN & CROOKESMOOR
1989/90	
1990/91	
1991/92	
1992/93	STEEL INN
1993/94	VINE ATHLETIC

DIVISION 6

1984/85	ABNEY HOUSE
1985/86	LONGLY BC
1986/87	SWANN MORTON
1987/88	COLT SATELLITES
1988/89	ANGEL FC

DIVISION 7

1986/87	FIVE ARCHERS

KO CUP

1976/77	BALL ALBION
1977/78	
1978/79	
1979/80	
1980/81	
1981/82	
1982/83	
1983/84	
1984/85	ARUNDEL WMC
1985/86	
1986/87	
1987/88	WOODHOUSE WEST END
1988/89	
1989/90	SHAKESPEARE HOTEL
1990/91	QUEEN HOTEL (MOSB)
1991/92	SHEFFIELD POLYTECHNIC
1992/93	
1993/94	
1994/95	SOUTHEY SOCIAL
1995/96	OWLERTON OLD BOYS
1996/97	
1997/98	
1998/99	HORSESHOE

SHEFFIELD SUNDAY SCHOOL FOOTBALL LEAGUE

By Chris Eyre

This competition started out as the Sheffield Sunday School Football Union in 1887/88 and was a cup competition before becoming a league competition in 1890/91. By the 1892/93 season the word Union had been replaced by League, under which title it was known until it finished (like so many competitions) at the start of the Second World War. It restarted again for one season only in 1947/48 and the competition never ran again.

The competition started on an idea by G W Sharman, the President of the Oak Street Sunday School football team. His idea was to form a competition to create friendly intercourse between clubs, and as far as possible, remove the present objection connected with playing ordinary cup-ties and having to strip in public houses and play on public house grounds.

Nineteen clubs were at the first meeting held on 23rd March 1887 at the Montgomery Hall library. Mr Sharman was elected Chairman of the meeting and C Thornhill, the Oak Street secretary, was elected Secretary of the competition.

The clubs in attendance agreed that the competition should be open to Sunday Schools belonging to any religious denomination or temperance. It was noted that £10 had been guaranteed to purchase a silver shield or cup to be held by the winning club.

The next meeting on 8 July went further, when they set the entry fee at 5/-, but the Committee was empowered to make further financial calls should the need arise. They also decided that no club playing in the competition would be allowed to strip in a public house or play on any ground where intoxicants are sold. However, the biggest rule was in respect of which players were allowed to play for a team. Each member of the team must have made 7 afternoon attendances out of 13 at the Sunday School in the previous quarter. If there were no afternoon services, then morning attendances would count.

The draw for the first round took place on 23rd September, when 12 clubs entered the competition. Four first round games were fixed up and four clubs given byes into the second round. One of the first round games, Oak Street v Mount Tabor, had to be replayed following a protest in respect of one of the Oak Street players, Oak Street winning the replay. One of the best teams in the competition and eventual winners of the first competition was Carbrook Reform. The press report on their first round game against Portmahon gave the score as 15 plus 2 dismissed goals to 0

League football had started in the area when the Sheffield & District League was formed in 1889. The competition decided to follow this format and moved their competition into a league, with Rotherham St Peters being the first winner. The competition became very popular and the number of teams in the competition continued to increase. By the 1895/96 season, there were 25 teams, split into two divisions. The top team in each division played each other for the overall champions and were awarded the Silver Shield.

In 1910, a 2nd team competition was started for players under the age of 16 and in 1921/22 an Associates (teams not allowed to be full members of the main competition) was started.

The silver shield, which is now in the ownership of myself, having been purchased at auction in 2013, only had space for 22 winners on it, so a new, large wooden shield was obtained for the winners of the competition in 1910. The silver shield was mounted at some stage onto a cushioned wooded surround, and was then presented to the winners of the 2nd team competition. I have not traced if any trophy was obtained for the winners of the Associates competition, however it is possible that one from the Sheffield Free Church League could have been used.

For three seasons during the First World War (1915/16 to 1917/18) the league joined up with the Sheffield Free Church League to be known as the Sheffield Sunday School and Free Church League. The Free Church League did not start again after the war and the Free Church name was dropped from the tittle. The main trophy from the Free Church League was taken down South by the Competition Secretary during the war, and was returned to Sheffield nearly 100 years later and is now played for by the Sheffield Fair Play League.

Sunday School Shield 1887

SHEFFIELD SUNDAY SCHOOL FOOTBALL LEAGUE

1887/88	CARBROOK REFORM
1888/89	CARBROOK REFORM
1889/90	DARNALL CONGREGATION
1890/91	ROTHERHAM ST PETERS
1891/92	HEELEY ST PETERS
1892/93	OAK ST SUNDAY SCHOOL HEELEY
1893/94	STOCKSBRIDGE CHURCH
1894/95	ROTHERHAM PARISH CHURCH
1895/96	ROTHERHAM PARISH CHURCH
1896/97	THORPE HESLEY PARISH CHURCH
1897/98	KENT ROAD MISSION
1898/99	BRUNSWICK MISSION
1899/00	MEADOW HALL PM
1900/01	WYCLIFFE CONGREGATIONAL
1901/02	HEELEY FRIENDS
1902/03	WYCLIFFE CONGREGATIONAL
1903/04	WYCLIFFE CONGREGATIONAL
1904/05	WYCLIFFE CONGREGATIONAL
1905/06	OXFORD STREET U M
1906/07	BRUNSWICK MISSION
1907/08	HEELEY FRIENDS
1908/09	SHARROW REFORM BROTHERHOOD
1909/10	ALL ST MISSION
1910/11	HEELEY ST PETERS
1911/12	ST JOHNS CHURCH INSTITUTE
1912/13	ST JOHNS CHURCH INSTITUTE
1913/14	GRENOSIDE B C & OWLERTON WES REFORM – (JT)
1914/15	HEELEY FRIENDS
1915-19	AMALGAMATED WITH FREE CHURCH LEAGUE –See below
1919/20	ST JOHNS CHURCH INSTITUTE
1920/21	ST MICHAELS
1921/22	MEERSBROOK CONGREGATIONAL
1922/23	ST BARTHOLOMEWS
1923/24	HEELEY FRIENDS
1924/25	HAWKSLEY PM
1925/26	ANNS ROAD PM
1926/27	HAWKLEY PM
1927/28	HAWKLEY PM
1928/29	QUEENS STREET CONGREGATIONAL
1929/30	HEELEY FRIENDS
1930/31	HEELEY FRIENDS
1931/32	QUEEN STREET CONGREGATIONAL
1932/33	HEELEY FRIENDS
1933/34	HEELEY FRIENDS
1934/35	ALLEN STREET METHS
1935/36	BIRLEY CARR
1936/37	BRUNSWICK MISSION
1937/38	DARNALL CONGREGATIONAL
1938/39	GRENOSIDE SPORTS
1939/40	GRENOSIDE SPORTS
1947/48	MEERSBROOK BROTHERHOOD

2nd TEAM COMPETITION DIVISION for under 16 teams

1909/10	OAK STREET
1910/11	OAK STREET
1911/12	SHARROW REFORM BROTHERHOOD
1912/13	ST JOHNS INSTITUTE
1913/14	ST JOHNS INSTITUTE
1914/15	HEELEY FRIENDS
1915-21	NO COMP
1921/22	DARNALL REFORM WESLEYANS
1922/23	QUEENS STREET CONGREGATIONAL
1923/24	CHAPELTOWN PM
1924/25	CHAPELTOWN PM

ASSOCIATES DIVISION

1921/22	MALIN BRIDGE
1922/23	FRANKLIN STREET
1923/24	CARBROOK REFORM
1924/25	BALDWIN ST CONGS
1925/26	HODGSON STREET
1926/27	WICKER CONGS

SHEFFIELD SUNDAY SCHOOL & FREE CHURCH LEAGUE

Due to the war, several leagues in the area amalgamated to pool the teams left due to call up of their players. The Sheffield Sunday School League amalgamated with the Sheffield Free Church League, bringing in amended rules for the competition. The Sunday School League restarted in 1919 under its own name.

1915/16	HARTSHEAD 2ND
1916/17	GRENOSIDE BC
1917/18	HEELEY FRIENDS
1918/19	HEELEY FRIENDS

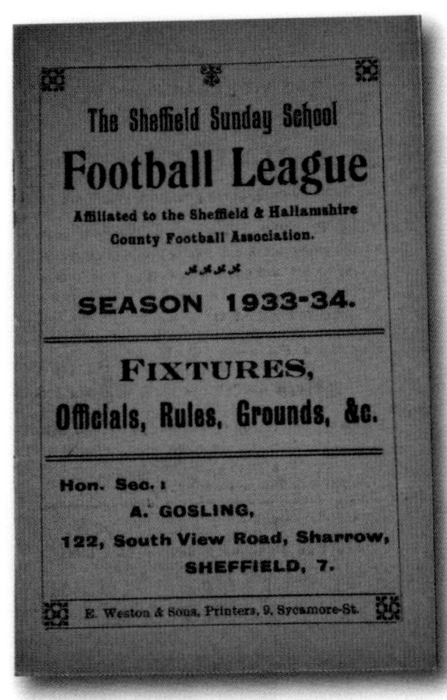
The Sheffield Sunday School
Football League
Affiliated to the Sheffield & Hallamshire County Football Association.
SEASON 1933-34.
FIXTURES,
Officials, Rules, Grounds, &c.
Hon. Sec.:
A. GOSLING,
122, South View Road, Sharrow,
SHEFFIELD, 7.
E. Weston & Sons, Printers, 9, Sycamore-St.

Sheffield Sunday School Football League Handbook for season 1933-34

SOUTH YORKSHIRE AMATEUR LEAGUE

LEAGUE CUP

1983	DARNALL WELLINGTON
1984	HURLFIELD YC
1985	WINDSOR FC
1986	STANNINGTON COLLEGE A
1987	JORDANTHORPE OB A
1988	STANNINGTON COLLEGE
1989	STANNINGTON UTD
1990	LDS
1991	ELM TREE
1992	ELM TREE
1993	CASTLE COLLEGE
1994	DE LA SALLE OB
1995	GATE 13
1996	BURNCROSS
1997	HILLSBOROUGH
1998	HILLSBOROUGH
1999	HILLSBOROUGH
2000	FORUM
2001	BURNCROSS
2002	SILKSTONE UTD
2003	EVEREST
2004	SHEFFIELD BANKERS
2005	CROSS SCYTHES
2006	GRIMETHORPE ATHLETIC
2007	GRIMETHORPE ATHLETIC
2008	GLEADLESS
2009	FURNACE
2010	NEW BOHEMIANS
2011	JUBILEE SPORTS
2012	NORTH GAWBER COLLIERY
2013	NORTH GAWBER COLLIERY
2014	BYRON HOUSE
2015	SHEFFIELD MEDICS
2016	SHEFFIELD MEDICS

LEAGUE SHIELD

2009	BOYNTON SPORTS

LEAGUE WINNERS TO 1983/84

LEAGUE CHAMPIONS

1933/34	ROTHERHAM BROOM SPORTS		
1934/35	ROTHERHAM YMCA		
1935/36	ROTHERHAM YMCA		
1936/37	DIV	A	ROTHERHAM YMCA
		B	OLD FIRPARNIANS
1937/38	DIV	A	FULWOOD
		B	PENISTONE CHURCH
1938/39	DIV	A	FULWOOD
		B	WOODSEATS METHS
1939-46	NO COMPETITION – WAR		
1946/47	FULWOOD		
1947/48	SHEFFIELD UNIVERSITY		
1948/49	SHEFFIELD UNIVERSITY		
1949/50	SHEFFIELD TRAINING COLLEGE		
1950/51	SHEFFIELD TRAINING COLLEGE		
1951/52	RAVENS		
1952/53	SHEFFIELD TRAINING COLLEGE		
1953/54	OLD EDWARDIANS		
1954/55	SHEFFIELD CLUB		
1955/56	SHEFFIELD TRAINING COLLEGE		
1956/57	SHEFFIELD TRAINING COLLEGE		
1957/58	SHEFFIELD TRAINING COLLEGE		
1958/59	OLD FIRPARNIANS		
1959/60	OLD FIRPARNIANS		
1960/61	SHEFFIELD TRAINING COLLEGE		
1961/62	OLD FIRPARNIANS		
1962/63	ELECTRICITY SPORTS		
1963/64	SHEFFIELD TRAINING COLLEGE		
1964/65	SHEFFIELD TRAINING COLLEGE		
1965/66	SHEFFIELD TRAINING COLLEGE		
1966/67	SHEFFIELD TRAINING COLLEGE		
1967/68	HOLLINSEND AMATEURS		
1968/69	NO CHAMPIONS		
1969/70	OLD FIRPARNIANS		
1970/71	OLD EDWARDIANS		
1971/72	ABBEYDALE OB		
1972/73	CROSSPOOL		
1973/74	CROSSPOOL		
1974/75	TRUSTEE SAVINGS BANK		
1975/76	HOLLINSEND AMATEURS		
1976/77	WOODBOURN		
1977/78	MEYNELL SPORTS		
1978/79	EARL FRANCIS		
1979/80	EARL FRANCIS		
1980/81	OLD EDWARDIANS		
1981/82	HOLLINSEND ALBION		
1982/83	STANNINGTON COLLEGE		
1983/84	STANNINGTON COLLEGE		

DIVISION TWO

1937/38	PENISTONE CHURCH
1938/39	WOODSEATS METHS
1952/53	PUBLIC WORKS
1953/54	OLD CENTRALIANS
1954/55	DE LA SALLE OB
1955/56	SHEFFIELD TRANSPORT A
1956/57	SHEFFIELD UNIVERSITY
1957/58	ELECTRIC SPORTS
1958/59	HOLLINSEND AMATEURS
1959/60	
1961/62	SHEFFIELD BANKERS
1962/63	CROFT HOUSE
1963/64	DE LA SALLE OB
1964/65	OUGHTIBRIDGE
1965/66	SHEFFIELD TEACHERS
1966-1969	NO COMPETITION
1969/70	SHEFFIELD EDUCATION
1970/71	WOODTHORPE
1971/72	
1972/73	DORE
1973/74	WADSLEY CHURCH
1974/75	ASH HOUSE
1975/76	PARK
1976/77	MEYNELL SPORTS
1977/78	MIDDLEWOOD HOSPITAL
1978/79	FIRPARNIANS
1979/80	STANNINGTON COLLEGE
1980/81	JORDANTHORPE OB
1981/82	DARNALL WELLINGTON
1982/83	ECCLESFIELD
1983/84	WOODTHORPE YC

South Yorkshire Amateur Football League

formed 1933

www.thefa.com/full-time/syal

Official Club Directory

2007-2008

Sanctioned by
Sheffield & Hallamshire
County Football Association Limited

South Yorkshire Amateur Football League Handbook for season 2007-2008

DIVISION THREE

1952/53	MILLSPAUGH
1953/54	OLD CESTREFELDIANS
1955/56	GREENHILL METHS
1956/57	NETHER EDGE OLD BOYS
1957/58	HOLLY GUILD
1958/59	ENGLISH STEEL CORPORATION
1959/60	
1960/61	
1962/62	SHEFFIELD BANKERS "B"
1962/63	HOLLINSEND AMATEURS
1963/64	SHEFFIELD OUGHTIBRIDGE
1964/65	SHEFFIELD TEACHERS
1965/66	SANDERSONS SPORTS
1966-1969	NO COMPETITION
1969/70	WOODTHORPE
1970/71	SANDERSONS SPORTS
1971/72	
1972/73	WADSLEY CHURCH
1973/74	PUBLIC WORKS DEPT
1974/75	CLUB 66
1975/76	MEYNELL SPORTS
1976/77	MIDDLEWOOD HOSPITAL
1977/78	WADSLEY BRIDGE SPORTS
1978/79	STANNINGTON COLLEGE
1979/80	OLD CESTREFELDIANS
1980/81	HURLFIELD YC
1981/82	DIXCEL SPORTS
1982/83	ESCALOPIANS
1983/84	HANDSWORTH METHS

DIVISION 4

1962/63	OUGHTIBRIDGE
1963/64	SHEFFIELD TEACHERS
1964/65	SANDERSONS SPORTS
1965/66	COLLEY YS
1966-1969	NO COMPETITION
1969/70	LONGLEY BC
1970/71	SWAN
1971/72	
1972/73	
1973/74	
1974/75	MEYNELL SPORTS
1975/76	ECCLESFIELD
1976/77	
1977/78	BROWN BEAR
1978/79	DIXCEL TISSUES
1979/80	HURLFIELD YC
1980/81	GLEADLESS
1981/82	RED GROUSE
1982/83	HANDSWORTH METHS
1983/84	MIDDLEWOOD

LEAGUE WINNERS 1984/85 ONWARDS

PREMIER LEAGUE

1984/85	HURLFIELD YC
1985/86	SHEFFIELD FOUNDRY WMC
1986/87	DIXCEL SPORTS
1987/88	DE LA SALLE OB
1988/89	DE LA SALLE OB
1989/90	SHEFFIELD GAS
1990/91	FREEDOM 90
1991/92	STANNINGTON UTD
1992/93	DIXCEL SPORTS
1993/94	ELM TREE
1994/95	MARKET INN
1995/96	BURNCROSS
1996/97	BURNCROSS
1997/98	ELM TREE
1998/99	HILLSBOROUGH
1999/2000	FORUM
2000/01	HOLLINSEND AMATEURS
2001/02	FULLFLOW FAIRWAY
2002/03	SILKSTONE UNITED
2003/04	CROSS SCYTHES
2004/05	JUBILEE SPORTS
2005/06	JUBILEE SPORTS
2006/07	GRIMETHORPE ATHLETIC
2007/08	ASTON FC
2008/09	GLEADLESS
2009/10	JUBILEE SPORTS
2010/11	GLEADLESS
2011/12	JUBILEE SPORTS
2012/13	NORTH GAWBER COLLIERY
2013/14	BYRON HOUSE
2014/15	GRIMETHORPE SPORTS
2015/16	SHEFFIELD MEDICS

DIVISION ONE

1984/85	RED GROUSE
1985/86	GRANVILLE SPORTS 85
1986/87	PHOENIX "A"
1987/88	GRADE A JOINERY
1988/89	SHEFFIELD GAS
1989/90	HOLLINSEND ALBION
1990/91	SHEFFIELD MEDICS & DENTALS
1991/92	STOCKSBRIDGE PARK STEELS
1992/93	ELM TREE
1993/94	BURNCROSS
1994/95	MIDLAND BANK
1995/96	OUGHTIBRIDGE WMSC
1996/97	HILLSBOROUGH
1997/98	RAILWAY
1998/99	BRADWAY
1999/2000	WOMBWELL MAIN

DIVISION ONE (continued)

2000/01	DIV 1A SILKSTONE UTD
	DIV 1B JUNCTION
2001/02	JUBILEE SPORTS
2002/03	PHOENIX ALL STARS
2003/04	NO COMPETITION
2004/05	YEW TREE
2005/06	GRIMETHORPE ATHLETIC
2006/07	KIVETON PARK
2007/08	ASTON FC
2008/09	BOYNTON SPORTS
2009/10	SHEFFIELD MEDICS
2010/11	ROYSTON
2011/12	NORTH GAWBER COLLIERY
2012/13	DODWORTH MW

DIVISION TWO

1984/85	GRANVILLE SPORTS 85
1985/86	PHOENIX FC
1986/87	D S TOOLING
1987/88	SHEFFIELD ACADEMICALS
1988/89	MIDLAND BANK
1989/90	MELCHESTER ROVERS
1990/91	STOCKSBRIDGE PARK STEELS
1991/92	ELM TREE
1992/93	RECORD TOOLS (CASTLE INN – per base)
1993/94	GATE 13 AFC
1994/95	DAVY FC
1995/96	HILLSBOROUGH
1996/97	CROOKES WMC
2008/09	SURUD UNITED
2009/10	MANOR CASTLE

DIVISION THREE

1984/85	PHOENIX FC
1985/86	D S TOOLING
1986/87	SHEFFIELD ACADEMICALS
1987/88	MIDLAND BANK
1988/89	MELCHESTER ROVERS
1989/90	MANPOWER RANGERS
1990/91	ELM TREE

SHEFFIELD SPORTS & ATHLETIC FOOTBALL LEAGUE

The league started in 1918 with just one division. However it appears that the league may have run the previous year as the Bird League

In 1924 it appears that a Second Division was added which was classified as the Junior section. This may have been for under 18/21 players only, or for less senior teams which were not allowed into the original division. It appears the original league was reclassified the Senior Division, a title it retained until the league ceased in 2007.

It appears that in 1931 the Junior section stopped running and the league's senior side expanded and was split into two divisions called Premier and Senior Divisions. I would expect the new set up to have incorporated some of the teams from the former Junior division, but most may have joined the S&H Junior League which was running at this time.

Like most leagues at the time, the final winners were not always the top team in the league. This was because the top four teams played off in semi-finals and a final game with the overall winners of the final receiving the cup. This was something this league did until 1968. Originally it would be the top 4 placed teams when all the league games had been played, but later on, a cut off date (usually mid March) was brought in with the top 4 teams at that date going into the play offs. This was to encourage teams to get their games played.

After the war, three identical silver cups (hallmarked 1945) were purchased and I believe this was the start of a third division known as the Senior Division 2, which ran until 1997. These were possibly used as league winners trophies rather than top 4 ones.

With the new division starting in 1945 or 1946, it now appears that the league had trophies for the top team in each division, and the Kenning Cup - which was presented to the league by Kennings Motors in 1947 - was used initially for the winners of the Premier Division..

Another division, known as Senior Division 3, started in 1967 and ran until 1978. It was re-introduced for one year in season 1988/89 (possibly when another league folded)

The league's cups have been moved around between divisions over the years (See notes) so it is hard to say who won which trophy in later years.

TOP 4 PLAY OFF COMPETITIONS ORIGINAL COMPETITION

1918/19	SANDERSON'S SPORTS
1919/20	WASHFORD SPORTS
1920/21	WASHFORD SPORTS
1921/22	PARK GRANGE
1922/23	PARK GRANGE
1923/24	INDUSTRY SPORTS
1924/25	INDUSTRY SPORTS
1925/26	INDUSTRY SPORTS
1926/27	VICTORIA FC
1927/28	FRIENDSHIP SPORTS
1928/29	CROFT HOUSE
1929/30	OSTRICH FC
1930/31	CARBROOK HALL SPORTS

JUNIOR SECTION

1924/25	ATLAS & NORFOLK
1925/26	CENTRAL L.O.G.T
1926/27	ECCLESFIELD JUNIORS
1927/28	ATTERCLIFFE BOYS
1928/29	ATTERCLIFFE BOYS
1929/30	PYEBANK JUNIOR
1930/31	WOODBOURNE ALLIANCE

TOP 4 PLAY OFF COMPETITIONS PREMIER DIVISION

1931/32	TINSLEY PARK STEELS
1932/33	ST PHILIPS C & I
1933/34	ST PHILIPS C & I
1934/35	PARK GARDENERS
1935/36	NETHERTHORPE INST
1936/37	NETHERTHORPE INST
1937/38	STOVIN ATH
1938/39	STOVIN ATH
1939-1947	NO COMPETITION
1947/48	LITTLE MATLOCK
1948/49	SHIREGREEN AMS
1949/50	PARK VILLA
1950/51	WINCOBANK & BLACKBURN
1951/52	WINCOBANK & BLACKBURN
1952/53	MANOR SOCIAL
1953/54	GLEADLESS HIMW
1954/55	PARK VILLA
1955/56	PARK VILLA
1956/57	WOODHOUSE FC
1957/58	MORTON VILLA
1958/59	PARSON CROSS
1959/60	PARAGON CINEMA
1960/61	PARAGON CINEMA
1961/62	PARK FC
1962/63	BOYNTON SPORTS
1963/64	NORMANTON SPRINGS MW
1964/65	LOXLEY VILLA "A"
1965/66	CROSS DAGGERS
1966/67	POMONA STREET
1967/68	BOYNTON SPORTS

TOP 4 PLAY OFF COMPETITIONS
SENIOR DIVISION

1931/32	GRAHAM'S SPORTS
1932/33	OLD BROWN COW
1933/34	STOVIN ATHLETIC
1934/35	MANOR UNITED
1935/36	GLEADLESS HIMW
1936/37	MANOR FC
1937/38	CARBROOK ALLIANCE
1938/39	SHIREGREEN R. R
1939/40	MARSHALL'S SPORTS
1940-1944	NO COMPETITION – WAR
1944/45	KAYSER ELLISON'S
1945/46	BURNABY STREET WMC
1946/47	LITTLE MATLOCK
1947/48	CROOKES FC
1948/49	PARK & ARBOURTHORNE WMC
1949/50	WINCOBANK & BLACKBURN
1950/51	SHEFFIELD LOCO WMC
1951/52	PARK ROVERS
1952/53	GLEADLESS HIMW
1953/54	BOYNTON SPORTS
1954/55	BELLHOUSE WMC
1955/56	PARSON CROSS
1956/57	MILLSPAUGH UTD
1957/58	PARSON CROSS
1958/59	PARAGON CINEMA
1959/60	WOODTHORPE ALLIANCE
1960/61	BIRLEY AMATEURS
1961/62	NORFOLK SPORTS
1962/63	LOXLEY VILLAGE
1963/64	ALBERT SPORTS
1964/65	JUBILEE SPORTS
1965/66	BRIGHTSIDE FC
1966/67	SPORTSMAN FC
1967/68	OXLEY PARK SPORTS

LEAGUE CHAMPIONS
PREMIER DIVISION

1947/48	LITTLE MATLOCK
1948/49	PARK VILLA
1949/50	LEAVYGREAVE SPORTS
1950/51	PARK VILLA
1951/52	PARK VILLA
1952/53	WINCOBANK & BLACKBURN
1953/54	PARK VILLA
1954/55	PARK VILLA
1955/56	PARK VILLA
1956/57	WOODHOUSE FC
1957/58	MORTON VILLA
1958/59	MORTON VILLA
1959/60	BRIGHTSIDE FC
1960/61	PARAGON CINEMA
1961/62	CHELSEA PARK
1962/63	NORMANTON SPRINGS
1963/64	LOXLEY VILLA "A"
1964/65	LOXLEY VILLA "A"
1965/66	LOXLEY VILLA "A"
1966/67	POMONA STREET
1967/68	BOYNTON SPORTS
1968/69	JUBILEE SPORTS
1969/70	OXLEY PARK
1970/71	JUBILEE SPORTS
1971/72	ST PHILIPS C & I
1972/73	HACKENTHORPE YC
1973/74	CROOKES WMC
1974/75	MORTON VILLA "A"
1975/76	CARTER LODGE YC
1976/77	HANDSWORTH CROSS KEYS
1977/78	SICEY HOTEL
1978/79	BRADWAY
1979/80	SHIREGREEN ARMS
1980/81	FREEDOM SPORTS
1981/82	BALL INN UTD
1982/83	VULCAN ATHLETIC
1983/84	ECCLESFIELD RED ROSE
1984/85	NORTHERN GENERAL SC
1985/86	BLACKSTOCK
1986/87	JUBILEE SPORTS
1987/88	BAGSHAWE ARMS
1988/89	INDUSTRY INN
1989/90	JUBILEE SPORTS
1990/91	NORTHERN GENERAL SC
1991/92	EARL OF ARUNDEL
1992/93	NORTHERN GENERAL SC
1993/94	EARL OF ARUNDEL
1994/95	EARL OF ARUNDEL
1995/96	EARL FULLFLOW
1996/97	WOODHOUSE WEST END
1997/98	EARL FULLFLOW
1998/99	EARL FULLFLOW
1999/00	FULLFLOW FAIRWAYS
2000/01	JUBILEE SPORTS
2001/02	HILLSBOROUGH WMC
2002/03	BOYNTON SPORTS
2003/04	SICEY FC
2004/05	SICEY FC
2005/06	WINDSOR WALL
2006/07	WYBOURN

LEAGUE CHAMPIONS SENIOR DIVISION – 1

1947/48	EAGLE SPORTS
1948/49	
1949/50	
1950/51	
1951/52	TURTON PLATTS
1952/53	CONCORD ATH
1953/54	BOYNTON SPORTS
1954/55	
1955/56	PARSON CROSS
1956/57	SHEFFIELD JAGUARS
1957/58	PARSON CROSS
1958/59	CHELSEA PARK
1959/60	GRENOSIDE SPORTS
1960/61	CLUBLAND FC
1961/62	LOPHAM STREET METHS
1962/63	LITTLE MATLOCK
1963/64	GRIMESTHORPE SPORTS
1964/65	JUBILEE SPORTS
1965/66	POMONA SPORTS
1966/67	WADSLEY BRIDGE SPORTS
1967/68	GLEADLESS H.I.M.W "A"
1968/69	HYDE PARK RANGERS
1969/70	ANDERSONS SPORTS
1970/71	HACKENTHORPE FC
1971/72	ATTERCLIFFE SA
1972/73	CARLTON
1973/74	ST MARYS
1974/75	NORFOLK PARK "A"
1975/76	LANE END WMC
1976/77	SHIREGREEN ARMS
1977/78	MOSBOROUGH TRINITY
1978/79	VULCAN ATHLETIC
1979/80	OLD BRADLEY WELL
1980/81	BRADWAY
1981/82	SES
1982/83	SPORTSMAN FC
1983/84	BIRLEY UTD
1984/85	FULWOOD ATHLETIC
1985/86	JUBILEE SPORTS
1986/87	NEW ROYAL
1987/88	PENGUIN
1988/89	PUNCHBOWL (CROOKES)
1989/90	BOYNTON SPORTS
1990/91	MANOR ELMS
1991/92	SPRINGWOOD
1992/93	SHEFFIELD LANE TOP
1993/94	WEST LANE
1994/95	BAGSHAWE ARMS
1995/96	TINSLEY WIRE
1996/97	WINCOBANK BARROW
1997/98	JUBILEE SPORTS
1998/99	JUNCTION
1999/00	ELM TREE
2000/01	HILLSBOROUGH WMC

LEAGUE CHAMPIONS SENIOR DIVISION – 2

1947/48	PARK VILLA
1948/49	
1949/50	
1950/51	
1951/52	PARK ROVERS
1952/53	GLEADLESS H.I.M.W
1953/54	HARTLEY SPORTS
1954/55	PARK FC
1955/56	CROOKESMOOR UTD
1956/57	MILLSPAUGH UTD
1957/58	SPA FC
1958/59	PARAGON CINEMA
1959/60	SPORTSMAN FC
1960/61	BIRLEY ARMS
1961/62	BRUNSWICK ROVERS
1962/63	WASHINGTON WORKS
1963/64	ALBERT SPORTS
1964/65	LOXLEY VILLAGE "B"
1965/66	NORFOLK SPORTS
1966/67	SPORTSMAN FC
1967/68	WRAGG SPORTS
1968/69	MORTON VILLA "A"
1969/70	ST STEPHENS
1970/71	SOUTHEY SOCIAL
1971/72	ROYAL OAK
1972/73	ST MARYS
1973/74	DARNALL BAPTIST
1974/75	BEEHIVE
1975/76	BRADWAY
1976/77	SICEY HOTEL
1977/78	OLD BRADLEY WELL
1978/79	FREEDOM SPORTS
1983/84	WOODHOUSE MILL WMC
1984/85	WARREN "B"
1985/86	GOLDEN KEYS 85
1986/87	OLD CROWN UTD
1987/88	NORFOLK RANGERS
1988/89	JOHN CARR
1989/90	GEORGE & DRAGON
1990/91	GRIMESTHORPE BC
1991/92	SHEFFIELD LANE TOP
1992/93	HIGH GREAVE
1993/94	NOT AWARDED
1994/95	TINSLEY WIRE
1995/96	WINCOBANK BARROW
1996/97	WOODMAN

LEAGUE CHAMPIONS SENIOR DIVISION – 3

1951/52	MANOR SOCIAL
1952/53	ST PHILIPS SOCIAL
1967/68	BEIGHTON MW
1968/69	ST STEPHENS
1969/70	SOUTHEY SOCIAL
1970/71	STANNINGTON ROSE & CROWN
1971/72	ST MARYS
1972/73	DARNALL BAPTIST
1973/74	OWLERTON ST JOHNS
1974/75	WOODSEATS ATHLETIC
1975/76	MOSBROROUGH TRINITY
1976/77	PITSMOOR CENTENNIALS
1977/78	JONAS WOODHEAD
1988/89	GUNSTONES

SID HILL – GERRY YOUNG TROPHIES

This competition was for clubs knocked out in either the preliminary or first round of the League KO Cup Competition

WINNERS – SID HILL TROPHY

RUNNERS UP GERRY YOUNG TROPHY

	WINNERS	RUNNERS UP
1988/89	PUNCHBOWL (Crookes))	CANNON HALL
1989/90	MOTEC	FOXHILL COMMUN
1990/91	SPRINGWOOD	JUBILEE SPORTS
1991/92	SHIREGREEN WMC	TINSLEY WIRE
1992/93	EARL OF ARUNDEL	SHEFF POLY STAFF
1993/94	BOYNTON SPORTS	NOT AWARDED
1994/95	TINSLEY WIRE	I E P BRAMAH
1995/96	WOODHOUSE WE	PAVEWAY DESIGNS
1996/97	WALESWOOD HOTEL	BOYNTON SPORTS
1997/98	FIGHTING COCK	FORGEMASTERS "A"
1998/99	EARL FULLFLOW	FARM ROAD S &SC
1999/00	JUBILEE SPORTS	NORWICH UNION
2000/01	HILLSBOROUGH WMC	HUNTSMAN
2001/02	FARM ROAD S & SC	GOLDEN PLOVER
2002/03	FARM ROAD S & SC	GLEADLESS RGERS
2003/04	FARM ROAD S &SC	NEWFIELD PRINCE
2004/05	NAILMAKERS ARMS	OLIVE GROVE
2005/06	MILLMOOR JUNIORS	WINDSOR WALL
2006/07	BOYNTON SPORTS	WYBOURN

BENEVOLENT CUP

	WINNERS	RUNNERS UP
1949/50	PARK VILLA	WINCOBANK & BLACKBURN
1950/51	SHEFFIELD LOCO WMC	WINCOBANK & BLACKBURN
1951/52	WINCO & BLACKBURN	PARK ROVERS
1952/53	MANOR SOCIAL	GLEADLESS H.I.M.W
1953/54	GLEADLESS H.I.M.W	BOYNTON SPORTS
1954/55	BELLHOUSE WMC	PARK VILLA
1955/56	PARK VILLA	PARSON CROSS
1956/57	WOODHOUSE FC	MILLSPAUGH UTD
1957/58	PARSON CROSS	MORTON VILLA
1958/59	PARAGON CINEMA	PARSON CROSS
1959/60	WOODTHORPE ALLCE	PARAGON CINEMA
1960/61	BIRLEY AMT	PARAGON CINEMA
1961/62	PARK FC	NORFOLK SPORTS
1962/63	BOYNTON SPORTS	LOXLEY VILLAGE
1963/64	NORMANTON SPG MW	ALBERT SPORTS
1964/65	LOXLEY VILLA "A"	JUBILEE SPORTS
1965/66	CROSS DAGGERS	BRIGHTSIDE FC
1966/67	POMONA STREET	SPORTSMAN FC
1967/68	BOYNTON SPORTS/OXLEY PARK SPORTS - JOINT WINNERS	
1968/69	JUBILEE SPORTS	BOYNTON SPORTS
1969/70	OXLEY PARK	JUBILEE SPORTS
1970/71	JUBILEE SPORTS	HYDE PARK RANGS
1971/72	ST PHILIPS C & I	HACKENTHORPE FC
1972/73	HACKENTHORPE YC	ST PHILIPS C & I
1973/74	CROOKES WMC	MORTON VILLA
1974/75	ROYAL OAK	MORTON VILLA
1975/76	CARTER LODGE	GREENLAND RD WMC
1976/77	HANDS'TH CROSS KEYS	NORFOLK PARK "A"
1977/78	SICEY HOTEL	BRADWAY
1978/79	HENRY BOOT	SICEY HOTEL
1979/80	SHIREGREEN ARMS	FREEDOM SPORTS
1980/81	BALL INN UTD	FREEDOM SPORTS
1981/82	MOSBOROUGH TRIN	BALL INN UTD
1982/83	VULCAN ATH	BRADWAY

LEAGUE KO CUP

From 1983 the former Benevolent Cup Competition was known as the League KO Cup

	WINNERS	RUNNERS UP
1983/84	ECCLESFIELD RED ROSE	MOSBOROUGH TRINITY
1984/85	NORTHERN GENERAL SC	BIRLEY HOTEL
1985/86	HIGH NOON	SAMUEL PLIMSOL
1986/87	TDR TRANSMISSIONS	BAGSHAWE ARMS
1987/88	SHEFFIELD POST OFFICE	ROYAL OAK MOSBOROUGH
1988/89	INDUSTRY INN	HIGH GREAVE "A"
1989/90	JUBILEE SPORTS	EARL OF ARUNDEL
1990/91	NORTHERN GENERAL SC	ROYAL
1991/92	EARL OF ARUNDEL	NORTHERN GENERAL
1992/93	MORTON VILLA	GUEST & CHRIMES
1993/94	MORTON VILLA	SHEFF HALLAM UNIVERSITY STAFF
1994/95	JUBILEE SPORTS	SHEFFIELD LANE TOP
1995/96	GUEST & CHRIMES	WINCOBANK BARROW
1996/97	WOODMAN	WOODHOUSE WEST END
1997/98	EARL FULLFLOW	TINSLEY WIRE
1998/99	JUBILEE SPORTS	JUNCTION
1999/00	FULLFLOW SPORTS	JUNCTION
2000/01	ELM TREE	JUBILEE SPORTS
2001/02	TOMO FC	DOUBLE TOP
2002/03	BOYNTON SPORTS	HILLSBOROUGH WMC
2003/04	BOYNTON SPORTS	FORGEMASTERS "A"
2004/05	SICEY FC	WYNSOR WALL
2005/06	FARM ROAD S &SC	PENGUIN
2006/07	WYBOURN	PENGUIN

Sports and Athletic League Kenning Cup

Sports and Athletic League Division One

Sports and Athletic League Handbook
for season 1952-53

Sports and Athletic League Division Two

TINSLEY CHARITY CUP

The competition was started in 1918 by returning soldiers to raise funds for war orphans. The original rules stated that all teams must be located within 5 miles of Tinsley Church

Was there originally a cup & what happened to it? A shield was presented by G Vickers (now in the Malay States) in May 1922, so what has happened to this?

Picture of Arbourthorne Community from 1971/72 shows that original shield had been enlarged by an attachment to original one. Picture from 1970/71 shows just original shield.

A cup appears to have been used from 1978/79 when the competition appears to have been taken over by Sheffield Amateur League

1918/19	EDGAR ALLENS
1919/20	SIR GEORGE GOODINSON LODGE
1920/21	TINSLEY UM
1921/22	ATTERCLIFFE UTD
1922/23	ATTERCLIFFE UTD
1923/24	ATTERCLIFFE FC
1924/25	ATTERCLIFFE
1925/26	ATTERCLIFFE VICTORY
1926/27	GREENLAND WMC
1927/28	GREENLAND WMC
1928/29	LOPHAM ST UM
1929/30	CARBROOK REFORM
1930/31	CARBROOK HALL SPORTS
1931/32	TINSLEY PARK COLLIERY SPORTS
1932/33	TINSLEY PARK MW
1933/34	TINSLEY SPORTS
1934/35	CATCLIFFE JUNIORS
1935/36	TINSLEY PARK WMC
1936/37	SANDERSONS SPORTS
1937/38	TINSLEY PARK WMC
1938/39	ATTERCLIFFE RADICALS
1939/40	ATTERCLIFFE RADICALS
1940/41	TINSLEY PARK COLLIERY MW
1941/42	ATTERCLIFFE RADICALS
1942/43	ATTERCLIFFE RADICALS
1943/44	ATTERCLIFFE RADICALS
1944/45	
1945/46	CROOKES WMC
1946/47	CROOKES WMC v AQUADUCT or ARUNDEL
1947/48	
1948/49	TRAVELLERS SPORTS
1949/50	EFFINGHAM SPORTS
1950/51	SHIREGREEN WMC
1951/52	SHIREGREEN WMC
1952/53	BELLHOUSE ROAD WMC
1953/54	ALBERT SPORTS
1954/55	PARK VILLA
1955/56	
1956/57	TRAVELLERS SPORTS or WINCOBANK & BLACKBURN
1957/58	BELLHOUSE ROAD WMC
1958/59	BELLHOUSE ROAD WMC
1959/60	BRIGHTSIDE
1960/61	CROOKES WMC
1961/62	PARSON CROSS
1962/63	TRAVELLERS SPORTS
1963/64	TRAVELLERS SPORTS
1964/65	BOYNTON SPORTS
1965/66	BELLHOUSE ROAD WMC
1966/67	AEI or HANDSWORTH ROVERS
1967/68	ST PATRICKS or EDGAR ALLEN
1968/69	NEW CROSS
1969/70	
1970/71	ECCLESFIELD RED ROSE
1971/72	ABOURTHORNE COMMUNITY
1972/73	WINDSOR BL
1973/74	
1974/75	WINDSOR BL
1976/77	WINDSOR BL
1977/78	NO COMPETITION

Now run by Sheffield Amateur League – A new trophy (Cup) appears to have been used from 1978/79

1978/79	BELLHOUSE ROAD WMC
1979/80	ST PATRICK'S
1980/81	STELLA WORKS
1981/82	INDUSTRY INN
1982/83	BRADLEY WELL
1983/84	BALL INN UTD
1984/85	ST NATHANEALS
1985/86	ST PATRICK'S
1986/87	NEW STUBBIN COLLIERY

End of Amateur League

1987/88	FORTYFOOT
1988/89	NEW STUBBIN COLLIERY
1989/90	AURORA UTD
1990/91	OUGHTIBRIDGE WMC
1991/92	INDUSTRY INN
1992/93	FRECHEVILLE CA
1993/94	KIVETON PARK
1994/95	FRECHEVILLE CA
1995/96	DEERSTALKER
1996/97 TO 1999/2000	NO COMPETITION

Now run by Meadowhall Sunday League in 2000 after several years of not running.

2000/01	STANNINGTON BULLS
2001/02	DEERSTALKER
2002/03	BRUNSWICK ATH "A"
2003/04	CHAPELTOWN
2004/05	COLLEY WMC
2005/06	HANDSWORTH OLD CROWN
2006/07	ARUNDEL ESC
2007/08	PACK HORSE INN
2008/09	ARBOURTHORNE EA
2009/10	ARBOURTHORNE EA
2010/11	RAWSON SPRING
2011/12	RAWSON SPRING
2012/13	CITY TAXIS
2013/14	PENISTONE CHURCH
2014/15	JACK-IN-A-BOX
2015-16	MILLMOOR JUNIORS U21

S & H CFA
WHARNCLIFFE CHARITY CUP

The cup is engraved Wharncliffe Charity Challenge Cup, presented to the Sheffield Football Association as an annual Challenge Cup by Edmund Montagu, 1st Earl of Wharncliffe – 1879.

The cup is silver and has 3 handles attached to it.

The cup is stamped Lions head (Victoria)/Lion/Head & B which indicates London 1877.The maker is shown as Arradi, Panton Street, London.

The Cup is engraved with the winners' names with a base being used since 1971 to record the winners up to it ceasing to be played for in 1984.

The cup has been played for in both League and KO Cup format.The proceeds each year were given to local charities.

1879	WEDNESDAY
1880	HEELEY
1881	WITHDRAWN ON CUP – (see Note 1)
1882	WEDNESDAY
1883	WEDNESDAY
1884	LOCKWOOD BROTHERS
1885	HEELEY
1886	WEDNESDAY
1887	STAVELEY
1888	WEDNESDAY
1889	STAVELEY
1890	STAVELEY
1891	NO FINAL PLAYED – (See Note 2)
1892	NO FINAL PLAYED – (See Note 3)
1893	Void – (See Note 4)
1894	SHEFFIELD UNITED
1895	MEXBOROUGH TOWN
1896	BARNSLEY ST PETERS
1897	SHEFFIELD UNITED RES – (Not on Cup)
1898	NO COMPETITION
1899	NO COMPETITION
1900	WEDNESDAY RES
1901	MONK BRETTON
1902	SHEFFIELD UNITED RES
1903	SHEFFIELD WEDNESDAY RES
1904	SHEFFIELD UNITED RES
1905	SHEFFIELD WEDNESDAY RES
1906	SHEFFIELD WEDNESDAY RES
1907	SHEFFIELD UNITED RES
1908	SHEFFIELD WEDNESDAY RES
1909	SHEFFIELD WEDNESDAY RES
1910	BARNSLEY RES
1911	SHEFFIELD WEDNESDAY RES
1912	SHEFFIELD UNITED RES
1913	GAINSBOROUGH TRINITY
1914	ROTHERHAM COUNTY
1915	SHEFFIELD WEDNESDAY RES
1916	WORKSOP TOWN – (Not on Cup)
1917-1919	NO COMPETITION
1920	RETFORD TOWN – (See Note 5)
1921	ROTHERHAM COUNTY RES
1922	SHEFFIELD WEDNESDAY RES
1923	DONCASTER ROVERS RES
1924	SHEFFIELD UNITED RES
1925	SHEFFIELD WEDNESDAY RES
1926	SHEFFIELD UNITED RES
1927	DONCASTER ROVERS RES
1928	SHEFFIELD UNITED RES
1929	DONCASTER ROVERS RES
1930	SHEFFIELD UNITED RES
1931	SHEFFIELD WEDNESDAY RES
1932	SHEFFIELD UNITED RES
1933	SHEFFIELD WEDNESDAY RES
1934	DONCASTER ROVERS RES
1935	NORTON WOODSEATS
1936	NO COMPETITION
1937	SHEFFIELD UNITED "A"
1938	SHEFFIELD WEDNESDAY "A"
1939	SHEFFIELD WEDNESDAY "A"
1940	NO COMPETITION
1941	THURCROFT MAIN
1942	ROYAL ARMY SIGNAL CORPS
1943	ROYAL ARMY SIGNAL CORPS
1944	ROYAL ARMY SIGNAL CORPS
1945	THORNCLIFFE WELFARE
1946	THORNCLIFFE WELFARE
1947	THORNCLIFFE WELFARE
1948	VOID ON CUP – (See Note 6)
1949	STOCKSBRIDGE WORKS
1950	HOYLAND COMMON ATH
1951	AUGHTON JUNIORS
1952	PENISTONE CHURCH
1953	BEIGHTON MW
1954	THORNCLIFFE REC
1955	BROWN BAYLEYS STEELS/ GREENHILL METHS–SHARED CUP
1956	THURCROFT MAIN
1957	SHEFFIELD WEDNESDAY "A"
1958	SHEFFIELD WEDNESDAY "A"
1959	SHEFFIELD WEDNESDAY "A"
1960	THORNCLIFFE REC
1961	HARWORTH CI
1962	RETFORD TOWN
1963	HARWORTH CI
1964	SWALLOWNEST MW
1965	MALTBY MW
1966	FRECHEVILLE CA
1967	FRECHEVILLE CA
1968	CHARLTON UNITED
1969	SWALLOWNEST MW
1970	THURCROFT WELFARE
1971	HALLAM
1972	ECCLESFIELD RED ROSE
1973	CHARLTON UNITED
1974	HEELEY
1975	KIVETON PARK
1976	HARWORTH CI
1977	NORTON WOODSEATS
1978	MOSBOROUGH TRINITY

Doncaster Rovers 1922-23 Medal

S & H CFA WHARNCLIFFE CHARITY CUP (continued)

1979	CHARLTON TAVERN
1980	MALTBY MW
1981	NO COMPETITION
1982	NO COMPETITION
1983	FRECHEVILLE CA
1984	KIVETON PARK

Note 1 SFA withdrew the cup because 3 of the 4 semi finalists had played players involved in the Zulu games. However Wednesday and Exchange did play each other in a so-called final on behalf of Medical charities. Exchange won 2-0.

Note 2 4 teams entered – Wed v Utd 2-1 & Staveley v Kilnhurst 3-1. No final played and Committee ordered competition to be stood over indefinitely.

Note 3 Wed could not agree on ground for final against Utd, so no final played. Wed instead played Bolton Wanderers and money raised donated to local charities.

Note 4 Sheffield United and Sheffield Wednesday drew 0-0 in the final. No reply so committee decided competition not won.

Note 5 Maltby Main won the cup and their name is inscribed on it. However it appears that they played an ineligible player and so the cup was awarded to Retford Town.

Note 6 Hoyland Common won the final but they had played a Pro player and so were dismissed. The competition was then cancelled and Void put on the Cup. Beat Penistone Church, but Morris was a pro with Nottingham Forest who had transferred to Gainsborough in Jan 1948. Club fined £5/5/0d and player £1/1/0d due to his honesty.

WOODHOUSE HOSPITAL CUP

1905/06	WOODHOUSE
1906/07	
1907/08	HANDSWORTH ROVERS
1908/09	WOODHOUSE
1909/10	BEIGHTON REC
1910/11	HANDSWORTH ROVERS
1911/12	HANDSWORTH ROVERS
1912/13	HANDSWORTH ROVERS
1913/14	BEIGHTON REC
1914/15	HANDSWORTH ROVERS
1915/16	CRAVENS SPORTS
1916/17	HOLLINSEND
1917/18	
1918/19	WOODHOUSE
1919/20	WOODHOUSE
1920/21	HANDSWORTH WMI
1921/22	HANDSWORTH WMI or WOODHOUSE
1922/23	HANDSWORTH or WOODHOUSE
1923/24	ATTERCLIFFE
1924/25	ANSTON ATHLETIC
1925/26	TREETON READING ROOM
1926/27	TREETON READING ROOM
1927/28	WOODHOUSE WMC
1928/29	INTAKE SPORTS
1929/30	WOODHOUSE BRUNSWICK
1930/31	WOODHOUSE BRUNSWICK
1931/32	SHEFFIELD UTD "A"
1932/33	SHEFFIELD UTD "A"
1933/34	WOODHOUSE ALLIANCE
1934/35	WOODHOUSE WEST END
1935/36	SWALLOWNEST
1936/37	WOODHOUSE MILL WELFARE
1937/38	SWALLOWNEST

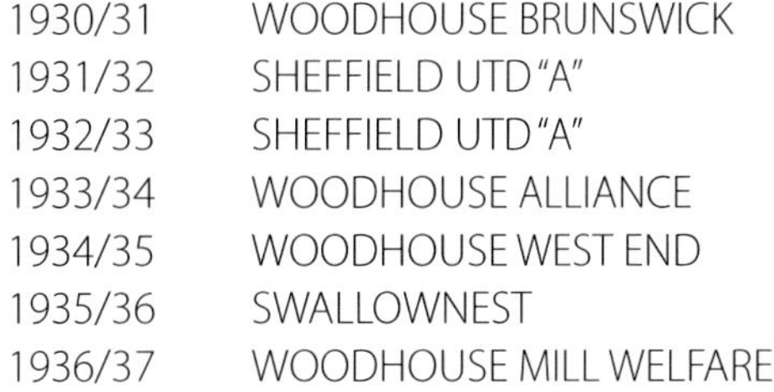

Wharncliffe Charity Cup Winners Medal won by Thorncliffe Welfare 1946-47

Sheffield & District Works Sports Association

PREMIER LEAGUE

The competition was run by the Sheffield & District Works Sports Association, who started in 1919.

This competition was the most senior competition and was open age.

The original trophy was a wooden shield with a silver centre and small silver shields round the outside. A new cup was presented in 1954 by J Brennan, chairman of the Works Council. This cup was sold by ELR in October 2010 for £140.

1919/20	WM COOKS SPORTS
1920/21	SANDERSONS SPORTS
1921/22	KAYSER ELLISON
1922/23	HOWELLS SPORTS
1923/24	HOWELLS SPORTS
1924/25	TURTON PLATTS
1925/26	HOWELLS SPORTS
1926/27	G P O
1927/28	SHEFFIELD FORGE
1928/29	NUNNERY COLLIERY
1929/30	SHARDLOWS SPORTS
1930/31	TINSLEY PARK COLLIERY
1931/32	CITY SURVEYORS
1932/33	CITY SURVEYORS
1933/34	SANDERSONS SPORTS
1934/35	INDUS SPORTS
1935/36	ATLAS & NORFOLK
1936/37	HAMPTONS SPORTS
1937/38	DAVY UNITED
1938/39	DAVY UNITED
1939/40	TINSLEY PARK MW
1940-44	NO COMPETITION
1944/45	L&NE RAILWAY
1945/46	SANDERSONS SPORTS
1946/47	SHARDLOWS
1947/48	PARRAMORE SPORTS
1948/49	EDGAR ALLEN
1949/50	
1950/51	EFFINGHAM WORKS
1951/52	THORNCLIFFE WELFARE
1952/53	BROWN BAYLEYS
1953/54	JESSOPS SPORTS
1954/55	METRO VICKERS
1955/56	JESSOPS SPORTS
1956/57	THORNCLIFFE REC
1957/58	OSBORN SPORTS
1958/59	OSBORN SPORTS
1959/60	DAVY UNITED
1960/61	ARTHUR LEE & SONS
1961/62	CRAVENS SPORTS
1962/63	(Competition cancelled due to bad weather)
1963/64	CITY SURVEYORS
1964/65	CITY SURVEYORS
1965/66	CITY SURVEYORS
1966/67	A E I
1967/68	TELEPHONE SPORTS
1968/69	TELEPHONE SPORTS
1969/70	
1970/71	TINSLEY WIRE
1971/72	SHARDLOWS SPORTS
1972/73	STANLEY TOOLS
1973/74	TWIL
1974/75	
1975/76	BONE CRAVENS
1976/77	
1977/78	DORMER SPORTS
1978/79	
1979/80	
1980/81	THORNCLIFFE
1981/82	BAYFIELD
1982/83	GPO
1983/84	WHITBREAD
1984/85	
1985/86	
1986/87	AURORA UTD
1987/88	WHITBREAD SPORTS
1988/89	WHITBREAD SPORTS
1989/90	WHITBREAD SPORTS
1990/91	WHITBREAD SPORTS
1991/92	WHITBREAD SPORTS
1992/93	JUBILEE SPORTS
1993/94	JUBILEE SPORTS

Works Premier League Winners Medal 1948-49
Won by Edgar Allen

BEATTY LEAGUE

The competition was run by the Sheffield & District Works Sports Association, who started in 1919.

This competition was second in line in seniority after the Premier League and was an open age competition.

There was more than one division at various times, so I assume there would have been a play off to win the league trophy.

There was a large wooden shield for the winning team. This was presented by Earl Beatty in May 1920 to the Association. The shield has a silver football scene in the middle and a silver plaque below to mark the fact that Earl Beatty was the "Admiral of the Fleet" at the time he donated it. It was sold for £520 at ELR auctions in October 2010.

There are various-sized shields on the wooden shield with the names of most of the winners on.

1919/20 HABERSHONS SPORTS
1920/21 SHEFFIELD SPORTS CLUB
1921/22 EFFINGHAM SPORTS
1922/23 WARD & PAYNE
1923/24 SHEFFIELD FORGE
1924/25 BEDFORD SPORTS
1925/26 WARD & PAYNE
1926/27 METRO VICKERS
1927/28 NUNNERY COLLIERY
1928/29 SHIPMANS SPORTS
1929/30 THORNTON SPORTS
1930/31 THORNTON SPORTS
1931/32 JOHN WOOD SPORTS
1932/33 INDUS SPORTS
1933/34 BEDFORD SPORTS
1934/35 SHEFFIELD STEEL FOUNDRY
1935/36 JOHN WOOD SPORTS
1936/37 CITY SURVEYORS
1937/38 ATLAS & NORFOLK
1938/39 HADFIELDS SPORTS
1939/40 CROWN WORKS
1940/41 JOHN WOOD SPORTS
1941-44 NO COMPETITION
1944/45 OSBORNS REGANT
1945/46 BALFOURS SPORTS
1946/47 EFFINGHAM SPORTS
1947/48 JESSOPS SPORTS
1948/49 BEDFORD SPORTS
1949/50 B&C CO-OP
1950/51 TINSLEY WIRE
1951/52 BALFOURS SPORTS
1952/53
1953/54 CLEANSING DEPT
1954/55 JUBILEE SPORTS
1955/56 JUBILEE SPORTS
1956/57 BRIGHTSIDE FOUNDRY
1957/58 SHEFFIELD GAS
1958/59 HADFIELDS SPORTS
1959/60 ARTHUR LEE SPORTS
1960/61 CRAVEN SPORTS
1961/62 STANLEY WORKS
1962/63 (Competition cancelled due to bad weather)
1963/64 SCIMITAR SPORTS
1964/65 KIVETON WIRE WORKS
1965/66 UNITED COAL & COKE
1966/67 BEDFORD SPORTS
1967/68 DORMER SPORTS
1968/69 EDGAR ALLEN SPORTS
1969/70 TINSLEY WIRE
1970/71 SHARDLOWS
1971/72 S C CLEANSING
1972/73 TELECOM SPORTS
1973/74 FORWARD SPORTS
1974/75 DORMER SPORTS
1975/76 DAVY ROLL
1976/77 MARSHALL SPORTS
1977/78 RECORD SPORTS
1978/79 THORNCLIFFE
1979/80 WHITBREAD
1980/81 BAYFIELD SPORTS
1981/82 SHEFFIELD POST OFFICE
1982/83 ECLIPSE SPORTS
1983/84 DORMER SPORTS
1984/85 SHEFFIELD POST OFFICE
1985/86 TINSLEY WIRE
1986/87 STANLEY TOOLS
1987/88 SHEFFIELD POLY
1988/89 UNBRAKO
1989/90 RECORD MARPLE
1990/91 TELECOM SPORTS

Sheffield Works Sports Ass. Beatty Shield

HAIG LEAGUE

The competition was run by the Sheffield & District Works Sports Association, who started in 1919.

This competition was third in line in seniority after the Premier League & Beatty League.

It was for players who were between 18 – 20, but players had to be under 20 on 1 September at the commencement of the season

It is possible that the original trophy could have been presented by the 1st Earl Haig – Field Marshall Douglas Haig – to match up with the one presented by Earl Beatty at the same time.

I have not found the original trophy – but I now have the 2 new cups which were obtained in 1958 for the First and Second Divisions. As there was a Third Division later, then I assume a cup was purchased for that.

The Second Division one was presented by J Brennan. He was the Chairman of the Works Council and a representative from William Jessop & Sons Ltd

Both cups were sold in 2010 by ELR – the First Division for £90 and the Second for £85.

The competition was stopped at the start of the Second World War and replaced by the Minor Competition.

ORIGINAL TROPHY WINNERS

1919/20	W COOKS
1920/21	W COOKS
1921/22	W COOKS
1922/23	ATLAS & NORFOLK
1923/24	(HOWELLS or CRESCENT STEELWORKS)
1924/25	HADFIELDS SPORTS
1925/26	ATLAS & NORFOLK
1926/27	HADFIELDS SPORTS
1927/28	ATLAS & NORFOLK
1928/29	ATLAS & NORFOLK
1929/30	ATLAS & NORFOLK
1930/31	HADFIELDS SPORTS
1931/32	NO COMPETITION
1932/33	NO COMPETITION
1933/34	NO COMPETITION
1934/35	ATLAS & NORFOLK
1935/36	HAMPTON SPORTS
1936/37	HAMPTON SPORTS
1937/38	HAMPTON SPORTS – (Unbeaten for 3 years)
1938/39	BRIGHTSIDE SPORTS

RESTARTED COMPETITION

1957/58	SILICA SPORTS

THEN NEW TROPHIES AND SEVERAL DIVISIONS

DIVISION 1

1958/59	SILICA SPORTS
1959/60	DAVY UNITED
1960/61	DARWINS
1961/62	KIVETON PARK WIRE WORKS
1962/63	(started - not finished due to bad winter)
1963/64	CRAVENS SPORTS
1964/65	BEDFORDS SPORTS CLUB
1965/66	HALLAM STEEL
1966/67	EDGAR ALLEN
1967/68	DYSON SPORTS
1968/69	INTAL WORKS
1969/70	UNITED COAL & COKE
1970/71	DIXCEL TISSUES
1971/72	DAVY UNITED
1972/73	ROTARY ELECTRIC
1973/74	DAVY ROLL
1974/75	HAMPTON SPORTS
1975/76	PARRAMORE SPORTS
1976/77	ROTHERWOOD
1977/78	SANDERSON KAYSER
1978/79	MIDLAND BANK
1979/80	CRAVENS SPORTS
1980/81	AURORA SPORTS
1981/82	DORMER SPORTS

DIVISION 2

1958/59	DAVY UNITED
1959/60	DARWIN SPORTS
1960/61	KIVETON PARK WIRE WORKS
1961/62	FLATHER
1962/63	(started but not finished due to bad winter)
1963/64	NUNNERY COLLIERY
1964/65	WOODHEAD COMPONENTS
1965/66	SHEFFIELD SMELTING CO
1966/67	DYSON SPORTS
1967/68	INTAL WORKS
1968/69	ABATTOIR
1969/70	E M G B
1970/71	BAIGENT & BIRD
1971/72	ROBSONS
1972/73	EDGAR ALLEN
1973/74	HAYDEN NILOS
1974/75	PARRAMORES SPORTS
1975/76	ROTHERWOOD
1976/77	SANDERSON KAYSER
1977/78	SHEFFIELD POST OFFICE
1978/79	TELEPHONE SPORTS
1979/80	SNOW & CO

DIVISION 3

1959/60	KIVETON PARK WIRE
1960/61	STANDARD STEEL
1961/62	HADFIELDS SPORTS
1962/63	(started but not finished due to bad winter)
1963/64	WOODHEAD COMPONENTS
1964/65	DYSON SPORTS

DIVISION 4 - DRAKE CUP?

1960/61	ATLAS & NORFOLK
1961/62	ENGLISH STEEL CORP

DRAKE LEAGUE

The competition was run by the Sheffield & District Works Sports Association, who started in 1919.

This competition was fourth in line in seniority after the Premier League, Beatty League & Haig League

It was for players who were under 18 on 1st September at the commencement of the season

The competition is also referred to as for the Prince Albert Cup. This trophy believed to still be held by the Sports Association.

1919/20	EDGAR ALLEN
1920/21	T FIRTH
1921/22	JONAS & COLVER
1922/23	VICKERS
1923/24	CAMMELLS
1924/25	ATLAS & NORFOLK
1925/26	ATLAS & NORFOLK
1926/27	HADFIELDS SPORTS
1927/28	ATLAS & NORFOLK
1928/29	ATLAS & NORFOLK
1929/30	HADFIELDS SPORTS
1930/31	ATLAS & NORFOLK
1931/32	NO COMPETITION
1932/33	ATLAS & NORFOLK
1933/34	STOCKSBRIDGE WORKS
1934/35	STOCKSBRIDGE WORKS
1935/36	STOCKSBRIDGE WORKS
1936/37	ATLAS & NORFOLK
1937/38	STOCKSBRIDGE WORKS (Team unbeaten for 5 Seasons)
1938/39	STOCKSBRIDGE WORKS
1939/40	ATLAS & NORFOLK
1940-46	NO COMPETITION
1946/47	THORNCLIFFE WELFARE
1947/48	DAVY UNITED
1948/49	SHEFFIELD FORGE
1949/50	THORNCLIFFE WELFARE
1950/51	E.S.C – LEAGUE & CUP
1951/52	ATLAS & NORFOLK - LEAGUE & CUP
1952/53	ATLAS & NORFOLK - LEAGUE & CUP
1953/54	THORNCLIFFE - LEAGUE & CUP
1954/55	DAVY UTD - LEAGUE ATLAS & NORFOLK - CUP
1955/56	E.S.C - LEAGUE SHEFFIELD FORGE - CUP
1956/57	THORNCLIFFE - LEAGUE
1957-60	NO COMPETITION
1960/61	ATLAS & NORFOLK - LEAGUE E.S.C - CUP
1961/62	E.S.C – LEAGUE & CUP
1962/63	BROWN BAYLEYS – LEAGUE THORNCLIFFE - CUP

RALEIGH LEAGUE

The competition was run by the Sheffield & District Works Sports Association, which started in 1919.

This competition was fifth in line in seniority after the Premier League, Beatty League, Haig League & Drake League

It was for players who were under 16 on 1 September at the commencement of the season

This league appears to have stopped at the start of World War II and never restarted

1919/20	J BROWN
1920/21	T FIRTHS
1921/22	EDGAR ALLEN
1922/23	CAMMELLS
1923/24	VICKERS
1924/25	ATLAS & NORFOLK
1925/26	ATLAS & NORFOLK
1926/27	ATLAS & NORFOLK
1927/28	HADFIELDS SPORTS
1928/29	HADFIELDS SPORTS
1929/30	ATLAS & NORFOLK
1930/31	ATLAS & NORFOLK
1932-36	NO COMPETITION
1936/37	ATLAS & NORFOLK
1937/38	ATLAS & NORFOLK
1938/39	ATLAS & NORFOLK
1939/40	HAMPTONS SPORTS

Works Leagues, Raleigh League Runners-Up Medal for season 1922

WORKS MINOR COMPETITION

At the start of World War II the Association decided to cancel the Haig League which was for 18-20 year-olds and replace it with the Works Minor Competition. A new cup was presented by Mr S. R. Alsop of Tinsley Park M.W.

Some limited competition may have been played during the War, with the leagues restarting for season 1945/46.

1939/40	CLEANSING DEPARTMENT
1940-45	NO COMPETITION
1945/46	SWIFT ATHLETIC
1946/47	TINSLEY WIRE
1947/48	NUNNERY COLLIERY
1948/49	W T FLATHERS
1949/50	SHEFFIELD FORGE
1950/51	
1951/52	Div 1 - INITIAL WORKS
	Div 2 GREENSIDE FOUNDRY
	& EAGLE FOUNDRY - JOINT
1952/53	LITTLE LONDON WORKS
1953/54	THORNCLIFFE
	LITTLE LONDON WORKS - JOINT
1954/55	OSBORN SPORTS
1955/56	HADFIELDS SPORTS
1956/57	SHEFFIELD GAS CO
1957/58	TEMPERED SPORTS
1958/59	HALL & PICKLES
1959/60	CRAVEN SPORTS
1960/61	DAVY UNITED
1961/62	DARWIN SPORTS
1962/63	(Competition cancelled due to bad weather)
1963/64	KIVETON WIRE WORKS
1964/65	BEDFORD SPORTS
1965/66	BEDFORD SPORTS
1966/67	CITY SURVEYORS
1967/68	E.S.C.
1968/69	STELLA WORKS
1969/70	
1970/71	CLEANSING DEPARTMENT
1971/72	UNITED COAL & COKE
1972/73	STELLA WORKS
1973/74	ESC
1974/75	DAVY ROLL
1975/76	MARSHALL SPORTS
1976/77	
1977/78	ROTHERWOOD

A S LEE CUP COMPETITION

The competition was run by the Sheffield & District Works Sports Association, who started in 1919.

I have found reference to two cup competitions (KO Cup and AS Lee Cup), but I assume that they are both the same

A.S. Lee Cup
A cigarette lighter engraved to H. Hopkinson dated 1945-46 which brings up a slight problem where, supposedly, there were no games played that year. Strange!

KO CUP/A S LEE CUP

1926/27	G P O
1927/28	NO COMPETITION
1928/29	THORNTON SPORTS
1929/30	THORNTON SPORTS
1930/31	NUNNERY SPORTS
1931/32	SPEAR & JACKSON
1932/33	CORNISH PLACE SPORTS
1933/34	SPEAR & JACKSON
1934/35	EDGAR ALLEN
1935/36	STEEL PEECH & TOZER
1936/37	TRUBRITE SPORTS
1937/38	NO COMPETITION
1938/39	THORNCLIFFE IRONWORKS
1939/40	THORNCLIFFE IRONWORKS
1940/41	TINSLEY PARK
1941-46	NO COMPETITION
1946/47	SHARDLOWS
1947/48	EDGAR ALLEN
1948/49	JUBILEE SPORTS
1949/50	ATLAS & NORFOLK
1950/51	
1951/52	TINSLEY WIRE IND
1952/53	METRO - VICKERS
1953/54	THORNCLIFFE
1954/55	BROWN BAYLEYS
1955/56	SHEFFIELD FORGE
1956/57	DORMER SPORTS
1957/58	TELEPHONE SPORTS
1958/59	TELEPHONE SPORTS
1959/60	TELEPHONE SPORTS
1960/61	DAVY UTD
1961/62	SHARDLOWS
1962/63	TEMPERED SPORTS
1963/64	CITY SURVEYORS
1964/65	CITY SURVEYORS
1965/66	
1966/67	
1967/68	
1968/69	TELEPHONE SPORTS
1969/70	
1970/71	
1971/72	BRAMAHS
1972/73	
1973/74	
1974/75	SHARDLOW SPORTS
1975/76	STELLA WORKS
1976/77	
1977/78	
1978/89	
1979/80	
1980/81	
1981/82	
1982/83	
1983/84	DORMER SPORTS
1984/85	
1985/86	
1986/87	TINSLEY WIRE
1987/88	BRAMAHS
1988/89	SHEFFIELD POLY
1989/90	WHITBREAD
1990/91	SHEFFIELD POLY
1991/92	WHITBREAD
1992/93	JUBILEE SPORTS
1993/94	JUBILEE SPORTS

THE WRAGG CHALLENGE CUP

The history of this League or Cup Competition (as it appears to have been at various stages), was somewhat shrouded in mystery for many years. At various times the Cup has been played for on a league basis, a straight knockout competition, and a midweek evening league competition, with the clubs drawn from other competitions by invite only.

The competition believed they were formed in 1892, initially being called the Attercliffe Licensed Victuallers League, However, that league only started running in seasons 1904/05. However it now appears that the competition started off as the Lewis Cup, which was a straight knockout competition in the Attercliffe area. This competition has been traced back to the 1892/93 season. The first cup was won outright by Baldwin Street Sunday School for winning it two years in succession as per the competition rules. The second cup lasted until 1903 when Nelson won it 3 years in a row, obviously the rules having been changed. However somebody else may have won another cup during the period 1895 to 1900, but results are hard to find in the press.

In 1903, the present cup was donated by their Secretary at the time, Walter Wragg of Wragg Cycles of Darnall. He was an S&H FA Council member and had been Secretary for the Lewis Cup. He put an advert in the Sheffield newspapers asking for entries for the new Wragg Challenge Cup, stating it was formerly the Lewis Cup Competition, indicating that a new trophy had been obtained because Nelson had kept the previous one as per competition rules

The Wragg Cup is still used today, being presented to the winners of the Premier Division.

At the end of the 1985/86 season, the league was down to nine clubs and several of these indicated that they would not enter for the following season. Chairman, Geoff Burgess outlined to the Committee about an Over 35 League that was in operation in County Durham. The Committee gave it some consideration before deciding to give it a try. The league has never looked back, and now also run an Over 45 section..

WRAGG CUP COMPETITION

1904 ECCLESFIELD CHURCH
1905 ROTHERHAM MAIN
1906 THORPE HESLEY
1907 KIMBERWORTH
1908 THORPE HESLEY
1909 THORPE HESLEY
1910 WARREN UTD/THORNCLIFFE UTD (Joint)
1911 BEIGHTON RECREATION
1912 BEIGHTON RECREATION
1913 MEADOWHALL
1914 WOODBOURNEROAD WR
1915 CAMMELLS SPORTS
1915-1919 NO COMP – WAR
1920 DARNALL OLD BOYS
1921 DARNALL OLD BOYS
1922 WOODHOUSE
1923 TREETON READING ROOM
1924 INDUSTRY SPORTS
1925 HOWELLS SPORTS
1926 ATTERCLIFFE FC
1927 ECCLESFIELD UTD
1928 RAWMARSH ATH
1929 LOPHAM ST UM FC
1930 WOODHOUSE BRUNSWICK
1931 TINSLEY PARK SPORTS
1932 HANDSWORTH UTD
1933 DINNINGTON ATH
1934 ST PHILIPS C&I & HALL SPORTS (Joint)
1935 ST PHILIPS C & I
1936 CROOKES WMC
1937 SILVERWOOD COLLIERY & CROOKES WMC (JT)
1938 INTAKE SPORTS
1939 ST PHILIPS C & I
1940 NORMANTON SPRINGS
1940- 1946 NO COMP – WAR
1947 WOODHOUSE WEST END
1948 TRAVELLERS SPORTS
1949 TRAVELLERS SPORTS
1950 TRAVELLERS SPORTS
1951 ECCLESFIELD COLLEY ROVERS
1952 MANOR SOCIAL
1953 SHEFFIELD ROVERS
1954 HANDSWORTH ROVERS
1955 MANOR SOCIAL
1956 MANOR SPORTS
1957 MANOR CASTLE
1958 ALBERT SPORTS
1959 MANOR SOCIAL
1960 PARAGON CINEMA
1961 ARUNDEL WMC
1962 ARUNDEL WMC
1963 KIVETON PARK COLLIERY UTD
1964 ARUNDEL C & I
1965 SPRINGWOOD
1966 ARUNDEL C&I
1967 WALKLEY/ SPRINGWOOD HOTEL (Joint)
1968 WALKLEY

WRAGG CUP COMPETITION (cont)

1969 MIDHILL WMC
1970 WOODHOUSE WEST END
1971 WOODHOUSE WEST END
1972 BRINSWORTH WMC
1973 BRINSWORTH WMC
1974 INTAKE F & SC
1975 INTAKE F & SC
1976 SHEFFIELD LANE TOP WMC
1977 FORTY FOOT
1978 FORTY FOOT
1979 STOCKSBRIDGE WORKS
1980 WOODHOUSE
1981 COBRAS
1982 CHAPELTOWN WMC
1983 JUNCTION FC
1984 JUNCTION FC
1985 SHIREGREEN WMC
1986 NORFOLK RANGERS

OVER 35 LEAGUE DIVISION ONE

1987 TAVERN 86
1988 DIV A - DARNALL LIBERALS
DIV B - TAVERN 86
1989 TAVERN 86
1990 TAVERN 86
1991 BLACK BULL TAVERNERS
1992 HORTICULTURAL
1993 HORTICULTURAL
1994 HORTICULTURAL
1995 HORTICULTURAL

DIVISION TWO

1989 DAVY FC
1990 STRADBROKE PSALTERS
1991 CONYERS CODGERS
1992 HOMESTEAD
1993 BARREL INN
1994 HILLTOP
1995 WICKERSLEY OLD VILLAGE

DIVISION THREE

1992 HARROW VOYAGERS
1993 HILLTOP
1994 WICKERSLEY OLD VILLAGE
1995 KENDRAY WMC FOSSILS

DIVISION FOUR

1994 KENDRAY WMC FOSSILS
1995 HANDSWORTH WMC

NEW SET UP OF DIVISIONS

To assist speedier promotion through the divisions it was decided that A & B divisions would be used with promoted clubs going from B to A and then into the Premier Division

PREMIER DIVISION

1996 HORTICULTURAL
1997 DAVY McKEE
1998 DAVY McKEE
1999 HILLTOP
2000 HATFIELD BLUE BELL
2001 TOMTREDDLEHOYLE
2002 TOMTREDDLEHOYLE
2003 TOMTREDDLEHOYLE
2004 FC MALIN
2005 TOMTREDDLEHOYLE
2006 TOMTREDDLEHOYLE
2007 NORTON WOODSEATS
2008 TELECOM SPORTS
2009 TELECOM SPORTS
2010 SHEFFIELD FC
2011 SHEFFIELD FC
2012 SHEFFIELD FC
2013 SHEFFIELD FC
2014 SHEFFIELD FC
2015 SHEFFIELD FC
2016 SHEFFIELD FC

DIVISION 1A

1996 KENDRAY WMC FOSSILS
1997 WINGFIELD AFC
1998 PHOENIX FC
1999 CLOWNE TOWN
2000 THURCROFT CORINTHIANS
2001 SCS BALL
2002 HIGHAM MINERS FOSSILS
2003 AVESTA POLARIT
2004 WICKERSLEY OLD VILLAGE
2005 WARD GREEN
2006 TELSTAR
2007 DUNSCROFT VETS
2008 GAWBER ROAD
2009 WARD GREEN WARRIORS
2010 UNITY DEARNE
2011 JUBILEE SPORTS
2012 AFC STANNINGTON
2013 MOSBOROUGH TRINITY
2014 ELSECAR DYNAMOES
2015 CARIBBEAN SPORTS

DIVISION 1B

1996 HANDSWORTH WMC
1997 TOMTREDDLEHOYLE
1998 RAILWAY TAVERN BENTLEY
1999 HORTICULTURAL
2000 DEMI VETS
2001 FC MALIN
2002 CLOWNE TOWN
2003 RAILWAY TAVERN BENTLEY
2004 AUGHTON BLACK BULL
2005 STOCKSBRIDGE PS VETS
2006 TELECOM SPORTS
2007 WICKERSLEY OLD VILLAGE
2008 THE MINSTHORPE
2009 NORTON WOODSEATS
2010 OUTO KUMPU S&S CLUB
2011 KINSLEY OLD BOYS
2012 PENISTONE CHURCH
2013 ANSTON FC
2014 DEARNESMAN
2015 FOSSILS

DIVISION 2A

1996 WINGFIELD AFC
1997 MOSELEYS ARMS
1998 SHEFFIELD CO-OP SOCIETY
1999 STOCKSBRIDGE PARK STEELS VETS
2000 HIGH GREEN CLUB
2001 ROSSINGTON MAIN
2002 CONYERS CODGERS
2003 AFC DRONFIELD
2004 FLETCHERS
2005 PEACOCK
2006 DUNSCROFT VETS
2007 GAWBER ROAD
2008 WARD GREEN WARRIORS
2009 UNITY DEARNE
2010 JUBILEE SPORTS
2011 AFC STANNINGTON
2012 BRINSWORTH WHITEHILL
2013 PLOUGH RANGERS
2014 HANDSWORTH
2015 EARL GREY

DIVISION 2B

1996 TOMTREDDLEHOYLE
1997 CO-OP CLUB
1998 THORNE DEMI VETS
1999 BIRLEY
2000 SILKSTONE UTD
2001 DRONFIELD WOODHOUSE
2002 HOLLINSEND AMATEURS
2003 KIMBERWORTH WILTON
2004 ROYAL OAK BLACKBURN
2005 TELECOM SPORTS
2006 BRADWAY OVER 35S
2007 THE MINSTHORPE
2008 SWINTON STATION
2009 PENISTONE CHURCH
2010 KINSLEY OLD BOYS
2011 JACK IN BOX
2012 ANSTON FC
2013 ECCLESFIELD VETS
2014 NO COMPETITION
2015 SWINTON ATHLETIC

SEASON 2015/16

The league structure was change with now only four divisions, the winners being as follows

PREMIER SHEFFIELD FC
DIVISION 1 PLOUGH RANGERS
DIVISION 2 MOSBOROUGH TRINITY
DIVISION 3 ROYSTON CROSS

OVER 40 & 45 DIVISIONS

With many of the players now over 40, it was decided to start an over 40's division for season 2011/12. This age level was increased to over 45 for season 2014/15

DIVISION 1A

2012 HALLAM 1860 OLD BOYS
2013 MINSTHORPE
2014 HALLAM 1860 OLD BOYS
2015 HALLAM 1860 OLD BOYS
2016 FOSSILS VETS

DIVISION 1B

2013 FOSSILS VETS
2014 WICKERSLEY OVER 45'S
2015 MALIN FC
2016 PENISTONE CHURCH VETS

THE TOPHAM CHALLENGE TROPHY

2012 HALLAM 1860 OLD BOYS
2013 THE MINSTHORPE
2014 HALLAM 1860 OLD BOYS
2015 HALLAM 1860 OLD BOYS
2016 FOSSILS VETS

THE TOPHAM RUNNERS UP CUP

2012 THE MINSTHORPE
2013 HALLAM 1860 OLD BOYS
2014 BRAMPTON BULLS HEAD
2015 FOSSILS VETS
2016 HALLAM 1860 OLD BOYS

SID BUTTERFIELD MEMORIAL TROPHY

This Competition is for teams who are knocked out of the Knock out Cup in the first round. The winners get this Sid Butterfield Memorial Cup and the runners up get the Sid Butterfield Memorial Shield

CUP

1994	HORTICULTURAL
1995	NOT PLAYED
1996	EDENTHORPE IDEAL INS
1997	STAG OLD BOYS
1998	DEARNE COMMUNITY OB
1999	MELCHESTER
2000	WICKERSLEY OLD VILLAGE
2001	WICKERSLEY OLD VILLAGE
2002	RAILWAY TAVERN BENTLEY
2003	MOSBOROUGH TRINITY
2004	NORFOLK ARMS
2005	CLOWNE TOWN
2006	AUGHTON BLACK BULL
2007	THURCROFT CORINTHIANS
2008	SWINTON STATION
2009	THE MINSTHORPE
2010	OLD EDWARDIANS
2011	THE MINSTHORPE
2012	HIGH GREEN PACKHORSE
2013	ECCLESFIELD VETS
2014	DEARNESMAN VETS 35
2015	AUGHTON VILLAGE
2016	HSBC BANK FC

SHIELD

1994	HILL TOP
1995	NOT PLAYED
1996	WICKERSLEY OLD VILLAGE
1997	HILL TOP
1998	HALLAMSHIRE HOTEL
1999	WICKERSLEY OLD VILLAGE
2000	PENISTONE CHURCH
2001	AUGHTON BLACK BULL
2002	WICKERSLEY OLD VILLAGE
2003	FORGEMASTERS
2004	MOSBOROUGH TRINITY
2005	WICKERSLEY OLD VILLAGE
2006	OLD EDWARDIANS
2007	THE ACORN
2008	ST JAMES VETS
2009	PLOUGH RAGGY LADS
2010	HANDSWORTH TURF TAVERN
2011	TIBSHELF TOWN
2012	WARD GREEN WARRIORS
2013	OUGHTIBRIDGE FC
2014	UPTON RUGBY CLUB
2015	KILLAMARSH JUNIORS
2016	SWINTON STATION

WRAGG KNOCKOUT CUP

This trophy was presented to the League by former Sheffield Wednesday player Derek Dooley in 1963.

1964	INTAKE F & SC
1965	INTAKE F & SC
1966	SPRINGWOOD
1967	PUNCH BOWL
1968	WALKLEY FC
1969	MIDHILL WMC
1970	WOODHOUSE WEST END
1971	WOODHOUSE WEST END
1972	DIAL HOUSE WMC
1973	BRINSWORTH WMC
1974	COLLEY YC
1975	ARUNDEL C & I
1976	SHEFFIELD LANE TOP
1977	STELLA WORKS
1978	SPEAR & JACKSON
1979	SHEFFIELD LANE TOP
1980	EARL MARSHALL
1981	COBRAS FC
1982	EARL MARSHALL
1983	NORFOLK PARK
1984	NOT PLAYED
1985	TOWN END ROAD WMC
1986	BRITANNIA FC
1987	TAVERN 86
1988	TAVERN 86
1989	TAVERN 86
1990	HORTICULTURAL
1991	THREE FEATHERS
1992	HORTICULTURAL
1993	BLACK BULL TAVERNERS
1994	HORTICULTURAL
1995	HORTICULTURAL
1996	HILLTOP
1997	JUVE' WADSLEY
1998	DAVY FC
1999	DAVY FC
2000	TOMTREDDLEHOYLE
2001	HATFIELD BLUE BELL
2002	TOMTREDDLEHOYLE
2003	TOMTREDDLEHOYLE
2004	TOMTREDDLEHOYLE
2005	TOMTREDDLEHOYLE
2006	TOMTREDDLEHOYLE
2007	GAWBER ROAD
2008	GAWBER ROAD
2009	TELECOM SPORTS
2010	SHEFFIELD FC
2011	MOSBOROUGH TRINITY
2012	SHEFFIELD FC
2013	SHEFFIELD FC
2014	SHEFFIELD FC
2015	SHEFFIELD FC
2016	SHEFFIELD FC

STEEL PEECH & TOZER – INTER DEPARTMENTAL COMP

This Competition was played for by the various departments and workshops within the Steel Peech & Tozer group between

1937/38 and 1983/84

1937/38	BAR MILL
1938/39	STRIP MILL
1939/40	TEMP FINISHING BANKS
1940/41	TEMP MELTING SHOP
1941/42	TEMP COGGING MILL
1942/43	NO COMPETITION
1943/44	GUN SHOP
1944/45	NO COMPETITION
1945/46	NO COMPETITION
1946/47	FUEL & LAB
1947/48	TEMP COGGING MILL
1948/49	TEMP MELTING SHOP
1949/50	NEW SPRING SHOP
1950/51	ICKLES ELECTRICIANS
1951/52	ICKLES ELECTRICIANS
1952/53	TYRE MILL
1953/54	TEMP COGGING MILL
1954/55	TEMP FINISHING BANKS
1955/56	TEMP ELECTRICIANS
1956/57	TEMP FINISHING BANKS
1957/58	TEMP MELTING SHOP
1958/59	TEMP FINISHING BANKS
1959/60	TEMP MELTING SHOP
1960/61	TEMP FINISHING BANKS
1961/62	TEMP COGGING MILL
1962/63	ENGINEERS
1963/64	TEMP COGGING MILL
1964/65	TEMP COGGING MILL
1965/66	TEMP MELTING SHOP
1966/67	TEMP COGGING MILL
1967/68	COST DEPT
1968/69	TEMP FINISHING BANKS
1969/70	TEMP FINISHING BANKS
1970/71	COMPUTER APPLICATIONS
1971/72	BAR MILL
1972/73	TEMP FINISHING BANKS
1973/74	PARKGATE WIRE DEPT
1974/75	TEMP FINISHING BANKS
1975/76	-
1976/77	-
1977/78	THRYBERGH BAR MILL
1978/79	-
1979/80	THRYBERGH BAR MILL
1980/81	BRINSWORTH HOT STRIP MILL
1981/82	11" MILL
1982/83	ALDWARKE FINISHING BANKS
1983/84	NEW ICKLES MACHINE SHOP

Steel Peech & Tozer
Inter Departmental Competition

STEEL PEECH AND TOZER'S TEAM.—Back row: E. Fawcus, H. Hollings, J. Casey, S. A. Smith, J. Wright, K. Jones, S. Smith. Front row: A. Guest, H. Howells R. Bates, E. Cardwell, E. Webb.

YORKSHIRE LEAGUE

Season	Division One
1920–21	Bradford Park Avenue reserves
1921–22	Houghton Main
1922–23	Bradford Park Avenue reserves
1923–24	Methley Perseverance
1924–25	Brodsworth Main
1925–26	Methley Perseverance
1926–27	Harrogate
1927–28	Goole Town
1928–29	Bradford Park Avenue reserves
1929–30	Bradford City reserves
1930–31	Leeds United "A"
1931–32	Huddersfield Town "A"
1932–33	Selby Town
1933–34	Huddersfield Town "A"
1934–35	Selby Town
1935–36	Selby Town
1936–37	Selby Town
1937–38	York City reserves
1938–39	Sheffield Wednesday "A"
1939–45	Competition suspended due to WWII
1945–46	Thorne Colliery
1946–47	Goole Town
1947–48	Sheffield United "A"
1948–49	Goole Town reserves

Yorkshire League Cup
Runners Up Trophy for season 1952-52

Season	Division One	Division Two
1949–50	Goole Town reserves	Retford Town reserves
1950–51	Sheffield Wednesday "A"	Stocksbridge Works
1951–52	Stocksbridge Works	Farsley Celtic
1952–53	Selby Town	Huddersfield Town "A"
1953–54	Selby Town	Rawmarsh Welfare
1954–55	Stocksbridge Works	Hull City "A"
1955–56	Stocksbridge Works	Rawmarsh Welfare
1956–57	Stocksbridge Works	Retford Town
1957–58	Stocksbridge Works	East End Park WMC
1958–59	Retford Town	Yorkshire Amateur
1959–60	Farsley Celtic	Grimethorpe Miners Welfare
1960–61	Sheffield Wednesday "A"	Hallam

Season	Division One	Division Two	Division Three
1961–62	Stocksbridge Works	Bridlington Trinity	Farsley Celtic reserves
1962–63	Stocksbridge Works	Wombwell Sporting Association	Farsley Celtic reserves
1963–64	Bridlington Trinity	Rawmarsh Welfare	Keighley Central
1964–65	Wombwell Sporting Association	Stocksbridge Works	
1965–66	Wombwell Sporting Association	Norton Woodseats	
1966–67	Bridlington Town	Hull Brunswick	
1967–68	Bridlington Trinity	Lincoln United	
1968–69	Farsley Celtic	Rawmarsh Welfare	
1969–70	Rawmarsh Welfare	Dinnington Athletic	
1970–71	Lincoln United	North Ferriby United	Stocksbridge Works
1971–72	Winterton Rangers	Barton Town	Leeds Ashley Road
1972–73	Mexborough Town	Leeds & Carnegie College	Hall Road Rangers
1973–74	Lincoln United	Thackley	Pickering Town
1974–75	Ossett Albion	Bridlington Town	Stocksbridge Works
1975–76	Emley	Guiseley	Rawmarsh Welfare
1976–77	Winterton Rangers	Sheffield FC	Bentley Victoria Welfare
1977–78	Emley	Kiveton Park	Yorkshire Amateur
1978–79	Winterton Rangers	Ossett Albion	York Railway Institute
1979–80	Emley	Barton Town	Hall Road Rangers
1980–81	Leeds Ashley Road	Ossett Albion	Bradley Rangers
1981–82	Emley	Harrogate Town	Pontefract Collieries

THE THOMAS YOUDAN FOOTBALL COMPETITION

By CHRIS EYRE (S&HCFA Area Historian)

On the front page of the Sheffield & Rotherham Independent newspaper on 16 February 1867 an advert indicated that the first series of 6 games were to be played that day for a Cup (actually a claret jug) presented by Thomas Youdan, a local theatre owner, to the clubs of the town and neighbourhood. It was stated that every game was to commence punctually at 3 o'clock and there was to be no waiting for players. In fact there was an error in the advert as the heading called it the Youdan Football Club rather than Cup. Obviously this error could be excused as this was the first time a football cup had been played for.

12 prominent teams from the Sheffield area took part in The Youdan Cup competition, which is now accepted as being the first ever football cup competition in the World. The teams involved were Broomhall, Fir Vale, Garrick, Hallam, Heeley, Mackenzie, Milton, Norfolk, Norton, Pitsmoor, Wellington and the United Mechanics. Note that Sheffield FC did not play in this competition as they refused to play local area clubs after a fallout with Hallam in 1860.

Over the following weeks there were reports on the games with the cup draw for the second round. These were tucked away in the general news columns and not under the sport section which at that time was more to do with horse racing, hunting, rabbit coursing and pigeon shooting.

This was the early days of football and many people had probably never seen or taken part in a game. To this end the report in the Telegraph several days after the first series of games indicated as much. The report stated those of the spectators who were not familiar with the usages of football players were not a little astonished at the unequivocal, but good humoured, roughness displayed, especially when a "charge" took place, and it was particularly gratifying to see that notwithstanding the severe collisions, the heavy tumbles, and the scarred shins, perfect friendliness invariably prevailed; and after a "charge" a collision, and a downfall, the prostrated would instantly spring to their feet and resume the game in the heartiest and the most determined and enthusiastic spirit.

THE ROUGE SYSTEM

No official rules for the Competition have been found, but I expect that there was a mixture of different area rules, but mainly incorporating the Sheffield Club rules.

However there was one big difference to the Sheffield Clubs rules used for the Youdan Cup competition. The competition used what was called the rouge system. Instead of having the goal posts 8 yards apart, the goal posts were only 4 yards apart. Another 2 posts were erected a further 4 yards either side of these posts, these being called rouge posts. Those familiar with Australian Rules football today will see that set up still being used. The idea of the game was to score goals between the middle 2 posts to win the game. However with only 4 yards to aim at, most games tended to finish without a goal being scored and so no winner. The idea of the rouge post was that if the ball was kicked between the goalpost and the rouge post and was then touched onto the ground by an attacking player, a rouge was scored. If the game then finished without any goals being scored or an even number of goals scored by both teams, then the number of rouges scored decided who had won the match. The rouge helped decide the winners of several of the games in the Youdan competition. The importance of touching down the ball was realised by the clubs, and was emphasised by the fact that most of the teams in the competition selected a local athlete to play for them. His main job appeared to be to act as a sprinter and chase after the long kicked balls to score the rouge.

FIRST SERIES (ROUND)

The United Mechanics were drawn against Norton at Norton. It was advised that a bus would leave the Surrey Arms, Granville Street at half-past one o'clock, punctually. You have to remember that the bus would have been a horse drawn wagon or carriage. The game finish in Norton's favour by 2 goals and 6 rouges to nothing.

Hallam FC, whose nickname even today is the Countrymen because of the distance out of Sheffield they played, were drawn at home against Heeley. A bus was to leave Heeley Bridge at one o'clock from the bottom of Ecclesall Road at half past one. Hallam won by 2 goals and 2 rouges to 1 rouge.

Two games took place at the orphanage at Cremorne. Mackenzie beat Garrick by 1 goal and 1 rouge to nothing. In the other game Milton beat Wellington by 2 goals and 5 rouges to nothing.

Norfolk took on Fir Vale at Norfolk Park. Norfolk won by 2 goals and 4 rouges to nothing.

The final game was between Broomhall and Pitsmoor at Broomhall's ground on Ecclesall Road. The game was well contested with Broomhall winning by scoring 2 rouges to nothing.

SECOND SERIES (ROUND)

Details of the second series of games was again on the front pages of the Sheffield Telegraph and Sheffield & Rotherham Independent papers. It indicated that at the last Committee meeting (when the draw was done) it was resolved "That the Referee shall have power to award a free kick to the opponents of any club, which makes more than three fouls or kicks-out, when the ball is being thrown in, if he (the Referee) considers those fouls or kicks-out to be intentional. I assume that this was to stop an early version of time wasting when a club was in front. Also a note indicated that the rules to drawn games and adjournments was as before, which became unexpectedly important in this round.

Mackenzie entertained Milton at the orphanage. In a close game Mackenzie managed to win by 1 rouge to nothing. However Green, who it was reported was well known as a "pedestrian", in charging one of the Milton players broke his collar bone. Unaware of the nature of his injury he had sustained, he went on playing for some time though suffering intense pain. A collection on his behalf in the club house after the game realised "sufficient for present wants and doubtless something will be awarded to him out of the weekly funds whilst he is unable to work".

The Norfolk against Broomhall game was fixed for Norfolk. The game was a well contested one and after playing the specified time neither team had scored so it was agreed to play an extra hour. After 2 minutes Norfolk managed to kick a goal and so won and ended the match. This was the first golden goal in football, over 130 years before FIFA brought it in for a trial period to settle games.

Norton played against Hallam at Norton. The game resulted in a tie with neither team able to score despite a further hour being played. The match was resumed on the following Monday and brought to a conclusion after an hour of very rough play when Hallam scored a rouge. The game on the Monday is often looked on as the first ever replay. However, having read the wording of the press reports many times, I take the view that the clubs went back to finish the game, with the first point scored being the winner rather than playing a full game against. In my mind it was the second golden goal winner and not the first as is also often indicated.

THE SEMI –FINAL

With three teams now left in the Competition the draw was made and in was decided that Hallam would play Mackenzie in the first match on Saturday 2 March at Bramall Lane cricket ground, with the winners playing Norfolk, who had been lucky to receive a walk over in what would have been the second semi final. The crowd were charged an entry fee of 3d.

Play had not long begun before Hallam kicked a rouge and they soon followed up this success by kicking another. Changing ends at half time they scored another 2 rouges in the second have, having a very active man up front to make the touch downs to complete the rouges. The press report indicated that there was some good play in the game, although it was evident from the commencement that Hallam had the advantage, their side being of a much more bulky specimen of humanity than their opponents, and were also as active in "the pedal" department, being both fleet of foot and sure kickers. Hallam certainly showed the best play, but there was far too much playing the opponents instead of the ball, as there generally is in these matches, thus giving the advantage to heavy roughs over the lighter players.

THE FINAL

The final between Hallam and Norfolk was fixed for Shrove Tuesday 5 March, again at Bramall Lane cricket ground with a 3 o'clock start, with J Tomlinson of Broomhall club appointed the referee to assist the two umpires J Berley junior of Heeley club and J Ullyett of Fir Vale club. The entry fee was again 3d each, but Ladies were to be allowed in free of charge. It is reported that the competition had caught the imagination of the Sheffield area people, and over 2,000 attended the match.

The press report indicated that the teams were equal, both in ability and size. The score was level at half time and ends were changed. 5 minutes before the end of the 90 minutes play, Hallam scored a rouge, the touch down being made by Ash, who was a fine sprinter. This score riled Norfolk as they had only a few minutes more to play. Norfolk went into a "burster" and the Hallam players were floored in all direction. In doing this they exposed their goal, and a player to whom they have awarded the sweet name of "Treacle" secured a second rouge for Hallam, immediately after which time was called making Hallam the first winner of a football cup played for in a style of football similar to what as we know today.

PLAY OFF

After the success of the competition it was decided at short notice that there would be a second place play off between Norfolk and Mackenzie's. Again this match took place at Bramall Lane cricket ground, on Saturday 9 March. The game was a closely contested game with Norfolk eventually winning by 1 rouge to nil

THE CUP

However one mystery remains. The claret jug was won by Hallam FC, but then what happened to it over the next 130 years? In 1997, Hallam FC received a letter from a Scottish antiques dealer which stated that he had obtained the Youdan Cup and were Hallam FC interested in purchasing it back. Negotiations took place and the jug re-united with Hallam FC for £2,000. Today, it is claimed that it is worth nearly one million pounds.

The Youdan Cup, first ever football trophy

FIRST ELECTRIC LIGHT MATCH

The 1878/79 season was the season that football history was made by the Sheffield FA. They organised the first football match under electric lights at Bramall Lane on Monday 14 October 1878.

The two teams were selected from local players with J C Clegg being captain of the red team and his brother W E Clegg captain of the blue team with the Association's two Vice Presidents R W Dickenson and W Skinner the Umpires and the Association's Secretary W Peirce-Dix as the Referee.

The game kicked off at 7.30pm with the best players in the area having been selected by the Association to make it a competitive game. The blue team eventually ran out winners by 2-0, with Tomlinson holding the record as the first man to score in a floodlit match. The scorer of the second goal is not recorded, perhaps the reporter was unable to see the other end of the ground.

THE TEAMS

Red

(Goal) P STACEY, (Backs) J HOUSELY, J HUNTER, E BUTTERY, F HINDE (Forwards) J C CLEGG, W MOSFORTH, A WOODCOCK, C STRATFORD, H E BARBER & G ANTHONY

Blue

(Goal) T LAWSON (Backs) W E CLEGG, R GREGORY, T BUTTERY, W H STACEY, (Forwards) G B MARPLES, A MALPAS, J TOMLINSON, E BARBER, P PATTERSON & T BISHOP

It is not reported in the minute books whose idea the game was, but it was run in conjunction with local businessman John Tasker of Taskers Sons & Co of Angel Street, Sheffield. He supplied, set up and controlled all the equipment used on the night. It is reported that the official attendance was 12,000 generating receipts of £300, but it is reported that possibly there were 20,000 in the ground, many getting in in the darkness. The £300 was split three ways, with the Bramall Lane grounds committee getting a share and the Sheffield FA getting back all out of pocket expenses. Taskers Sons & Co was allowed to claim up to £80 for out of pocket expenses, with any balance being split equally between the Association and Taskers Sons & Co.

The lighting power was supplied by two portable engines, one behind each goal. The lamps and reflectors were set up on 30 foot high wooden towers, one in each corner of the ground. They generated 8,000 candle power and were initially so bright that they had to be adjusted so that the players could see. It was reported that the power was so bright that some of the ladies in the crowd put up their umbrellas to protect themselves. The arc-lighting technology used in the lighting had actually been invented by Humphrey Davy in the early part of the 19th century when he used the technology in his famous Davy miners safety lamps.

The night proved a financial success and other electric light games followed in the following weeks at Chorley, Blackburn, Glasgow, Birmingham, The Oval and Trent Bridge. The first electric light rugby match was played 15 days after the Sheffield game when Broughton played Swinton in Manchester. Today we take games under floodlights for granted, but it was over 80 years after the first game in Sheffield before professional football games started to appear under floodlights. In fact it was the mid 1960's before all the Football League teams had floodlights, mainly encouraged by the introduction of the Football League Cup competition in 1961.

John Tasker's main business was actually boot and shoe making, which involved him with the rubber and leather industry. It is reported that he later added an engineering department which patented an armour plate grinding machine which at one time was responsible for making all the armour plating for the Royal Navy Ships.

He was able to turn his hand to almost anything from inventing a bouncy ball to a way of mending galoshes, using India rubber. Using rubber for wire insulation opened his eyes to electricity and he is credited with opening the first Sheffield telephone exchange.

Chapter Five

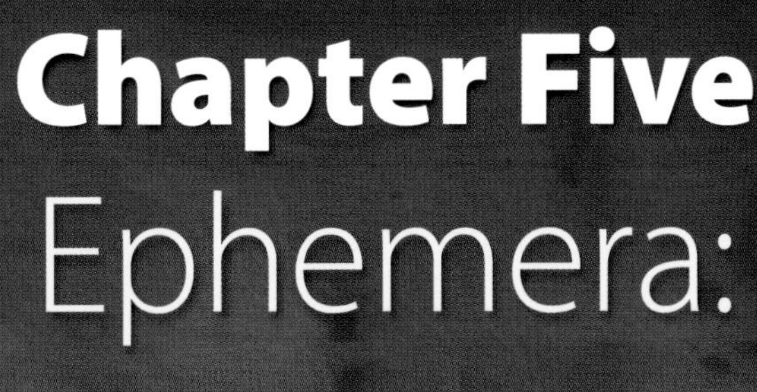

Ephemera: handbooks, programmes, newspaper clippings, advertisements etc

In library and information science, the term ephemera also describes the class of published documents which are meant to be thrown away after one use.
Large academic and national libraries and museums may collect, organize, and preserve ephemera as history.

Sheffield Football Ephemera
spanning over 130 years

The rise of organised football in Sheffield brought not only the glorious game to the masses but also a tidal wave of literature, handbooks, programmes, relevant Sheffield sport/football related advertising, articles from various local newspapers such as the Sheffield Star, Sheffield Telegraph and probably the most useful publication when it comes to the history of football in the city, the Sheffield Green'Un.

The following pages are adorned with images of all the aforementioned items but also with some of the individual and more personal items such as photographs of the local players themselves, public houses with teams proudly standing in front, individuals showing off their medals or standing with their trophies. Postcards specifically produced for that team, where just 11 or 12 cards were printed so that each player could have his own keepsake of a Cup Final or League Championship that they won.

This chapter also includes personal items that are from relatives who still greatly cherish some images of their great-grandfather, grandfathers, father, uncle or brothers so much that they will never part with them. These have been loaned to the authors of this book with the proviso that they are returned immediately after they have been scanned for use within this book.

Also on the next few pages are some rather glorious illustrations of players from the local leagues which appeared in the Sheffield Star newspapers during the 1920s and 1930s.

Robin Hood FC v Carbrook United FC playing at the Little Matlock ground which was situated in the lower Stannington area of Sheffield. Friendlies League game in 1968. Brian Kennedy and Dave Walker are the two Carbrook United players in the candy striped kit.

Sheffield Newspapers illustrations
of local team players in the 1929-30 season

Every week throughout the 1929-30 season the Sheffield newspapers produced illustrations of players who played in the local leagues - the next few pages depict just a small selection.

J Newbould,
Warren United FC

A Hutchinson
St Cuthberts FC

W Snape
Woodhouse FC

Isaac Marsh
Captain of Dinnington FC

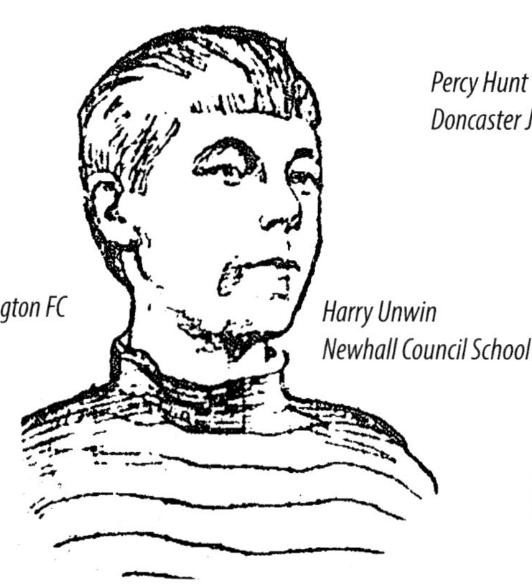

Harry Unwin
Newhall Council School

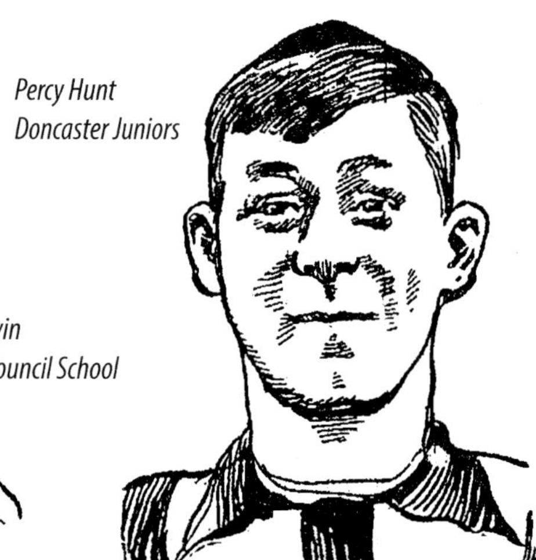

Percy Hunt
Doncaster Juniors

Captain
Aston FC

B Rigby
Firshill Old Boys FC

W Davis
Greasborough Rovers

Sheffield Newspapers illustrations
of local team players in the 1929-30 season

Hannigan
Hoyland F.C.

Ross
Hoyland F.C.

J. Clayton
Attercliffe Zion F.C.

A. Frost
Wadsley Bridge F.C.

Johnson
Tapton Hill
Congregational F.C.

Oscar Haynes
Normanton Springs F.C.

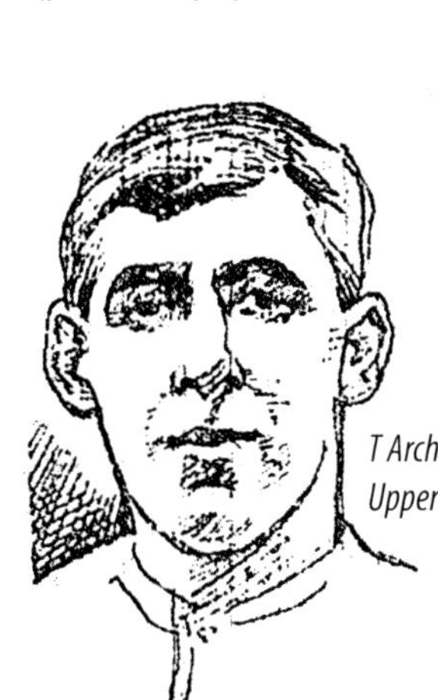

T Archer
Upperthorpe Unitarians F.C.

L Warriss
Croft House Settlement F.C.

A Burkitt
Beighton F.C.

Sheffield and Hallamshire County Football Association embroidered badge

Ephemera relating to Sheffield Football Club
Brendan Murphy's book 'From Sheffield with Love'
Entrance ticket for game at Don Valley Stadium, October 1997
Sheffield - The Home of Football booklet

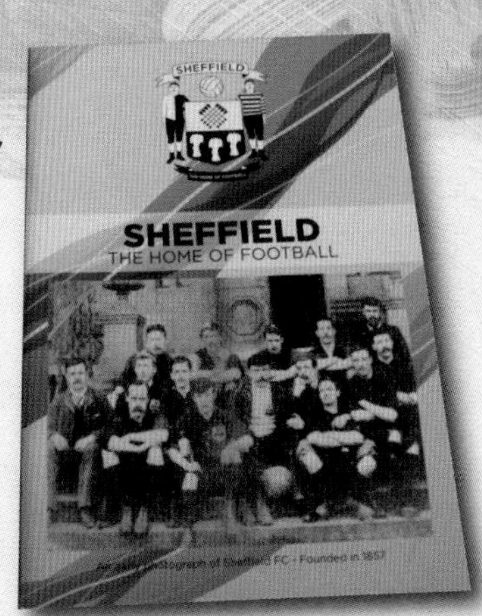

Ephemera from Hallam Football Club
'150 years of the Countrymen' booklet
Two team photographs showing Hallam FC in the 1950s

Two local teams playing at Concord Park, Shiregreen, Sheffield. c1969

SHEFFIELD SUNDAY SCHOOL LEAGUE.

RESULTS UP TO DATE.

DIVISION 1.

	P.	W.	L.	D.	Goals. F.	A.	Pts.
All Saints Church	21	16	0	6	75	14	37
Owlerton N.C.	21	17	1	3	83	14	37
All Saints Mission	20	11	4	5	60	19	27
Attercliffe Zion	21	10	4	7	45	29	27
Wycliffe	19	10	7	2	36	45	22
Oxford Street U.M.C.	17	7	4	6	29	20	20
Brightside Cong.	20	8	9	3	45	48	19
Grenoside B.O.	21	6	9	6	28	38	18
Hillsboro Tabernacle	19	7	8	3	33	32	17
Corby Street W.R.	21	3	12	6	20	60	12
Grimesthorpe P.M.	17	3	10	4	21	49	10
Attercliffe Church	20	3	16	1	34	60	7
Philadelphia W.R.	16	0	15	1	8	86	1

DIVISION 2.

	P.	W.	L.	D.	Goals. F.	A.	Pts.
Brunswick Mission	19	19	0	0	116	6	38
Heeley Friends	21	18	2	1	106	18	37
Sharrow Reform Bro.	22	15	6	2	53	31	32
Sharrow Lane N.C.	21	15	5	1	63	32	31
Heeley St. Peter's	20	14	4	2	79	23	30
St. Marie's	22	9	12	1	35	69	19
Old Street Mission	20	8	10	2	33	30	18
St. George's	21	6	14	1	22	69	13
Park Friends	18	5	11	2	21	34	12
Meersbrook Baptist	21	4	13	4	26	86	12
Hartshead 3rd Section	20	3	14	3	25	65	9
Ranmoor St. John's	21	3	16	2	26	73	8
Shalesmoor Guild	19	3	15	1	24	87	7

Clipping from the Green'Un showing the league tables of the Sheffield Sunday School League, circa 1920s

Play Up Dore! Booklet compiled by Dorne Coggins and Anne Slater extolling the achievements of the local Dore football club

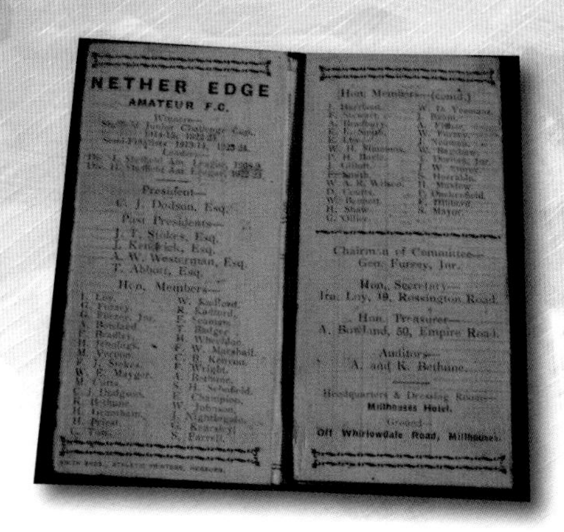
NETHER EDGE
AMATEUR F.C.
President—
C. J. Dodson, Esq.
Past Presidents—
J. T. Stokes, Esq.
J. Kendrick, Esq.
A. W. Westerman, Esq.
T. Abbott, Esq.
Hon. Members—
Hon. Members—(contd.)
Chairman of Committee—
Geo. Furesy, Jnr.
Hon. Secretary—
Ira. Ley, 19, Rossington Road.
Hon. Treasurer—
A. Rowland, 50, Empire Road.
Auditors—
A. and K. Bethune.
Headquarters & Dressing Rooms—
Millhouses Hotel.
Ground—
Off Whirlowdale Road, Millhouses.

Member's Card for Nether Edge Amateur Football Club Season 1926-27

Member's Card
NETHER EDGE
AMATEUR
FOOTBALL CLUB
*****
SEASON 1926-27

Packhorse Inn 1 Royal Earl 2

By Paul Webster
Meadowhall Sunday League

THE Meadowhall Sunday League showpiece Cup Final went the way of the favourites as Premier Division Royal Earl edged out Division One Packhorse Inn 2-1

However, it was anything but an easy ride for Earl who were made to work hard for the win by a Packhorse side that showed tremendous spirit on the night.

The Division One out outfit may have lacked the knowhow of a vastly experienced Earl side. But they played with great determination in a performance that departing manager Nathan Griffin, in his final game in charge, would have been immensely proud of.

Packhorse full-back and Arctic Monkeys guitarist Jamie Cooke kept Earl's danger man Ashley Burbeary in check for much of the night before tiring defender was substituted late on.

There was no doubt that on the night Earl were the worthy winners but it was a game in which they could never relax despite taking the lead inside the first 20 minutes, then adding a second early in the second half.

A goal 13 minutes from time made it an anxious finale where it took some fine clearing headers from man-of the match Ben Leonard, who edged out Packhorse Inn's industrious midfielder Chris Ledwood for the award. Leonard worked hard all evening with his box to box play then late in the game when Earl were under pressure, he put his head in where it hurts as the midfielder helped out his defenders to ensure Earl held onto their lead.

PACKHORSE INN LINE-UP

Wrightson
Cooke
Burns
J Thompson
Robinson
Spencer
Duty
Shepherd
Gibson
C Ledwood
Parkinson

SUBS

Senior
M Ledwood
Longston
Ashberry
A Thompson

Four minutes later Earl edged in front when Darren Schofield's long throw was taken on the chest by Ashley Longstaff who hit the ball on the turn as it dropped inside Wrightson's near post.

Packhorse were only inches away from an equaliser just past the half hour, Ryan Robinson's 30-yard free-kick hitting the cross bar with Earl keeper James Beddingham beaten, while at the other end Longstaff wasn't far away with a header that went just over the bar on the stroke of half-time.

Three minutes into the second half Earl had some breathing space with the second goal despite the appeals of the Packhorse players for handball.

ROYAL EARL LINE-UP

Beddingham
Cotton
Schofield
Baker
Colley
Furniss
Leonard
Goff
Longstaff
Bates
Burbeary

SUBS

Smith
Sutcliffe
Broomhead
Whitehead
Davenport

row angle despite the efforts of Robinson on the line to keep it.

It signaled a spell of Earl dominance but the third goal that would sealed the tie never came and they were suddenly found themselves having to defend when Packhorse pulled one back on 77 minutes.

A Free-kick from out of the right saw substitute Tom Senior send a lopping header beyond Beddingham. Earl had to defend a number of dangerous crossed and free-kick into the box, one of which saw Spencer send a 20-yard lob just over from the keeper's punch clear, while at the other end Bates hit the post after a Earl counter attack.

Final line-ups: The Packhorse Inn team (top) and Royal Earl (above)

Half page newspaper clipping from the Grass Roots Section of the Sheffield Star detailing the Meadowhall League Cup Final 2010 which was played at Bramall Lane

Local league game at Concord Park, Shiregreen, Sheffield. c1969

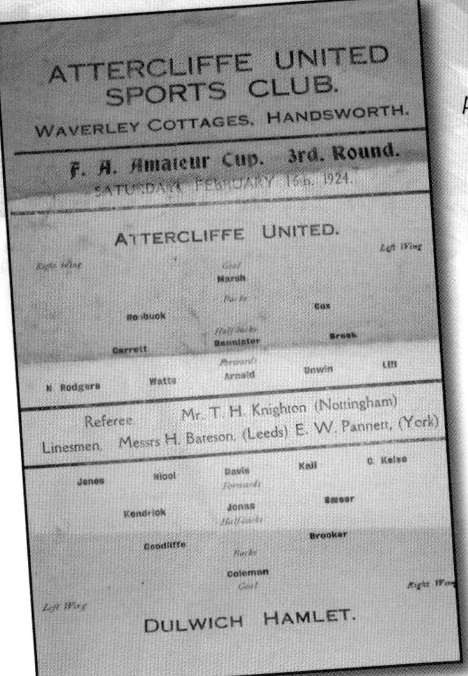
ATTERCLIFFE UNITED
SPORTS CLUB.
WAVERLEY COTTAGES, HANDSWORTH.

F. A. Amateur Cup. 3rd. Round.
SATURDAY, FEBRUARY 16th. 1924.

ATTERCLIFFE UNITED.

Right Wing — Left Wing

Goal
Marsh

Backs
Roebuck — Cox

Halfbacks
Carrett — Bannister — Brook

Forwards
N. Rodgers — Watts — Arnold — Unwin — Lill

Referee Mr. T. H. Knighton (Nottingham)
Linesmen Messrs H. Bateson, (Leeds) E. W. Pannett, (York)

Jones — Nicol — Davis — Kail — C. Kelso
Forwards

Kendrick — Jonas — Smear
Halfbacks

Goodliffe — Brooker
Backs

Coleman
Goal

Left Wing — Right Wing

DULWICH HAMLET.

Attercliffe United Sports Club versus Dulwich Hamlet Programme for 3rd round of FA Amateur Cup, February 1924

A Newspaper clipping showing Alf Ringstead, right, Sheffield United's Republic of Ireland International presenting the Tinsley Charity Shield to Ecclesfield Red Rose F.C. The Shield now seems to have been lost and a Cup has taken its place. Now played for within the Meadowhall League

Sheffield Foot-Ball Club: Rules, Regulation and Laws

Thos Pierson

RULES, REGULATIONS, & LAWS

OF THE

SHEFFIELD

FOOT-BALL CLUB,

A LIST OF MEMBERS, &c.

PRESIDENT:
FREDERICK WARD, ESQ.

VICE-PRESIDENT:
T. A. SORBY, ESQ. | M. J. ELLISON, ESQ.

COMMITTEE:
T. PIERSON, ESQ. | S. NEWBOULD, ESQ.
W. PREST, ESQ. | G. MOSELEY, ESQ.
F. FOWLER, ESQ.

HON. SEC. & TREASURER;
N. CRESWICK, ESQ.

1859.

This card was issued in the UK by "Ogden's" cigarettes in 1899. It depicts Mr. J. Fox a member of the Sheffield & Hallamshire F.A..

Wragg League Cups

Two local teams playing at Concord Park, Shiregreen, Sheffield. c1970s

SPORTS Equipment
Try the "Arcade" FIRST
SHEFFIELD & ECCLESALL CO-OPERATIVE SOCY. LTD.
"The Arcade," Ecclesall Road

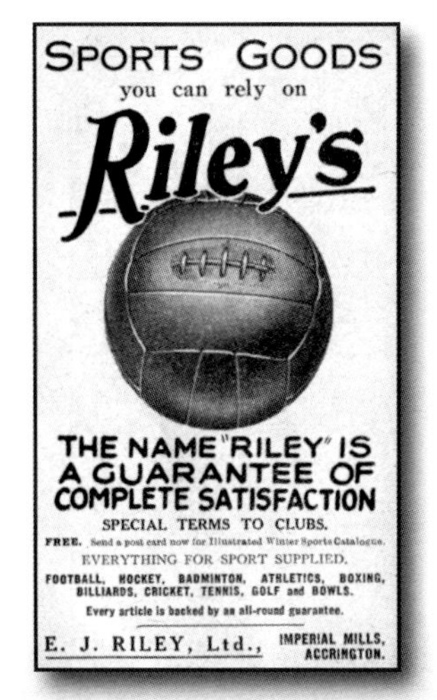

Advertisements within the Sheffield Telegraph handbook top left to right: Players cigarettes, Craven A advertised by Stan Matthews, Players cigarettes, Sheffield & Ecclesall Co-operative Society, bottom left to right: Thomlinson Greban Footballs, Riley's, Players cigarettes, Chelsea Royal Boot Dubbin and Ogden's Guinea Gold Cigarettes

A dramatic action image from a Meadowhall League Cup Final at Bramall Lane,

RULES OF
THE WRAGG FOOTBALL LEAGUE
AND
THE WRAGG CHALLENGE CUP
COMPETITIONS

Formed 1892

Affiliated to The Sheffield & Hallamshire
County Football Association

THE SHEFFIELD IMPERIAL
SUNDAY FOOTBALL LEAGUE
Established 1968

HANDBOOK
SEASON 1976/77

Sanctioned by: Sheffield & Hallamshire
County Football Association

SHEFFIELD AND HALLAMSHIRE
COUNTY FOOTBALL ASSOCIATION

AMATEUR LEAGUE

Directory and Fixtures
Season 1977/78

Chairman:
S. BUTTERFIELD, Esq.

Management Committee:
Messrs. R. Cowen, A. H. Holbrook,
J. Hogg, T. Lawton, J. Waters,
and E. J. N. Woolley.

Secretary:
E. KANGLEY, Esq.
40, Waingate, Sheffield S3 8LB
(Tel: Sheffield 27817)

Handbooks and Fixture Lists for various local leagues
Wragg League 1970-71, Sunday Imperial League1976-77, Amateur League1977-78,
Amateur League 1978-79, Sports & Athletic League 2005-06, The Yorkshire League 1969-70

SHEFFIELD and HALLAMSHIRE
COUNTY FOOTBALL ASSOCIATION

AMATEUR LEAGUE

DIRECTORY & FIXTURES
SEASON 1978/79

Chairman:
S. BUTTERFIELD, Esq.

Management Committee:
Messrs. G. DIGBY, K. A. GUNNEE,
J. HOGG, A. H. HOLBROOK,
T. LAWTON, K. PARSONAGE,
J. WATERS and E. J. N. WOOLLEY

Secretary:
G. THOMPSON
40, Waingate, Sheffield S3 8LB
Telephone: (0742) 27817

SHEFFIELD
SPORTS
AND
ATHLETIC
FOOTBALL
LEAGUE

OFFICIAL GUIDE
2005-2006
SEASON

Sponsored by
OWLERTON
STADIUM

THE
YORKSHIRE
LEAGUE

SEASON 1969-70

Handbooks and Programmes

Left: Nine Handbooks for

The Meadowhall Sheffield Sunday Football League

Below: Tinsley Charity Trophy

Final Programmes 2008, 2011, 2012

Below left: Six Meadowhall League Cup Final

Programmes covering 2008-2013

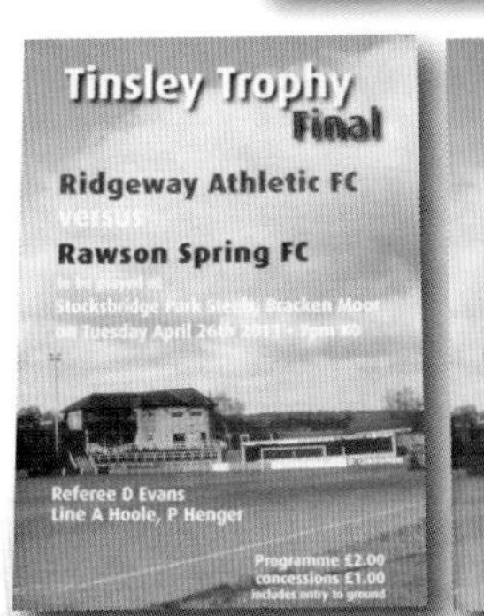

Meadowhall League Cup Final 2010 at Bramall Lane,
between Royal Earl FC and Packhorse Inn FC which Royal Earl won 2-1

Handbooks
Above: Six Handbooks for The Regional Alliance Sunday Football League covering seasons 2001 to 2007

League members Ties
Above: Three Sunday Regional Alliance League membership ties.
The tie on the right was during the period when Pickard Communication, a local print and publishing company, sponsored the League.

otball game played in Totley, Sheffield. The Cricket Inn looming in the background
Copyright Neil Theasby and licensed for reuse under this Creative Commons Licence

Sheffield and Hallamshire County Football Association Handbooks
Three Handbooks for seasons 1999-2000, 2000-2001, 2001-2002

Play Up Attercliffe
An old card produced around 1890s

SHEFFIELD LICENSED VICTUALLERS' LEAGUE.

RESULTS UP-TO-DATE.

	P.	W.	L.	D.	Goals. F.	A.	Pts.
Bellefield Inn	25	22	2	1	75	29	45
Great Britain Hotel	25	20	3	2	88	19	42
Black Horse Hotel	26	20	3	3	82	21	41
Royal Oak Hotel	26	17	5	4	81	28	38
Sawmill Tavern	25	17	8	0	74	28	34
Cricket Inn	25	11	11	3	67	42	25
Douglas Hotel	24	9	12	3	37	49	21
Porter Cottage	26	9	15	2	49	57	20
Bricklayers' Arms	24	6	13	5	34	59	17
Chequers Inn	24	7	14	3	39	68	17
Target Inn	22	7	14	1	33	68	15
Waggon & Horses Hotel	25	4	15	6	28	58	14
Chantry Arms	22	4	18	0	29	101	8
Coach & Horses Hotel	25	2	20	3	21	87	7

MATCHES FOR NEXT WEEK.

FINAL FOR L.V. SHIELD.

Bellefield v. Royal Oak or Great Britain. Monday at Sheaf House. Kick off at 5.30.

Sheffield Licensed Victuallers - League Winners Medal 1906-07
League Table from Green'Un c1906

Tommy Crawshaw, Sheffield Wed. and England and William Foulke, Sheffield United and England

Postcard produced by Furniss, Photo Series, Langsett Road, Sheffield

Ernest Nudger Needham. Cigarette card produced by Singleton & Cole's

Crookes Congs FC. Won AJ Sanders trophy 1936. Cigarette card produced by Ardath tobacco

A Benefit Match in aid of
MICK LIVERSIDGE
ALL STARS XI
VERSUS
SADDLE SELECT
KICK OFF 3.00p.m.
ON
Sunday 2nd April 1978
ON THE
Brightside & Carbrook Ground
Bellhouse Rd, Shiregreen
Programme
10p
Promoter Mr Edward Cox

Mike Liversidge, the author of this book in his somewhat inactive footballing days (right).

The programme, left, was for his benefit match in which Peter Swan, Gerry Young and Howard Wilkinson amongst other Wednesday and United players turned out for the Johnny Quinn's All Stars

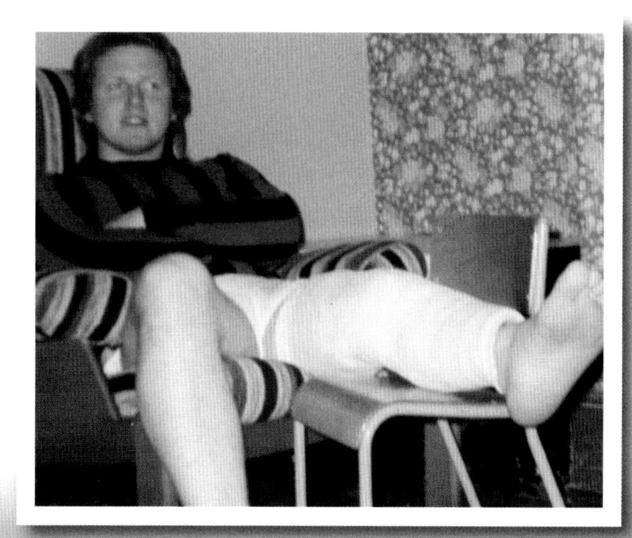

CHARITY FOOTBALL.

ATTERCLIFFE ALLIANCE CUP PAIRINGS.

Mr. L. Davies presided at the adjourned annual meeting of the Attercliffe Alliance Charity Competition, held at the Albert Inn, Attercliffe, last night.

In addition to the draw for the first round of the knock out competition, an important item discussed was the proposed revival of the League.

Following some discussion on the formation of the League, it was decided to hold the matter in abeyance until Monday night, 2 September, when, if sufficient entries have been obtained, fixtures will be made. In the meantime any club desirous of joining should communicate with Mr. D. Craddock, 295, Petre street, Sheffield.

The draw for the first rounds of the Charity Competition came out as follows:

PRELIMINARY ROUND.

Gas Co. v. Tinsley Park Colliery.
Penistone Church. v. Lopham Street U.M.
Tinsley Park Sports v. Attercliffe Church.

FIRST ROUND.

Nether Edge v. Ecclesfield Red Rose.
Victoria F.C. v. Roundel Street P.M.
Croft House v. Indus Sports.
Greenland W.M.C. v. Hollin Bush.
Gas Co. or Tinsley Colliery v. Penistone or Lopham Street.
Tinsley Sports or Attercliffe v. Turton Platts.
Metro-Vickers v. Ostrich Inn.
The Hall Sports v. Grimesthorpe R.M.C.

Clubs to mutually agree as to playing the matches, but the preliminary round must be played on or before 5 October, and the first round, 9 November.

Attercliffe Alliance Cup
Clipping from the Green'Un
Sheffield's Saturday sports paper

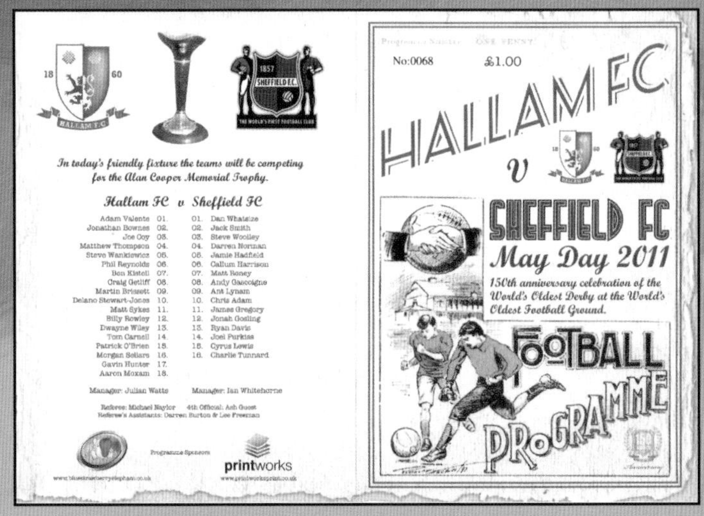

Hallam FC programme
May Day 2011, 150th Anniversary Game v Sheffield FC

Postcard showing player getting ready for a game!

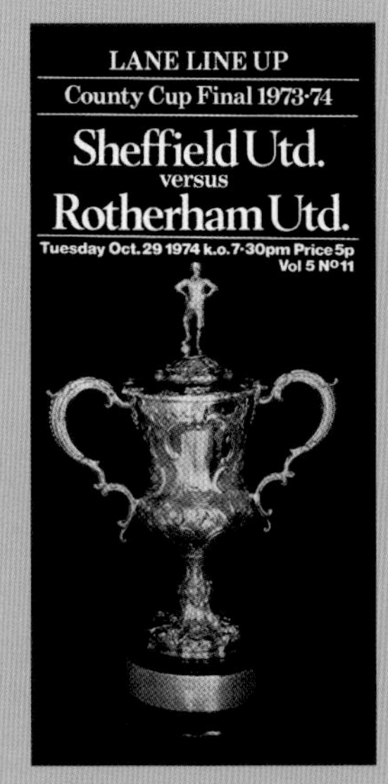

Sheffield County Cup Final
1973-74 Programme

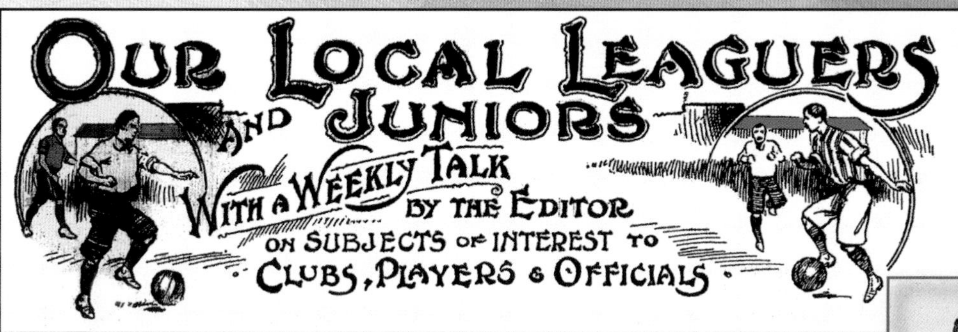

This page shows newspaper clippings from the Sheffield Sports Paper, ***The Green'Un***

ALF SAYS

Get t'Green 'Un fer football,
feightin' an' fishin' news,
an' ivery other soart o' sport,
If it's in t'Green 'Un, it's reight.

DUNCAN GILMOUR FOOTBALL CLUB

ANNUAL DANCE

TO BE HELD AT
NETHER EDGE HALL
NETHER EDGE ROAD
THURSDAY 16TH NOVEMBER 1950
7.30 P.M. TO 12 MIDNIGHT
KEN BINGLEY AND HIS BAND
BUFFET SPOT PRIZES BAR
Tickets 3/- Each

Duncan Gilmour Football Club Annual Dance Ticket at Nether Edge Hall 1950

Sir Arthur Matthews being introduced to the Atlas and Norfolk team before the start of their match with Shanks Athletic, the Scottish club, at Roe Lane. He is seen shaking hands with Haldane. With him is Harry Metcalfe, the Atlas and Norfolk Club chairman.

Atlas & Norfolk Department League Winners Medal 1926-27

Postcard: Attercliffe Boys FC. Note the large crowd

Attercliffe Charity Cup Final, won by the Kings Arms, situated on Attercliffe Road. Clipping from the Green'Un

MINOR FOOTBALL.

Attercliffe Charity Cup Final.

KING'S HEAD v. WOODBOURNE.

The above teams met in this attractive final tie on the sple.didly-equipped gound or the Handsworth W.M.C. All the proceeds were for charity, and as the "gate" would be close upon 4,000 when the sides appeared, the promoters were sure of handing over a good sum. Mr. J. Atkin had charge of the game.

Frith was a notable absentee from the King's Head side, but their opponents were at full strength, and as there was very little to select between the sides on the season's form, there was every prospect of a good game.

King's Head had the advantage of the wind, and for the first ten minutes they were much the superior side. All the danger came from Stainrod and Bean, and thrice Dyson had his goal seriously threatened. Twice Bean put the ball past the post, but later on the Woodbourne goalkeeper was very smart in dealing with a shot from Burton. Spooner followed this by shooting over the bar after which Woodbourne got into their stride. Pollard and his left wing working cleverly, with the result that the ball was crossed into the centre again, and Pollard tested Redfern with a very deceptive shot.

The Woodbourne half-back line did not appear to be able to master the King's forwards, and consequently their rear line was subject to heavy pressure, but Dyson and his backs defended in brilliant fashion.

The Woodbourne attacks were few and far between, but yet always appeared of a dangerous order, Ramsden, on the left wing, showing a fine turn of speed. It was from one of his dashes that Woodbourne made a great effort to obtain the lead, but their effort was beaten back by Redfern, who saved smartly on the line.

This was followed by a rapid rush to the other end, Burton leading the movement, and in order to stave off the attack Globe conceded a corner, but this brought no material advantage to the attackers, while a minute later Bean shot wide at the same end. The game was being fought at a hot pace, but the wind made ball control rather difficult, and thus the class of football was rather below what had been expected.

Half-time:—King's Head 0
Woodbourne 0

The game was restarted with Woodbourne on the attack, but the King's defence held firm, and after rather under 15 minutes from the interval, a long-looked for goal was registered. This fell to the Kings, who were stil lrather the cleverer side. Spooner was dribbling the ball down, when he was tripped and from the free-kick the ball went to BEAN, who, with a splendid first kick shot, dropped the ball just under the bar to defeat Dyson.

This naturally put a lot of life into the proceedings, and away rushed J. Robinson in a desperate effort to equalise, but Holbrook rushed across the field and got the ball away with a Strong kick. Later, a free kick to Woodbourne was well placed by C. Robinson, but eventually Redfern got the ball away after a great struggle near the post.

The King's continued to show the better methods forward, and Holmes, with a grand drive struck the bar. It was an anxious moment for the defenders, but Dyson was quick to realise the danger, and soon cleared. Five minutes from the end, however, the King's right got away, and a centre from Stainrod passed across the goal to the opposite wing, for FAIRIES to obtain possession and put on the second.

Result:—KING'S HEAD 2
WOODBOURNE 0

Craig, a William Hills FC player looking lonely on Concord Park. Tinsley Towers looming in the background, c2003

Sheffield football Postcards

Cartoon postcard showing Mr Charles Clegg pointing out that local teams should be playing in the FA Cup competitions. c1907

Sheffield football related publications also by Michael Liversidge

Stannington, Sheffield postcard showing a local football game being played on Lomas field

Manchester Football Museum postcard depicting Famous English Football Player of 1881 John Hunter of Heeley FC is standing 5th from left

Chris Eyre and Uriah Rennie at the Sandygate ground of Hallam Football Club reading the Sheffield F.C. Booklet

Old football postcards

These were commonplace in the mid to late part of the 19th century when football was in its youth. Most coloured cards of the day depicted Southern aristocratic sides. This changed when a northern side, Blackburn Olympic, brought the FA Cup back to the North of England in 1883.

Hurlfield, 2 down, win shield game

TWO goals to the good in 12 minutes, Beaver Hill were beaten 3-2 by Hurlfield School in the Clegg Shield on Brook School's ground today.

In spite of an injury to John Phoenix, which took him from half-back to forward line, and some courageous goalkeeping by Ernest Booth, they should have saved the game in the last quarter hour.

Hurlfield were without inside forward and captain Michael Vardy, who is hoping to start training again very soon following a broken ankle.

Using the swirling wind WELLS put Beavers into the lead in eight minutes from a pass by Phoenix. 'Keeper Booth, maybe surprised by the surge of the ball, was too far forward. Four minutes later Phoenix supplied a very good pass for LYCETT to score No. 2.

The first Hurlfield goal, smoothly worked on the left, came in 20 minutes, ABBOTT scoring and the equaliser came in 40 minutes with smart reading of the game by Hinch. Indeed, his effort from the left hand corner of the box was almost there before THOMAS completed the scoring technicality.

Goalkeeper Ellis must take responsibility for the goal that proved to be decisive in 51 minutes. He should not have lost hold as Thomas challenged for ABBOTT to score his second with the loose ball.

Clegg Shield Cup Final 1963
Result: Hurlfield 3 v Beaver Hill 2 - Played at Brook School ground
Newspaper clipping from the Sheffield Green'Un

Cigarette card showing a caricature of Harry Gooney who played for Newhall Road School, Sheffield Boys, England Boys, Sheffield United, Plymouth and Luton. For some reason, although signed by them, Harry never made an appearance for Plymouth or Luton

Triple Cup Winners, unknown team with their three trophies, taken from an old Sheffield published postcard

Green'Un

Football results on a Saturday night in Sheffield City Centre

Chapter Six

Sheffield Schools Football

Clegg Shield
Wednesday Shield
& United Shield

Clegg Shield

Wednesday Challenge Shield Medal 1912

United Challenge Shield Medal 1919

Len Badger Sheffield United played for Coleridge Road School football team which won the Clegg Shield Trophy in the late 1950s. Whilst at this school Len was selected to play for England Boys against Scotland in the 1960s. The England Schoolboys team also included David Pleat and Barry Fry while George Graham was playing for the Scotland team.

Len went on to play in over 500 Football League matches with 457 games for Sheffield United and 46 games for Chesterfield. Len Badger was born in the Tinsley Park/Darnall area of Sheffield

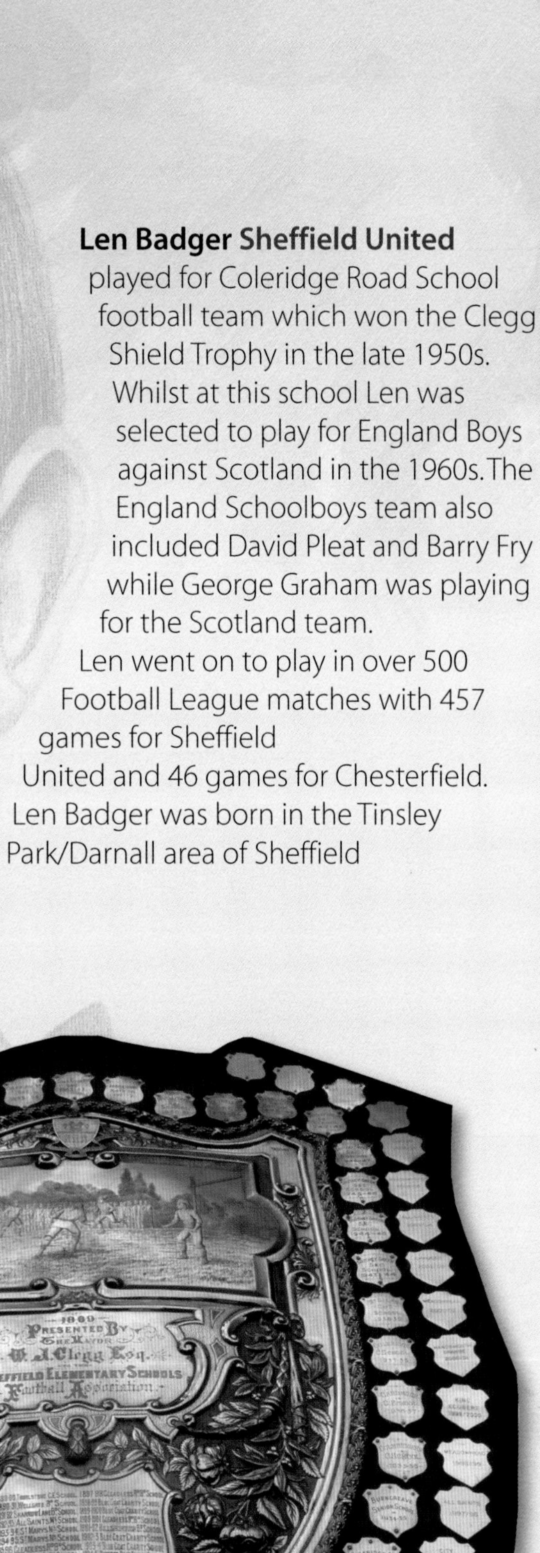

Sheffield Schoolboys Football

The Clegg Shield, the oldest school football trophy in the world, is still contested annually within the Sheffield area.

Over the last 125 years thousands of Sheffield and district teenagers have competed in this prestigious competition. Some will have memories of playing and probably losing in the earlier rounds, but some will hold winners medals of which there were only 11 given out every season. This means that over 1300 of these medals were presented to the young men and are probably still held in high regard by the players themselves or their families. It also means they are as rare as FA Cup Final medals, not as prestigious, obviously, but still equally rare.

In 1889 Alderman W. S. Clegg (father of the famous footballing Clegg Brothers) presented the Clegg Shield to be used for a football competition for the Elementary Schools within the City of Sheffield.

A World Cup winner, England Internationals and long serving Football League players have all taken part in this schoolboy competition: Harry Gooney, Fred Furness, Len Badger, Gordon Banks, Johnny Fantham, David Layne, Tony Kay, Brian Richardson, Graham Shaw and brother Bernard, Scott Sellars, John Beresford, Jamie Hoyland, Ray McHale, Kevin Davies and many more schoolboy players who have gone on to grace the professional ranks of the English Football League.

Coleridge Council School, winners of the Clegg Shield 1952-53
back: Mr Wragg, teacher. M Saxilby, K Hunthorpe, K Cooke, C Ellis, Mr Thomas, Headmaster
middle: B Habersham, C Yeardly, R Bradwell, K Allen, J Beecham, unknown, B Jacobs
front: D Slater, R White

Taken from the Sheffield Independent on Monday 31st March 1890

Clegg Challenge Shield, Final Tie

Thurlstone 2 v Rotherham 0

Played at Olive Grove

There was a capital attendance to witness this match. Thurlstone won the toss, and Alderman Clegg set the leather in motion. The Thurlstone lads were the first to attack, and then, after level spell they gained a couple of corners. Both teams at first played pretty football, but afterwards their play fell off. The Rotherham forwards then raced away but were stopped by Smith. Then Rotherham tried hard to score, in fact, for a time they continued a perfect state of siege, but the Thurlstone goalkeeper dealt with difficult shots in a most praiseworthy manner. Half Time arrived with no score having been made. Immediately after the restart the Rotherham right wing got possession, but the final shot was a poor attempt. Rotherham then had a try, and as a result of a neat run on the right, the ball was splendidly crossed to goal but it went outside. The Thurlstonians retaliated for a time, but in C. L. Cooper they found a back a lot too much for them, his play throughout the game being a marvel for one so young. Soon after the Thurlstone goal had had a narrow escape from downfall. The scene of play was transferred to the other end, where Thurlstone had a corner, which after a short struggle was converted into a goal. Ned Lake giving the leather the final touch, amid great enthusiasm. Returning to the fray the same team scored a second directly afterwards, a long, low shot by Kilner, passing through the posts. The whistle was blown immediately afterwards, and the Thurlstone boys were left the winners of the very first **CLEGG SHIELD**. The youthful footballers received quite an ovation on leaving the field, many of them being carried shoulder high by their admirers.

Thurlstone: Marsden, Smith, Hinchcliffe, Adams, Depledge, Sykes, Bowler, Jones, Kilner, Goddard, Lake.

Rotherham: Parkinson, Early, C.L.Cooper, Blackshaw, H.S. Cooper, Hemsell, Kenning, Banks, Clarke. Two of the Rotherham team names are sadly missed from the report.

Umpires: Messrs. Green & Fletcher.
Referee Mr. W. E. Clegg

Clegg Shield Winners

Thurlstone
the first winners of the Clegg Shield in 1890

Crookesmoor Council School
Won Clegg Shield in 1924-25

Burgoyne School
Won Clegg Shield in 1907

United and **Wednesday Shields**

The United and Wednesday Shields were inaugurated slightly later than the Clegg Trophy, in the early part of the 20th century.

The Clegg Shield made changes to its age group format over its early years. It was developed for 11-13 age group but later moved up slightly to the mid teens 14-16 years old, which is still the case today.

The United and Wednesday Shields were brought about to develop football for two younger age groups. They, as with the Clegg trophy, became annual schoolboy competitions for the young schoolboys of the local areas.

Over many years younger players throughout Sheffield & district competed for these two shields with even more gusto, than the Clegg trophy, as they perceived them as belonging to the two league teams; Sheffield United and Sheffield Wednesday which technically was the case as they were donated by these two famous clubs

These two competitions, as stated, started 15-20 years later than the Clegg Shield.

The United and Wednesday Shields also came to a finish quite a few years ago.

This does means that the shields were only competed for for around 50-60 years. Therefore, only 550-660 of each of the United and Wednesday medals were ever produced and presented to the young winners. Therefore, they are much rarer than the Clegg Shield medals. The Medals seemed to fluctuate in their quality. Some were produced in silver and hallmarked as such and some cast in bronze. This may have been winners medals in silver and runners-up medals in bronze.

Keep searching on e-bay and you may find a little gem. You can also find the odd postcards or photographic images of the school teams with their winners shield.

WEDNESDAY SHIELD

1895 THURLSTONE C.E.
1896 GLEADLESS ROAD BOARD
1897 BLUE COAT CH
1898 GLEADLESS ROAD BOARD
1899 SAINT EDMUNDS R.C.
1900 HILLSBOROUGH BOARD
1901 DUCHESS ROAD COUNCIL
1902 DUCHESS ROAD COUNCIL
1903 HILLSBOROUGH COUNCIL
1904 HILLSBOROUGH COUNCIL
1905 HILLSBOROUGH COUNCIL
1906 GLEADLESS ROAD COUNCIL
1907 CROOKESMOOR COUNCIL
1908 HILLSBOROUGH COUNCIL
1909 HILLSBOROUGH COUNCIL
1910 HILLSBOROUGH COUNCIL
1911 LOWFIELD COUNCIL
1912 TINSLEY COUNCIL
1913 LYDGATE COUNCIL
1914 TINSLEY COUNCIL
1915 HILLSBOROUGH R.C.
1916 DUCHESS ROAD COUNCIL
1917 HILLSBOROUGH COUNCIL
1918 HILLSBOROUGH COUNCIL
1919 MALIN BRIDGE COUNCIL
1920 OWLER LANE COUNCIL
1921 MANOR COUNCIL
1922 NEWHALL COUNCIL
1923 CROOKESMOOR COUNCIL
1924 NEWHALL COUNCIL
1925 OWLER LANE COUNCIL
1926 PYE BANK COUNCIL
1927 WOODBOURNE COUNCIL
1928 TINSLEY INTERMEDIATE
1929 SHIREGREEN COUNCIL
1930 CROOKESMOOR COUNCIL
1931 WOODBOURNE COUNCIL
1932 COLERIDGE ROAD COUNCIL
1933 ST VINCENTS RC
1934 BURNGREAVE COUNCIL
1935 COLERIDGE ROAD COUNCIL
1936 CARBROOK COUNCIL
1937 COLERIDGE ROAD COUNCIL
1938 BURNGREAVE COUNCIL
NO COMPETITION WWII
1946 ARBOURTHORNE NORTH SEC
1947 COLERIDGE ROAD COUNCIL
1948 MEYNELL ROAD SEC
1949 BURNGREAVE SEC & HUNTSMANS GARDENS (SHARED SHIELD)
1950 SHIRECLIFFE SCHOOL
1951
1952
1953
1954
1955
1956 DE LA SALLE

UNITED SHIELD

1908 WADSLEY BRIDGE COUNCIL
1909 HILLSBOROUGH COUNCIL
1910 WADSLEY BRIDGE COUNCIL
1911 ST MARYS C.E.
1912 SALE MEM C.E.
1913 WADSLEY C.E.
1914 HILLSBOROUGH R.C.
1915 TINSLEY C.E
1916 HILLSBOROUGH COUNCIL.
1917 HILLSBOROUGH COUNCIL
1918 HILLSBOROUGH R.C.
1919 ST BARNABUS C.E.
1920 WADSLEY C.E.
1921 WADSLEY C.E.
1922 WADSLEY C.E.L
1923 WADSLEY C.E.
1924 WADSLEY C.E.
1925 WADSLEY C.E.L
1926 WADSLEY C.E.
1927 WADSLEY C.E.
1928 HILLFOOT COUNCIL
1929 WADSLEY BRIDGE COUNCIL
1930 WADSLEY BRIDGE COUNCIL
1931 WADSLEY BRIDGE C.E.
1932 WADSLEY BRIDGE C.E.
1933 SALE MEM C.E.
1934 ST PATRICKS R.C.
1935 SALE MEM C.E.
1936 DARNALL C.E.
1937 CARBROOK C.E.
1938 CARBROOK C.E.
NO COMPETITION WWII
1946 HANDSWORTH COUNTY
1947 INTAKE COUNTY
1948 INTAKE COUNTY
1949 INTAKE COUNTY
1950 WINCOBANK COUNTY

United Shield

Hillsborough Council School
Won United Shield 1915-16

Tinsley Church of England School
Won United Shield 1915

Morley Street School *Won United Shield 1956-57*

Wednesday Shield

Shiregreen Council School
Won Wednesday Shield 1928-29

Shirecliffe School
Won the Wednesday Shield in 1949-50
The goalkeeper is Tony Kay, who later became, as a midfielder, a Sheffield Wednesday regular first team player and who was transferred, in a record deal, to Everton in 1962.
He was such an influential player that he captained both of these teams. He played in the Sheffield Wednesday side who finished 2nd in the year, 1961, that Spurs did the league and cup double with what was then a record number of points. When at Everton he went one better and won the First Division title (the Premier League to you and me now) in 1962-63.
He was also a full England international scoring on his debut against Switzerland, his only cap.

Tony Kay in his Everton strip

Tony Kay leading Sheffield Wednesday out followed by another English International Ron Springett

Clegg Shield winners

1890	THURLSTONE
1891	WELLGATE BOARD
1892	SHARROW LANE
1893	ALL SAINTS C E
1894	ST MARYS C E
1895	ST MARYS C E
1896	GLEADLESS ROAD BOARD
1897	ST MARYS C E
1898	GLEADLESS ROAD BOARD
1899	BLUE COAT CHURCH
1900	BLUE COAT CHURCH
1901	GLEADLESS ROAD BOARD
1902	HILLSBOROUGH BOARD
1903	BLUE COAT CHURCH
1904	BLUE COAT CHURCH
1905	DUCHESS ROAD COUNCIL
1906	ALL SAINTS CE
1907	BURGOYNE ROAD COUNCIL
1908	DUCHESS ROAD COUNCIL
1909	HILLSBOROUGH COUNCIL
1910	HILLSBOROUGH COUNCIL
1911	HILLSBOROUGH COUNCIL
1912	WALKLEY COUNCIL
1913	COLERIDGE ROAD COUNCIL
1914	MANOR COUNCIL
1915	DUCHESS ROAD COUNCIL
1916	HILLSBOROUGH COUNCIL
1917	HILLSBOROUGH COUNCIL
1918	HILLSBOROUGH COUNCIL
1919	HILLSBOROUGH COUNCIL
1920	OWLER LANE COUNCIL
1921	MANOR COUNCIL
1922	CROOKESMOOR COUNCIL
1923	NEWHALL COUNCIL
1924	NEWHALL COUNCIL
1925	CROOKESMOOR COUNCIL
1926	HUNTSMANS GDNS COUNCIL
1927	DUCHESS ROAD COUNCIL
1928	CARFIELD INTERMEDIATE
1929	CROOKESMOOR COUNCIL
1930	WADSLEY BRIDGE COUNCIL
1931	CROOKESMOOR COUNCIL
1932	BURNGREAVE COUNCIL
1933	NEWHALL COUNCIL
1934	COLERIDGE ROAD COUNCIL
1935	BURNGREAVE COUNCIL
1936	COLERIDGE ROAD COUNCIL
1937	CARBROOK COUNCIL
1938	COLERIDGE ROAD COUNCIL
	NO COMPETITION WWII
1945	SOUTHEY GREEN COUNCIL
1946	SOUTHEY GREEN COUNCIL
1947	SOUTHEY GREEN COUNCIL
1948	SOUTHEY GREEN COUNCIL
1949	SHIRECLIFFE SEC
1950	MEYNELL ROAD
1951	SOUTHEY GREEN
1952	ARBOURTHORNE NORTH
1953	COLERIDGE ROAD
1954	COLERIDGE ROAD
1955	SOUTHEY GREEN
1956	CROOKESMOOR COUNTY
1957	NORFOLK
1958	BURNGREAVE
1959	NEWFIELD
1960	
1961	MEYNELL ROAD
1962	NEWFIELD SCHOOL
1963	HURLFIELD
1964	HURLFIELD
1965	
1966	NEWFIELD SCHOOL
1967	WALTHEOF COMP
1968	NEWFIELD SCHOOL
1969	ABBEYDALE GRANGE
1970	
1971	
1972	
1973	CARTER LODGE
1974	KING ECGBERT
1975	CITY (LEAGUE CHAMPS)
1976	HERRIES
1977	HERRIES
1978	CHAUCER U16 (LGE CHAMPS)
1979	CHAUCER U16 (LGE CHAMPS)
1980	
1981	
1982	CHAUCER U16 (LGE CHAMPS)
1983	ASHLEIGH U16
1984	
1985	ABBEYDALE GRANGE
1986	??? – SHIELD MISSING
1987	HINDE HOUSE
1988	ROWLINSON
1989	ECCLESFIELD
1990	MEADOWHEAD
1991	MYERS GROVE
1992	KING EDWARDS
1993	CHAUCER
1994	HERRIES
1995	HIGH STORRS
1996	HINDE HOUSE
1997	CITY SCHOOL
1998	ALL SAINTS
1999	MEADOWHEAD
2000	KING ECGBERT
2001	HANDSWORTH GRANGE
2002	MEADOWHEAD
2003	CHAUCER
2004	ALL SAINTS
2005	MEADOWHEAD
2006	TAPTON
2007	
2008	WESTFIELD
2009	KING ECGBERTS
2010	BIRLEY COMMUNITY SCHOOL
2011	BIRLEY COMMUNITY SCHOOL
2012	CITY SCHOOL
2013	ECCLESFIELD SCHOOL
2014	KING ECGBERTS
2015	ECCLESFIELD SCHOOL
2016	WESTFIELD SCHOOL

All Saints - Clegg Shield winners

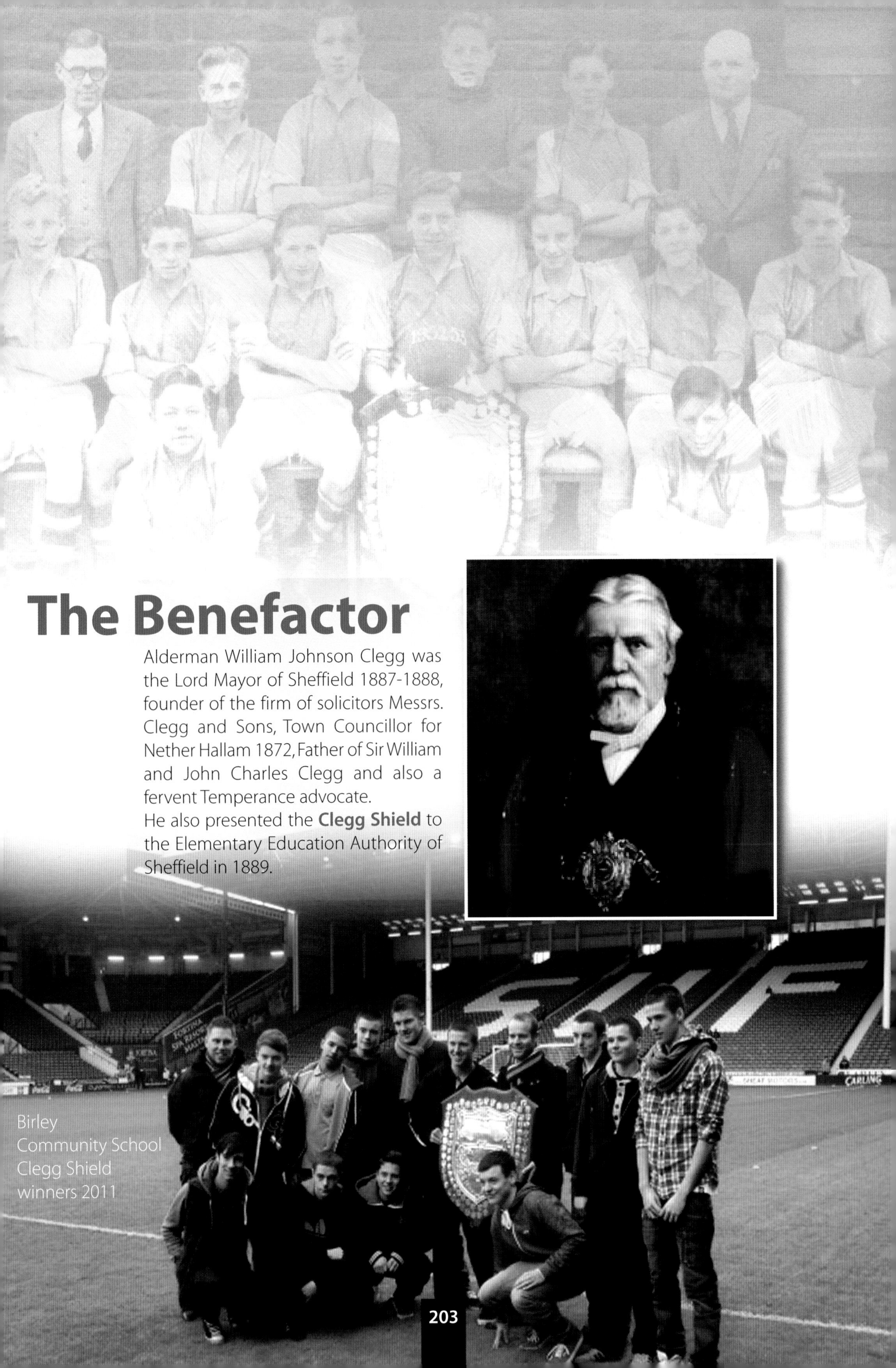

The Benefactor

Alderman William Johnson Clegg was the Lord Mayor of Sheffield 1887-1888, founder of the firm of solicitors Messrs. Clegg and Sons, Town Councillor for Nether Hallam 1872, Father of Sir William and John Charles Clegg and also a fervent Temperance advocate.
He also presented the **Clegg Shield** to the Elementary Education Authority of Sheffield in 1889.

Birley Community School Clegg Shield winners 2011

From Clegg Shield games to a Wembley World Cup Final

World Cup Winners Medal, won by Gordon, which was sold for over £120,000

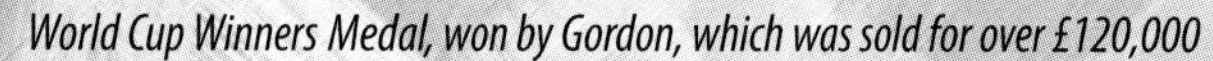

Sheffield Boys football team, pictures below, in the late 1950s. All of these young men will have, at some time in their school lives, played in the Clegg Shield Competition.

Gordon Banks who was in goal for this Sheffield Representative team, went on to play, and play well, in the 1966 World Cup Final following Bobby Moore up those famous Wembley steps to collect his Winners medal (pictured left).

Chapter Seven
Local Football Grounds

Pye Bank Recreation ground
Still getting in a game of football
whilst the flats are being demolished
©Adrian Wynn

Local Football Grounds

Hallam Football Club cup winners in the 1950s

Hallam F.C. , the oldest football ground in the world

Stocksbridge Cup Winners

Stocksbridge Park Steels ground

Woodbourne Alliance who played in this area of Sheffield some 80 years ago.

Woodbourne Road Athletics stadium

Sheffield City Police, Thursday Friendlies League - Six times Yorkshire Police League Champs

Niagara Football Pitches
Wadsley Bridge

Walkley F.C., c1950s

Bole Hills, Walkley, 1985
Looking over Malin Bridge and Wisewood
©Adrian Wynn

Jamie Vardy who played for three season at Stockbridge Park Steels

Stocksbridge FC ground

Unknown football team pictured in Concord Park

Pitch 14, Concord Park, Shiregreen

Stannington Village (Red/Black stripes) v Redmires

Lomas Football Field, Stannington Village.

Getting in a game of football anywhere you can!

Ponderosa Playing Fields, Upperthorpe area. Netherthorpe flats and University Tower in distance

Thorncliffe Playing Fields, High Green

William Hill FC - Sunday Regional Alliance League

Concord Park, Shiregreen - William Hill F.C.
versus Jack in a Box F.C., c2001

Sharrow FC celebrating their Meadowhall League Sunday cup win

Sharrow United F.C. versus William Hill c2001
At the Sheffield University Football Grounds.
William Hill. won the game 3-2.

Richard Tims Sheffield FC - Chairman of the World's Oldest Football Club

Sheffield FC playing under their floodlights at the Coach and Horses Ground, Dronfield

McKee Postcard

English Steel Corporation Sports Ground, Shiregreen Lane

Woodhouse West End WMC won Sheffield Junior League in season 1929

Stradbroke Playing Fields, home ground of Woodhouse West End for many years

Two local teams in action. Image taken by Graham Leary

Parson Cross Park, going for goal but well saved by the keeper

Tinsley Wire Industries, in 1959 they won the National Wiredrawers Cup

Ferrars Road, Tinsley

Graves Park FC, winners of the A.J. Sanders trophy in the early 1960s

Graves Park, South Sheffield, between the districts of Norton, Woodseats and Meadowhead.

They think it's all over...
It is now!

Thank you for reading our book.

Please feel free to make contact, by email, with the authors Michael Liversidge or Chris Eyre if you find any inaccuracies throughout this book. If your information is proved to be correct amendments will be made to the details if, or hopefully when, a reprint is scheduled.

email: mliversidge@pickards.org.uk or chris@cjeyre.co.uk